Patrick O'Brian is the author of the acclaimed Aubrey-Maturin tales and the biographer of Joseph Banks and Picasso. He translated many works from French into English, among them the first volume of Jean Lacouture's biography of Charles de Gaulle. In 1995 he was the first recipient of the Heywood Hill Prize for a lifetime's contribution to literature. In the same year he was awarded the CBE. In 1997 he was awarded an honorary doctorate of letters by Trinity College, Dublin. He died in January 2000 at the age of 85.

A BOOK OF VOYAGES

EDITED BY

PATRICK O'BRIAN

WITH DECORATIONS BY

JOAN BURTON

HARPER

Harper
An imprint of HarperCollins*Publishers*
77–85 Fulham Palace Road,
Hammersmith, London W6 8JB

www.harpercollins.co.uk

This paperback edition 2014
1

This facsimile edition first published by HarperCollins*Publishers* 2013

First published in Great Britain
by Home and Van Thal, London 1947

A catalogue record for this book
is available from the British Library

ISBN: 978 0 00 748712 7

Printed and bound in Great Britain by
Clays Ltd, St Ives plc

CONTENTS

FOREWORD

This collection of voyages has been made from some of those many seventeenth- and eighteenth-century books of travel that are no longer easily to be found. The Elizabethan voyages and the more famous later travellers have often been reprinted, and most public libraries can supply Hakluyt and Purchas, Dampier, Anson and Cook. The big eighteenth-century collections, however, have not found modern publishers, and it is not likely that they ever will, for they are inordinately long and their hundreds of maps and engravings would be far too costly to reproduce.

Nearly all these collections (and there were dozens of them) were designed to give a view of the known world: they were intended to act as a kind of encyclopaedic geography, and the voyages were often constrained to suit the system. The result of this treatment was undoubtedly useful at the time, but a determined editor would often mangle an interesting voyage cruelly, extracting commercial and geographical facts and relating them in a uniformly dull manner. A melancholy example was the Abbé Prevost, whose *Histoire Générale des Voyages* fills some twenty insipid quartos.

Of these collections perhaps the most enjoyable is that called Churchill's. It is an anonymously compiled work published in four handsome folio volumes by A. and J. Churchill in 1704; they brought out another edition in six volumes in 1732 and lastly an eight-volume edition in 1752. Churchill has the virtue of being the least systematic of the collections; when the original voyage is in English Churchill's editor leaves his author alone, or at the most makes no alteration more ambitious than modernizing the spelling, which is hardly offensive at this length of time. Churchill had access to several manuscripts, the most important being that of Sir William Monson's Naval Tracts, and he appears to have printed them with scholarly accuracy.

Most of the collections use much the same material, but as

Churchill shows most respect for his authors, I have used him as the main provider for this book, though I have gone to the original wherever there has been an earlier printed version.

The text is integral in the case of the complete voyages; I have given it exactly as I found it, down to the last inconsistency in spelling. The extracts have been edited, but the editing has been confined to excision, and every cut, except in Lady Craven's journey, is shown. There are no footnotes except those of the original authors. Editor's footnotes seem to me out of place in a work of this kind; they spoil the impression of reading the original text, they ruin the appearance of a page, and if they tell you anything new it is often annoyingly trivial. The only notes are short biographical and bibliographical remarks at the beginning of the accounts, and a list of sea-terms, taken from various eighteenth-century sources, at the end of the book.

Most books of voyages say in their prefaces that they intend to be useful. "Let us have no unnecessary ornamentation at the outset of a work in which we propose nothing but the weighty and the useful," begins one; they hardly ever speak of giving entertainment.

The intention of this book is quite different; its first aim is to give the reader pleasure. It makes no claim to being a scholarly work, and it has no didactic purpose. If the reader draws instruction or edification from it as well as pleasure that is his own affair, and beside the bargain.

PATRICK O'BRIAN.

PREFACE BY VARIOUS TRAVELLERS

. . . for thy more easier understanding, I have divided this
. . . into . . . parts . . . which being seriously perused,
doubtlesse thy Labour shall receive both profit and pleasure.
Accept them therefore with the same love, that I offer them
to thee, since they cost thee nothing but the reading, but how
deare soever they are to me. But understand me better, I
scorne to draw my Pen to the Ignorant Foole, for I contemne
both. To the Wise I know it will be welcome; to the profound
Historian yeeld knowledge, contemplation and direction: and
to the understanding Gentleman, insight, instruction, and
recreation: and to the true bred Poet fraternal love, both in
meane and manner. Now as touching the hissing of snakish
Papists, a tush for that snarling Crew; for as this Worke, being
sensed with experience and garnished with trueth, is more than
able to batter downe the stinging venome of their despitefull
Waspishness: so also they may clearely see therein, as in a
Mirrour, their owne blindnes, and the damnable errours of
their blind guiders, Deceivers and Idolaters: and above all the
cruel inflictions imposed upon me, by the mercilesse Inquisi-
tion of their profession in Malaga; which for Christ's sake I
constantly suffered, in Tortures, Torments, and Hunger.

And lastly, they may perceive God's miraculous Mercy, in
discovering and delivering me from such a concealed and
inhumane murther.

And now referring the well set Reader to the History it
selfe, where satisfaction lyeth ready to receive him, and
expectation desirous of deserved thankes: I come to talke with
the scelerate Companion: If thou beest a Villain, a Ruffian,
a Momus, a Knave, a Carper, a Critick, a Bubo, a stupid Asse,
and a gnawing Worme with envious Lips, I bequeath thee to a
Carnificiall reward, where a hempen Rope will soon dispatch
thy snarling slander, and free my toylesome Travailes and
now painefull Labours, from the deadly Poyson of thy sharpe
edged calumnies, and so goe hang thy selfe; for I neither will

respect thy Love, nor regard thy Malice: and shall ever and always remaine,

To the Courteous still Observant:

And to the Criticall Knave as he deserveth.

Wм. Lithgow

The Prologue to the Reader, from William Lithgow's *The Totall Discourse of the Rare Adventures, and Painefull Peregrinations of long nineteene yeares Travailes from Scotland . . . etc.* ed. 1640. Lithgow has recently been republished, so I have included none of his travels; however, he says what so many travellers feel on meeting with a doubtful reception at home, and says it with so much force and ability that he must be included: furthermore, I had the good luck many years ago to pick up a battered copy of the 1640 edition for fourpence, so I feel that I have a certain property in him.

There are some men, who will scarce believe anything but what they see, and at the same time will not stir an inch from home to be inform'd.

These sort of creatures are not to be satisfied as to the credibility of any thing beyond their own capacities. But for those who only seek a reasonable testimony and probability to believe things. . . .

(THE TRANSLATOR OF HAMEL,
A DUTCHMAN WRECKED OFF KOREA, 1653)

From

LADY CRAVEN'S

A JOURNEY THROUGH THE CRIMEA TO CONSTANTINOPLE

Lady Craven was the daughter of the fourth Earl of Berkeley; she was born in 1750, and in 1767 she was married to William Craven, afterwards the sixth Earl of Craven.

She and her husband did not agree; in 1780, after she had borne six children, they separated and Lady Craven left England. In the following years she travelled extensively: in a series of letters to her great friend the Margrave of Anspach she described France, Italy, Austria, Poland, Russia, Turkey and Greece, which she visited in turn. She published the letters in London in 1789.

Lord Craven died in 1791, and Lady Craven married the Margrave, whose wife had died shortly before.

From about 1777 until long after her marriage with the Margrave Lady Craven managed to attract a great deal of ill-natured scandal. Her beauty may have had as much to do with this as anything else, although it must be allowed that she was uncommonly indiscreet: she was exceptionally beautiful, as one may see from the portraits by Sir Joshua Reynolds, Romney and Vigée le Brun.

Lady Craven wrote some plays and her memoirs. Walpole, who admired her very much, printed her comedy *The Somnambule* at Strawberry Hill. Her memoirs appeared in 1826; if you enjoy reading the Lady Craven of the travels it is a mistake to read the Margravine's memoirs.

Lady Craven died at Naples in 1828.

This extract is taken from *A Journey through the Crimea to Constantinople. In a Series of Letters from the Right Honourable Elizabeth Lady Craven, to his Serene Highness the Margrave of Brandebourg, Anspach, and Bareith. Written in the Year* MDCCLXXXVI. *London: Printed for G. G. J. and J. Robinson, Pater-Noster Row.* MDCCLXXXIX. In order to get Lady Craven to her journey's end it was necessary to cut quite a lot out of her account, particularly the extraneous matter, like her copied history of the Crimea. It was a pity, but without it she would have been too long for inclusion. In this case I have not put in the usual dots—the scars of editing—which point the excisions, partly because they spoil the continuity of the text, which I have endeavoured to preserve, and partly because they would conflict very much with Lady Craven's own system of punctuation.

VIENNA, DECEMBER 14, 1785

I CAME, as I told you I was advised, by a new road; but I should imagine from the difficulties I met with it was the worst,—It is true, some of them were owing to rivers, which, swelled by the late rains, are become torrents which have carried whole villages and many miles of the road before them—

I set out from Venice on the 30th of last month, going by water to Mestre, where my coach and horses met me—

Trevisa, which is the place I next slept at, I arrived at with much difficulty; my coach drawn with ten horses and four oxen—and you can form to yourself no idea of the obstinacy, and provoking phlegm of a German postillion or postmaster—At one place, tired of the snail-like pace I went, I hired a traineau of a peasant, and went on before my carriage—It seems there is an order at every frontier town in Germany, not to suffer strangers who travel without post-horses, to leave the town without staying in it two hours—this the German post-master did not choose to tell me—nor did he refuse me another traineau and horses, but sat with two other fat Germans playing at cards, without deigning to give me any other answer

15

than *Patienza*, to any thing I could say to him—when I recollect the scene of these three fat men playing at cards, their figures, and all I said in Italian to persuade the man and his *patienza* I could die with laughing; however, in about an hour, an officer came in; who looking at me some time, said, *Parlez vous Français?—Mon Dieu, oui Monsieur*, says I; and I found, the post-master's deafness proceeded from his not being able to talk Italian very well, French not at all—so he took me for an impatient boy—and sent me to Coventry—When the gentleman called me Miladi, these three fat Germans deigned to look at me, for I must tell you that in this country, the respect paid to our sex is such, that it is enough for a woman to speak, she is obeyed immediately—and I had a traineau—and six horses for my coach ready in an instant. One night I slept at Klagenfurt, a large town, where one of the Emperor's unmarried sisters lives—I am arrived here at last, through a very beautiful country; but must observe, that whoever wrote L. M. ——'s Letters (for she never wrote a line of them) misrepresents things most terribly—I do really believe, in most things they wished to impose upon the credulity of their readers, and laugh at them—The stoves of this country, which she praises so much, are the most horrid invention you can conceive. The country people in Germany seem to fear the cold very much; the casements of their windows are double; and there being no chimney in the rooms, there is no vent for fumes of any sort—so that the breath of the inhabitants of them rests in drops of steam on all the tables, etc. and the stink and suffocating heat that assails the traveller's senses when he enters any room, particularly where people are, cannot be conceived. I do not believe the German women, of the lower order, are very gentle tempers—for several of them flew into the most violent passions, when I opened a door or window—and shut them again immediately—My only resource upon these occasions was to go out into the yard—

In this town, the German ladies are handsome, accomplished, and civil to a degree you have no idea of; several of them, besides possessing many other languages, read, write, and speak English well; most of the Germans are naturally musicians, and I am sure a young Englishman, with good manners, may every evening here pass his hours in a circle of handsome and accomplished women of the first rank—I have seen no place yet I should so much wish my son to come to as Vienna—Sir Robert Keith assures me he has presented above four hundred noblemen and gentlemen, young countrymen of mine, and has never had reason to complain of them, while we hear and see constantly the follies of the *Anglais* at Paris, where they go to ruin themselves, equally with the *Duchesse* or the *fille d'opera*, and only to be laughed at.

The ladies are tall and fair—more handsome than pretty— There is a great supper at Prince Galitzin's every Sunday night; and at Prince Par's every Monday; the first is the Russian minister, who does great honour to his court, by his sense and politeness here—

P.S. I cannot help adding, that the questions asked travellers by the guards at the frontier towns are most ridiculous—are you married or not?—Do you travel for your pleasure or upon business?—Your name and quality?—It put me in mind of a story told me by the Russian Minister at Venice, of a traveller who being asked his name, answered Boo hoo hoo hoo hoo— Pray, Sir, says the guard, how do you write that? That, Sir, replied the traveller, is your business, I have told you my name;—It is impossible, I think, to answer gravely to questions so perfectly absurd.

VIENNA, DECEMBER 15, 1785

I went with Madame Granieri, the Sardinian Minister's wife, to court. Nothing is more striking, than the variety of the officers' dresses in the Emperor's antichamber—The Hungarian and Polish I think beautiful, and I now am strengthened in the opinion I always had, that every nation ought to preserve the fashion of their country—and there is no necessity for mankind to ape one another in dress—

The Emperor gives a private audience for ladies that are presented to him. There was only myself and the lady who accompanied me that went into his room together. The Emperor was close to the door, and after bowing very civilly, he made us sit upon a sofa, and stood the whole time himself; I stayed three quarters of an hour; there is no occasion to fear staying too long; for when he cannot spare any more time for the audience, or for any other reason chooses to end it; he very civilly says, he will detain you no longer; you then get up, and go to the door, which he opens himself—and thus ends the presentation—The Emperor is like the Queen of France, and the only thing that *genéd* me at all was his not being seated—He converses politely and agreeably—

The first minister here, Prince Kaunitz—is a very extraordinary personage; he is reckoned an able minister and a good patriot; I see in him all that sincerity and frankness which are the constant attendants on a mind truly great—and I believe the welfare of the people at large is his delight; for he asked me what I thought of Vienna; I told him that I had not time to make many observations, but that there was an air of plenty and comfort among the lower sort of people very striking; *même les vendeuses de pommes ont l'air aisé mon Prince;* on my saying this, there was a smile upon his countenance, which I am sure came from his heart; and he condescendingly told me several particulars relative to the markets and provisions, one of which I cannot help thinking very necessary in all large cities—which is, that there is an inspector of the garden-stuff—another for meat—and so on, for all provisions exposed to sale; and if they are not found perfectly good they are flung away—And now we are upon the subject of provisions, I must say, that I never saw such a profusion of things, and those so excellent in their kind, as are served up at the tables here—Green peas, artichokes, and asparagus, I eat every day—The crawfish are as large as the Chichester lobsters; and the pheasants from Bohemia have a flavour you can form no idea of—Yet I do not think the people are gourmands; but they pique themselves on having the greatest abundance and the best sort of eatables of every kind. The forests and rivers of this country do not in a small degree contribute to the possibility of these things—for with us, our cooks cannot produce wild boar and venison, *gelinottes*, and *coqs de bruyères*; or crawfish as big as lobsters—

There is one thing here that shocks me, and that is, that every lower class of women paint white—and that even girls of ten years old going of errands in the street are painted—What their reason for so doing is I cannot guess; for the Germans are generally fair.

There are great assemblies here as in London; and I repeat it, there are women here with whom I could pass my life—

They have not the cold silent reserve of English women, nor the impertinent *interêt* for me, of the French ladies—

The public works (such as sweeping the streets, etc., etc.) are done by malefactors, who, chained two and two, perform their task attended by a guard—

P.S. You cannot buy a drug at the apothecaries here, without an order from a physician—A very prudent caution against the madness of those who choose to finish their existence with a dose of laudanum, or their neighbours with one of arsenic—

WARSAW, JANUARY 7, 1786

I got away as fast as I possibly could from Vienna; for if I had staid a week longer, I am convinced I should have staid the whole winter—

WARSAW, JANUARY, 1786

The entrance into the town of Cracow exhibits a melancholy proof that confusion ever ends in ruin—The system of government in Poland is of all others the surest source of confusion that ever yet was imagined by mankind—an elected King from the noble families, most of which think they have a right to royalty, and several really are entitled to it—

Dirty suburbs filled with Jews—and the Emperor's eagle, are the only objects that precede the gates of Cracow—these gates are pierced by many a ball. . . .

I had letters for several Polish ladies at Cracow—but I staid only to rest myself, and get a traineau made; for I was told I might go thus—but a couple of miles from the town I was obliged to take my coach off the sledge; and here I must observe, Sir, that the Prince Galitzin at Vienna, was very much mistaken, when he told me, he should advise me to have just such a coach as mine made, if I were not already mistress of such a one—

I hung more than once upon fir-trees; the track of the road being too narrow for my wide carriage—and when travellers come into Germany—I think they ought to part with their

French and English carriages—as the carriages of our northern countries are liable to inconveniences and accidents—

I staid two hours one night, so fastened with the hind-wheel upon a fir-tree, that six men could not stir it—and peasants were called to cut down the tree—before I could proceed—

When I arrived at Warsaw, I found my apartments had been warmed and ready two days before my arrival; the Comte de Stackelberg having bespoke them, by the desire of Prince Galitzin—and the Russian Minister C—— de S—— waited on me—He is sensible, and even witty—he presented me to the King, the day after my arrival, in the evening—The King received us in his study; I was accompanied by the Grand Marechal's wife, who is one of the King's nieces—You, Sir, do not speak better French and English than that amiable Sovereign—he told me he had been in England thirty years past, and asked me if Mr. W—— [alpole] was still living—not only living I replied, Sir; but in good spirits; for I have a charming letter in my pocket from him—He said, if there was nothing imprudent in his request, he would ask to see it. He imagined Mr. W.'s stile must be uncommon; I gave him the letter—he put it in his pocket after reading it, and told me, as his sister, the Princess of Cracovia did not understand English, he should translate it into French for her; and if I would dine with him two days after, he would read me his translation, which indeed surprized me—He must be a very elegant writer in every language he chooses to profess—I wish I had dared to have asked him for a copy—

I make visits in a new stile here—in the Comte de Stackelberg's coach and six—and a couple of equerries at the two coach windows on horseback—The Polish ladies seem to have much taste—magnificence—spirit and gaiety—they are polite and lively—excessively accomplished—partial to the English.

I have seen several dwarfs here—who with equerries stand in drawing-rooms of the great houses, and hear all the conversation that passes—an uncomfortable custom I think; and which in any other country would be dangerous; but here servants and dependants are the absolute property of the master—and their fidelity in general is equal to their subjection; to the credit of the Polish nobles, I believe there are few servants that, having proved for eight or ten years their attachment, are not dismissed with a pension for life. I found the French maid, the Princess C—— had from me, in this situation; nine years service had obtained a hundred pounds a year, and a farm of sixty acres of land for the rest of her life—she seems the happiest creature in the world—

I am sorry to quit this place so soon; not that there is anything in this flat country that would tempt me to see the beauties of it in the spring—but the King's acquaintance, with that of some of the ladies—and Monsieur de Stackelberg's conversation, I am sorry to quit.

PETERSBURGH, FEBRUARY 8, 1786

The road between Warsaw and this place is one insipid flat—except just in and about the town of Nerva, where I took a sledge and flew hither.

I am something like a country Miss, gaping at the window all day here—every creature that goes about the streets, seem as if they were in a violent hurry—they drive full gallop—traineaus with one horse ply at the corners of the streets as do our hackney-coaches and chairs—Mr. S—— informed me, it belonged to my dignity to have six horses to my coach, in order to pay my visits; and I beg you will imagine my surprise, when I found I had a coachman on the box, with three postillions, one to each pair of horses—and these sitting on the right-hand, I go thus, full gallop, running races with every other *attelage* that falls in my way—the streets are luckily wide—and custom makes the danger less than one should imagine.

PETERSBURGH, FRIDAY, FEBRUARY 18, 1786

I was to have been presented to the Empress next Sunday—but she graciously sent me word to come to the Hermitage on Thursday, where she keeps her court in the evening every week—and has alternately a French play or an Italian opera—I cannot conceive why this building which she has added to the palace is called the Hermitage; it is a long suite of rooms, full of fine pictures. You are not ignorant, dear Sir, of the many collections the Empress has purchased; among the rest Lord Orford's; Petersburgh is a chearful and fine looking town; the streets are extremely wide and long—the houses stucco'd to imitate white stone; none above three stories high—which certainly adds to the lively and airy appearance of them— I think, Sir, that not only the town, but the manner of living is upon too large a scale; the nobles seem to vie with one another in extravagancies of every sort, particularly in foreign luxuries and fashion—The fashion of the day is most ridiculous and improper for this climate; French gauzes and flowers were not intended for Russian beauties—and they are sold at a price here which must ruin the buyers.

There are buildings erected for the reception of Arts and Sciences of every kind; for artists or amateurs, though but the surplus of Italy, France and England, would find handsome encouragement and house-room from the Empress, whose respect for talents, and generosity to those who possess them, have induced some, and would many more, to fix in the present capital of this vast empire; but alas! Sir, eight months of winter; and the horrid cold I feel, must congeal the warmest imagination.

From Cherson, the new town on the Turkish frontiers, which is one thousand six hundred miles from hence, are brought many provisions; from Archangel likewise this town is provided, and from Astracan on the Caspian Sea, near two thousand miles, all the dainties, such as grapes, pease, beans, artichokes, are brought—It is natural to suppose, that the necessaries of life are dear, from these circumstances; but some of them are extremely cheap—and I believe Russia is one of the cheapest countries in the world to live in; if French wines and fashions, and English comforts can be dispensed with— To these last I never felt so much attachment as at this moment —*Dans le Ligne Anglais*, a quarter of this town, where the English merchants live, I find English grates, English coal, and English hospitality, to make me welcome, and the fireside chearful—

We are in the last part of the carnival and balls; those given by the Ambassadors are very superb—Mr. de Segur, and the Duc de Serra Capriola, the Neapolitan Minister, have each given one in a very magnificent style—

I was presented to the Grand Duchess the same night that I waited upon the Empress—She has since been brought to bed—There are some young Russian ladies very pretty and much accomplished—many of them sigh after a different climate from their own—here the houses are decorated with the most sumptuous furniture from every country—but you come into a drawing-room, where the floor is of the finest inlaid woods, through a staircase made of the coarsest wood in the rudest manner, and stinking with dirt—The postillions wear sheep-skins—and at a ball, when a nobleman has proposed his hand to a fair lady—he often kisses her before the whole company—

You may have heard much of Prince Potemkin; I see him everywhere, but he is reserved and converses very little with ladies—I was invited by him to dine in an immense palace he is building in the suburbs; the only room finished is too particular not to be described; it is three hundred feet in length, and on the side opposite the windows there are two rows of stone pillars, whose height and breadth are proportioned to the immense size of the room, which is an oblong square; in the centre of which on the side where the windows are, it is formed into a semi-circle or what we call a bow—which bow forms another large space independent of, though in the room; this space was laid out by his English gardener into a shrubbery with borders of flowers, hyacinths, and narcissuses—myrtles, orange-trees, etc., etc. were in plenty—We were seven or eight ladies, and as many men—immense stoves concealed by the pillars, were heated in order to make such a hall in such a climate supportable—but I came home quite ill with cold—It was there I heard that extraordinary music performed by men and boys, each blowing a straight horn adapted to their size—sixty-five of these musicians produce a very harmonious melody, something like an immense organ. The music, the room, the cold, all was gigantic. I sat by Prince Potemkin at dinner; but except asking me to eat and drink, I cannot say I heard the sound of his voice—

Justice obliges me to say, the Empress does all she can to invite politeness, science and comforts from other countries, to cheer these regions of ice—but, until she can alter the climate, I believe it is a fruitless trial—I am informed the spring, or rather the time of year we call spring, is more melancholy than winter here, so I shall hasten my departure; but a conversation I had with the Swedish Minister, a few days past, will make me give up entirely the thoughts of returning into Germany through

23

Sweden and Denmark—I shall in my next have the honour of repeating it to you.

I promised to give you an account of the conversation with the Minister, here it is—

M. S—— I have been told, that Miladi wishes to do me the honour of consulting me upon the journey she is about to take.

M—— Yes, Monsieur, people say that it is very risky to traverse these ice fields, and I desire to know how to do so because, whichever way I go, I wish to travel mostly in a traineau, as I detest the jolting of an ordinary carriage, and find a traineau very agreeable—

M. S—— Does Miladi know that, to travel from here to Sweden, a third horse is harnessed in front of the two others; at a very considerable distance in the dangerous parts—

M—— What do you mean by dangerous parts?—

M. S—— Where the ice is liable to break—and the horse is harnessed with very long cords; he is called the *enfant perdu*—because, if the ice cracks, the cords are quickly cut; the horse disappears for ever, and the travellers retrace their steps—

M—— As I have never started on a voyage in order to retrace my steps, and as it seems that I run the risk of becoming an *enfant perdu* myself, if I undertake this journey—I will put off my visit to your country for another occasion, *Monsieur l'Ambassadeur*; and so we talked of other things—

I shall now prepare every thing to visit the Crimea or rather the Tauride; I have been told it is a very beautiful country; and I confess I am not sorry this *enfant perdu* gives me a good excuse for turning my steps towards Constantinople—

I am speaking without any partiality, dear Sir; but I do not see here the prejudices of the English, the conceit of the French, nor the stiff German pride—which national foibles make often good people of each nation extremely disagreeable. I am assured the Russians are deceitful—it may be so; but as I do not desire to have intimacies, I am much better pleased to find new acquaintances pleasant and civil than morose or pert—

P.S. I am not a little surprised to hear people say: I shall inherit so many hundred peasants, or such a one lost a village—it is the number of men, and not of acres, that make a fortune great here; so that a plague or any distemper that would prove mortal to the peasants, would be death to the nobles' pockets likewise—

24

The Vicechancellor, Comte d'Osterman, is obliged to have a table for sixty foreigners every Wednesday; and a widow, Princess de Galitzin, a supper once a week—at Mons. d'Osterman's too, a ball every Sunday night. The Empress is at the expence of these dinners and suppers—and, I confess, I think it an excellent and royal idea, to be certain of having houses open for the entertainment of foreign ministers and strangers of distinction—There is a custom here which I think very abominable; noblemen, who are engaged to marry young ladies, make no ceremony, but embrace them in the midst of a large company at a ball—

I have mentioned to a few people my intention of seeing the Crimea; and I am told that the air is unwholesome, the waters poisonous, and that I shall certainly die if I go there; but as in the great world a new acquired country, like a new beauty, finds detractors, I am not in the least alarmed; for a person, not a Russian, who has been there on speculation, has given me so charming a description of it, that I should not be sorry to purchase a Tartarian estate.

MOSCOW, FEBRUARY 29, 1786

I left my coach at Petersburgh, and hired for myself and my small suite, the carriages of the country, called Kibitkas; they are exactly like cradles, the head having windows to the front which let down; I can sit or lay down, and feel in one like a great child, very comfortably defended from the cold by pillows and blankets—These carriages are upon sledges, and where the road is good, this conveyance is comfortable and not fatiguing; but from the incredible quantity of sledges that go constantly upon the track of snow, it is worn in tracks like a road; and from the shaking and violent thumps the carriage receives, I am convinced the hardest head might be broken. I was overturned twice; the postillions I fancy are used to such accidents; for they get quietly off their horse, set the carriage up again, and never ask if the traveller is hurt—Their method of driving is singular; they sit behind three horses that are harnessed abreast—a shrill whistling noise, or a savage kind of shriek is the signal for the horses to set off, which they do full gallop; and when their pace slackens, the driver waves his

25

right-hand, shrieks or whistles, and the horses obey. I would never advise a traveller to set out from Petersburgh as I have, just at the end of the carnival; he might with some reason suppose it is a religious duty for the Russian peasant to be drunk; in most villages I saw a sledge loaded with young men and women in such a manner, that four horses would have been more proper to draw it than one, which wretched beast was obliged to fly with this noisy company up and down the village, which is generally composed of houses in straight rows on each side of the public road—The girls are dressed in their holiday-clothes, and some are beautiful, and do not look less so from various coloured handkerchiefs tied over their forehead, in a becoming and *pittoresque* manner. The Russian peasant is a fine, stout, straight, well-looking man; some of the women, as I said before, are uncommonly pretty; but the general whiteness of their teeth is something that cannot be conceived; it frequently happened that all the men of the village were in a circle round my carriages—and rows of the most beautiful oriental pearl cannot be more regular and white than their teeth—It is a matter of great astonishment to me, how the infants outlive the treatment they receive, till they are able to crawl into the air; there is a kind of space or *entresol* over every stove, in which the husband, wife and children lie the greatest part of the day, and where they sleep at night—the heat appeared to me so great that I have no conception how they bear it; but they were as much surprised at me for seeking a door or window in every house I was obliged to go into, as I could possibly be at their living in a manner without air. The children look all pale and sickly, till they are five or six years old. The houses and dresses of the peasants are by no means uncomfortable; the first is generally composed of wood, the latter of sheep-skins; but trees laid horizontally one upon another makes a very strong wall, and the climate requires a warm skin for clothing—It might appear to English minds, that a people who are in a manner the property of their lord, suffer many of the afflictions that attend slavery; but the very circumstances of their persons being the property insures them the indulgence of their master for the preservation of their lives; and that master stands between them and the power of a despotic government or a brutal soldiery. Beside, my dear Sir, the invaluable advantage which these peasants have, as in paying annually a very small sum each, and cultivating as many acres of land as he thinks fit, his fortune depends entirely upon his own industry; each man only pays about the value of half-a-guinea a year—If his lord would raise this tax too high, or make their vassals suffer—misery and desertion would ruin his fortune, not theirs.

MOSCOW, MARCH 3, 1786

I believe I have not told you, that I am possessed of all the instructions to proceed upon this new journey in a very pleasant manner. The commanders at Krementchouck and at Cherson are informed of my intention to proceed to Perekop, where I shall enter into that peninsula called the Tauride . . . in which there is at present about thirty thousand of the Empress's troops, including five thousand Cossacks in her pay; which I am very curious to see. The Khan's palaces, noble Tartar houses, and others are prepared for her reception, in which I am assured I shall be received and treated perfectly well—

CHERSON, MARCH 9, 1786

I was obliged to put my kibitkas on wheels at a vile little town called Soumi, before I arrived at Pultawa—Notwithstanding there might have been many things worth stopping to look at in the immense town of Moscow, I was so impatient to meet the spring, that I would not send my name to any person whose civilities would have obliged me to stay. I cannot say that Moscow gives me any idea than of a large village, or many villages joined, as the houses stand at such a distance, and it is such a terrible way to go to visit things or people, that I should have made as many long journeys in a week, as there are days in one, had I staid—What is particularly gaudy and ugly at Moscow are the steeples—square lumps of different coloured bricks and gilt spires or ovals; they make a very Gothic appearance, but it is thought a public beauty here; a widow lady was just dead, who having outlived all the people that she loved, she left an immense sum of money to gild with the purest gold, the top of one of the steeples—

27

At Soumi I conversed with a brother of Prince Kourakin's and a Mr. Lanskoy, both officers quartered there; and to whom I was indebted for a lodging: they obliged a Jew to give me up a new little house he was upon the point of inhabiting—The thaw had come on so quickly that I was obliged to stay two days while my carriages were taken off the sledges—

There is no gentleman's house at Pultawa; I slept at my banker's, and walked all about the skirts of the town—

CHERSON, MARCH 12, 1786

This place is situated upon the Dneiper, which falls into the Black sea; the only inconvenience of the Docks here is that the ships, when built, are obliged to be taken with camels into that part of the channel deep enough to receive them—The town is not at present very large, though there are many new houses and a church built after pretty models; good architecture of white stone—There are no trees near this place; [Colonel] Korsakof is trying to make large plantations; the town is entirely furnished with fuel by reeds, of which there is an inexhaustible forest in the shallows of the Boristhenes, just facing Cherson—Rails, and even temporary houses are made of them—Korsakof, and a Captain Mordwinof, who both have been educated in England, will, I have no doubt, make a distinguished figure in the military annals of Russia; Mordwinof is a sea-officer, and superintends the ship-building here—there are some very pretty frigates on the stocks. Repninskai is the governor's name, and he has a young wife, who is very civil; my lodging is a large house built for a Greek Archbishop—but, being empty, was appropriated to my use: I have remonstrated here, but in vain, against having centinels, and the guard turning out as I pass through the gates. The Emperor's Consul has a wife who wears a Greek dress here; I think it by no means becoming—I have nothing but maps and plans of various sorts in my head at present, having looked over all such as my curiosity could induce me to ask for—The fortifications and plantations are executed here by malefactors, whose chains and fierce looks struck horror into my heart, as I walked over them, particularly when I was informed there are between three and four thousand—

28

Mordwinof informs me, the frigate which is to convey me to Constantinople is prepared, and is to wait my pleasure at one of the seaports in the Crimea, and that the Comte de Wynowitch, who commands at Sevastopole has directions to accommodate me in the best manner—

I went in a barge for about two hours down the Boristhenes, and landed on the shore opposite to that on which Cherson stands. A carriage and horses belonging to a Major who commands a post about two hours drive from the place where I landed were waiting, and these conveyed me to his house, where I found a great dinner prepared, and he gave me some excellent fresh-butter made of Buffalo's milk; this poor man has just lost a wife he loved, and who was the only delight he could possess in a most disagreeable spot, marshy, low, and where he can have no other amusement but the troops— From thence I crossed the plains of Perekop, on which nothing but a large coarse grass grows, which is burnt at certain periods of the year,—All this country, like that between Cherson and Chrementchruk, is called Steps—I should call it desart; except where the post-horses are found, not a tree not a habitation is to be seen—But one thing which delighted me much, for several miles after I had quitted Cherson, was the immense flocks of birds—bustards, which I took at a certain distance for herds of calves—and millions of a small bird about the size of a pigeon, cinnamon colour and white—droves of a kind of wild small goose, cinnamon colour, brown, and white.

Just without the fortress of Perekop I was obliged to send one of my servants to a Tartar village to get a pass; the servant whom I sent, whose ridiculous fears through the whole journey have not a little amused me, came back pale as death—He told me the chiefs were sitting in a circle smoaking, that they were very ill black-looking people—I looked at the pass, it was in Turkish or Tartarian characters. I saw there two camels drawing a cart—This village gave me no great opinion of Tartarian cleanliness, a more dirty miserable looking place I never saw—The land at Perekop is but six miles across from the sea of Asoph, or rather an arm of it called the Suash, to the Black Sea—The Crimea might with great ease be made an island; after leaving Perekop, the country is exactly like what we call downs in England, and the turf is like the finest green velvet—The horses flew along; and though there was not a horse in the stables of the post-houses, I did not wait long to have them harnessed; the Cossacks have the furnishing of the horses—and versts or mile-stones are put up; the horses were all grazing on the plain at some distance, but the instant they see their Cossack come out with a little corn the whole herd surrounds him, and he takes those he pleases—The posts were sometimes in a deserted Tartarian village, and sometimes the only habitation for the stable-keeper was a hut made under ground, a common habitation in this country, where the sun is so extremely hot, and there is no shade of any sort. To the left of Perekop I saw several salt lakes about the third post—it was a most beautiful sight. About sun-set, I arrived at a Tartarian village, of houses or rather huts straggling in a circle without fence of any kind—I stopped there and made tea; that I might go on, as far as I could that night—You must not suppose, my dear Sir, though I have left my coach and harp at Petersburgh, that I have not all my little necessities even in a kibitka—a tin-kettle in a basket holds my tea equipage, and I have my English side-saddle tied behind my carriage—What I have chiefly lived upon is new milk, in which I melt a little chocolate. At every place I have stopped at I asked to taste the water from curiosity, I have always found it perfectly good—

I can easily suppose people jealous of Prince Potemkin's merit; his having the government of the Tauride, or commanding the troops in it, may have caused the invention of a thousand ill-natured lies about this new country, in order to lessen the share of praise which is his due, in the attainment of preservation of it—but I see nothing at present which can justify the idea of the country's being unwholesome.

KARASBAYER, APRIL 4, 1786

About half an hour after ten last night I ordered my servants not to have the horses put to, as I intended to sleep; I had not an idea of getting out of it, as our Post was a vile Tartar village; in a few minutes the servants called me, and said, the General's nephew and son were arrived to meet me, and very sorry to find I had quitted Perekop, as they had orders to escort me from thence. I opened my carriage and saw two very pretty looking young men; I told them I should certainly not think of detaining them; and we set off, nor did I suspect that there were any persons with me but them: at — o'clock I let down the forepart of my carriage to see the sun rise; when, to my great surprise, I saw a guard of between twenty and thirty Cossacks, with an officer, who was close to the fore-wheel of the carriage; upon seeing me he smiled and pulled off his cap—his companions gave a most violent shriek, and horses, carriages, and all increased their pace, so that the horses in the carriage behind mine took fright, ran away, and running against my carriage very nearly overturned it; and when I asked what occasioned this event, I found my Cossack escort, seeing my carriage shut, thought I was dead; as a Cossack has no idea that a person in health can travel in a carriage that is not open, and the shout I had heard, the smile I had seen, was the surprise they had felt, that the young English princess, as they called me, was alive; as they believed it was only my corpse that was conveying to Karasbayar to be buried—They always ride with long pikes, holding the points upwards; the Tartars ride with pikes, but they hold the ends of theirs to the ground—About six I passed the Tartar town of Karasbayar, lying to the left—and arrived at the General's house, a very good one, newly built for the reception of the Empress; the General Kokotchki, his brother the governor, and almost all the general officers were up and dressed, upon the steps of the house I found myself in my night-cap, a most tired and forlorn figure, in the midst of well-powdered men, and as many stars and ribbons around me as if I had been at a birth-day at St. James's—I retired but rose again at one, dressed and dined, and looked about me; this house is situated near the river Karasou or Black-water, which bathes the lawn before the house, and runs in many windings towards the town; it is narrow, rapid, and very clear; this is a most rural and lovely spot, very well calculated to give the Empress a good opinion of her new kingdom, for so it may be called. I had a Cossack chief presented to me, a soldier-like white-haired figure, he wore a ribband and order the Empress had given him set round with brilliants—The general told me he was sorry he was not thirty years younger, as the Empress had not a braver officer in her service—In the evening, in an amazing large hall, several different bands of music played; and I heard the national songs of the Russian peasants—which are so singular that I cannot forbear endeavouring to give you some idea of them—One man stands in the midst of three or four, who make a circle round him; seven or eight make a second round those; a third is composed of a greater number; the man in the middle of this groupe begins, and when he has sung one verse, the first circle accompany him, and then the second, till they become so animated, and the noise so great, that it was with difficulty the officers could stop them—What is very singular they sing in parts, and though the music is not much varied, nor the tune fine, yet as some take thirds and fifths as their ear direct, in perfect harmony, it is by no means unpleasing—If you ask one of them why he does not sing the same note as the man before him—he does not know what you mean—The subjects of these ballads are, hunting, war, or counterfeiting the graduations between soberness into intoxication—and very diverting. As these singers were only young Russian peasants, they began with great timidity, but by little and little ended in a kind of wild jollity, which made us all laugh very heartily—The Governor's residence is not here, but at a place called Atchmechet; he is only come here to meet and conduct me through the Crimea; he is a grave sensible mild man. I am told he has conciliated the Tartars to their change of sovereign very much by his gentleness and firmness —To their honour, I find none would stay who could not bear the idea of taking the oaths of allegiance—but are gone towards Mount Caucasus—They have repented since, but it was too late—All the country here is downs except the borders of vallies, where rice is cultivated, and what the Tartars call gardens, which I call orchards—I cannot tell you, Sir, with what respect and attention I am treated here, and how good-naturedly all the questions I ask are answered—

There is an Albanian Chief here, though his post is at Balaklava, a sea-port; he is distinguished by the Empress likewise for his bravery; his dress differs much from the Cossack; it is something like the ancient Romans—he is an elderly man too. In a day or two I shall take my leave of this place for Batcheserai, the principal town and formerly the chief residence of the Khans.

In the evening I went in a carriage with the governor and general to Karasbayar—and on the road saw a mock battle between the Cossacks—As I was not apprised before-hand, I confess the beginning of it astonished me very much—I saw the Cossack guard on each side the carriage spring from their stirrups, with their feet on the saddle and gallop away thus with a loud shriek—The General smiled at my astonished looks—and told me the Cossack Chief had ordered an entertainment for me—and desired me to get out and stand on the rising part of the down, facing that where a troop of Cossacks was posted—which I saw advancing with a slow pace—a detached Cossack of the adverse party approached the troop, and turning round sought his scattered companions, who were in search like him of the little army—they approached, but not in a squadron, some on the left, some on the right, some before, some behind the troop—a shriek—a pistol fired, were the signals of battle—the troop was obliged to divide in order to face an enemy that attacked it on all sides—The greatest scene of hurry and agility ensued; one had seized his enemy, pulled him off his horse, and was upon the point of stripping him[1], when one of the prisoner's party came up, laid him to the ground, remounted his companion, and rode off with the horse of the first victor—Some flung themselves off their horses to tear their foe to the ground—alternately they pursued or were pursuing, their pikes, their pistols, their hangers all were made use of—and when the parties were completely engaged together, it was difficult to see all the adroit manoeuvres that passed—

I arrived at the town, and was led to the Kadi's house, where his wife received me, and no male creature was suffered to come into the room, except the interpreter and a young Russian nobleman only twelve years of age. This woman had a kind of turban on, with some indifferent diamonds and pearls upon it. Her nails were dyed scarlet, her face painted white and red, the veins blue; she appeared to me to be a little shrivelled woman of near sixty, but I was told she was not above fifty—She had a kind of robe and vest on, and her

[1]A Cossack if he can avoid it never kills his enemy before he has stripped him, because the spoils are his property, and he fears the blood should spoil the dress—

girdle was a handkerchief embroidered with gold and a variety of colours—She made me a sign to sit down; and my gloves seeming to excite much uneasiness in her I took them off—upon which she drew near, smiled, took one of my hands between her's, and winked and nodded as a sign of approbation—but she felt my arm up beyond the elbow, half way up my shoulder, winking and nodding—I began to wonder where this extraordinary examination would end—which it did there—Coffee was brought, and after that rose-leaves made into sweetmeats—both of which the interpreter obliged me to taste—the sweetmeats are introduced last, and among the Orientals they are a signal that the visit must end—Our conversation by the interpreter was not very entertaining—A Tartar house is a very slight building of one story only—no chair, table, or piece of furniture in wood to be seen—large cushions are ranged round the room, on which we sat or reclined—As the visit was at an end, I curtsied and she bowed.

BATCHESERAI, APRIL 8, 1786

In my way hither I dined at the Cossack Chief's post—and my entertainment was truly Cossack—a long table for thirty people—at one end a half-grown pig roasted whole—at the other a half-grown sheep, whole likewise—in the middle of the table an immense tureen of curdled milk—there were several side-dishes made for me and the Russians, as well as the cook could imagine to our taste—The old warrior would fain have made me taste above thirty sorts of wine from his country, the borders of the Don; but I contented myself with three or four, and some were very good. After dinner from the windows, I saw a fine mock battle between the Cossacks; and I saw three Calmoucks, the ugliest fiercest looking men imaginable, with their eyes set in their head, inclining down to their nose, and uncommonly square jaw-bones—These Calmoucks are so dexterous with bows and arrows that one killed a goose at a hundred paces, and the other broke an egg at fifty—The young Cossack officers tried their skill with them, but they were perfectly novices in comparison to them—they sung and danced, but their steps and their tones were equally insipid, void of grace and harmony.

34

When a Cossack is sick he drinks sour milk for a few days, and that is the only remedy the Cossacks have for fevers—

At night I lodged at a house that had belonged to a noble Tartar, where there is a Russian post, with about twelve hundred of the finest men I ever saw, and uncommonly tall. A Tartarian house has always another building at a little distance from it, for the convenience of travellers or strangers, whom the noble Tartar always treats with the greatest hospitality—Here the General parted from us. I proceeded in the Governor's carriage with him thus far; the rest of our company went to see Kaffa or Theodosia. I go to meet them tomorrow, at a place called Mangouss—We had only two Cossacks with us, as the General, to please the Tartars, never is escorted by a military party. Batcheserai is situated in so steep a valley, that some of the hanging pieces of rock seem ready to fall and crush the houses—About a mile from the town on the left, I saw a troop of well-dressed Tartars, there were above a hundred on horseback; the Kaima-Kan[1] was at the head of this company, who were come out to meet and escort us, but I who did not know this, asked the Governor if there was a Russian post here, which there is above the town, of a thousand men—There are five thousand Tartar inhabitants here; I do not believe there was a man left in his house, the streets being lined with Tartarian men on each side; their countenances were very singular, most of them kept their eyes fixed on the ground, as we passed; but some just looked up, and, as if they were afraid of seeing a woman's face uncovered, hastily cast their eyes downward again; some diverted at the novelty, looked and laughed very much—There is a great trade here of blades for swords, hangers, and knives—I am assured many made here are not to be distinguished from those of Damascus—

The Khan's palace is an irregular building, the greatest part of it is one floor raised upon pillars of wood painted and gilt in a fanciful and lively manner—the arch, or last doorway, has fine proportions, a large inscription in gilt letters is the chief ornament—I am told it was perfectly in ruins, but the Governor has had it repaired, new gilt, and painted for the Empress's

---

[1] That word means the Khan's first minister—a person called him cream of Tartar—which I fearing he should be told of, turned into the cream of the Tartars—which he said was no wonder; as he was so—

reception—Court within court, and garden within garden, make a variety of apartments where the Khan walked from his own residence to the Harem, which is spacious and higher than the other buildings—What I thought pretty enough was that several of the square places under his apartment were paved with marble, and have in the centre fountains which play constantly—My room is a square of more than forty feet, having two rows of windows one above the other on three sides, and it was with difficulty I found a place to have my bed put up in—

I never saw such a variety of colours—different coloured gold and silver mixed together—The Kaima-Kan, and two other principal Tartars, supped with us, and I find nothing can exceed the ignorance and simplicity of these people—The Kaima-Kan is the Khan's first minister—He is totally ignorant of the geography of his own country; and says that England and Petersburgh are the same thing—I am to dine with his sister tomorrow; she is married to a rich Tartar, who has given a certain yearly sum to possess, solely, the profits of the soap mines—For among the excellent productions of this peninsula, there is a mine of earth exactly like soap, and reckoned very good for the skin—the Turkish women consume a great quantity of it at Constantinople—and I am told this Tartar makes an immense income from it—I saw from the windows a kind of dome which raised my curiosity, and I am told it is a monument built to the memory of a Christian wife, which the Khan loved so tenderly that he was inconsolable for her loss; and that he had placed it there, that he might have the satisfaction of looking at the building which contained her remains. This Tartar Khan must have a soul worthy of being loved by a Christian wife I think—

SEVASTOPOLE, APRIL 12, 1786

I have been at Soudak, where the foundations yet remain of a very large town, which was rebuilt by the Genoese, on the descent of steep rocks—

To the left of the town there is a fine harbour—it is upon this southern part of the peninsula that vines are cultivated, and grow wild in great abundance—at present only a few private people there have vineyards of their own—There is little good wine made, and the Empress has indeed a Frenchman who seems to care only about the strength of the wine being sufficient to make brandy, which he distils in great quantities—He is settled at Soudak at present, and probably will make a great fortune, but not teach the culture of vines to the Russians—From Soudak I went to Atchmetchet, the residence of the Governor—

I find a thirty-six gun frigate, under the disguise of a merchant-ship, had been fitted out for me, and had been ready above a fortnight; I crossed an arm of the sea in the Comte de Wynowitch's barge to arrive here—

There were several Turkish boats in the harbour, but there was a line on the shore marked with fires which they were not permitted to pass—The Turks came to sell oranges, and every precaution is taken to prevent their communicating the plague; so that although they may come on shore, they are obliged to heap their oranges within the space allotted to them, and bargain at a distance—We were above thirty people at table, and I returned with my company to Sevastopole in carriages—I called just now the Turkish vessels boats—but I am told they are ships—a most dangerous sort of conveyance for men or merchandise in my opinion—long, narrow, and top-heavy—The frigate prepared for me seems a good ship—the three sea-officers who go with me, have never been at Constantinople; we go as merchants, for by a treaty between the Porte and Russia, trading vessels may come from the Black Sea into the Canal of Constantinople, but not men of war. We have a Greek pilot on board, who is to steer us safe, please Heaven. I am told we are not to be much more than two days in our passage.

PALAIS DE FRANCE, PERA, APRIL 20, 1786

I am safely arrived, dear Sir, and hasten to inform you how I made my voyage. I set out the 13th at five in the morning; Mr. de Wynowitch took me out of the harbour in a small frigate, and after seeing me safe in my cabbin took leave. He gave me a royal salute, and as his guns fired, we set sail with a fair wind; we had not been two days at sea before we were becalmed; and we lay three days and three nights, wishing for wind, which came on at last very fresh with rain—On the seventh day, the Greek pilot, the only person on board who had ever been at Constantinople, was dead drunk and incapable of speaking, much less of steering the ship—The officers were greatly alarmed, and there was a long consultation between them and the rest of the company—I luckily had a small map of the Black Sea, and the entrance of the Canal—which alone was our guide—As to me I had dressed myself in a riding habit, and had a small box in one hand, an umbrella in the other, and had told the captain I was determined to get into the boat and land on the Turkish shore, rather than lose sight of the Canal, or sail into it without being quite sure that we were right—There is a large rock on the European shore, which is so far distant from it that, unless a map or pilot directs the mariner, he must infallibly take it for the entrance of the Bosphorus, and several hundreds of Turkish boats are wrecked upon it yearly.

The gentlemen and officers stood all the morning upon deck, watching the shore; we had ran then above ninety leagues to the left, always seeing land, which was owing to the currents which had taken our ship during the three days calm, so much more to the right—As to me I stood between decks till the Captain told me to come and look at a village, church, or something—it was a Turkish Minaret, and a few moments afterward we saw that rock I dreaded so much, upon which there are about a thousand Turkish vessels that perish constantly every year, as the Turks forget as they leave it to the left in coming out, they must leave it to the right in going in—

To return to my voyage, Sir: you may judge how infinitely comfortable I felt, in being at anchor about six in the evening; escaped from all the dangers I had been threatened with upon the Black Sea; and the ugly circumstance that attended us when we were about to take our leave of it. I had so many birds, among which was a most beautiful milk-white small heron, that had taken refuge in the ship, that my cabbin looked like a bird-shop—We supped on board very comfortably, and I took some hours rest; and the next morning we put ourselves in the long-boat, and were rowed to Mr. de Bulkalow's house at Bouyukdere, but he was at Pera, so we were rowed by a Turkish boat down to Pera—The Bosphorus takes a sudden turn at Bouyukdere—I refer you to Mr. Gibbon, Sir, for his account of the singular situation of Constantinople, my pen will repeat feebly what he has described in language majestic as the subject deserves—But I am certain no landscape can amuse or please in comparison with the varied view, which the borders of this famed Straight compose—Rocks, verdure, ancient castles, built on the summit of the hills by the Genoese—modern Kiosks[1], Minarets, and large platane-trees, rising promiscuous in the vallies—large meadows—multitudes of people, and boats swarming on the shore and on the water; and what was particular, nothing to be seen like a formal French garden—The Turks have so great a respect for natural beauties, that if they must build a house where a tree stands, they leave a large hole for the tree to pass through and increase in size, they think the branches of it the prettiest ornament for the top of the house. The coast is so safe that a large fleet of Turkish vessels is to be seen in every creek, masts of which are intermingled with the trees, and a graceful confusion and variety make this living picture the most poignant scene I ever beheld.

Judge of Mr. de Bulakow's surprise, when he had opened his letters and read my name; he had scarcely time to offer me his services, when Mr. de Choiseul's people came and claimed me from their master, who had been prepared for three weeks before for my arrival, by Mr. de Segur at Petersburgh; and I confess, from the character I had heard of him, I was not at all sorry that he claimed my society as his *droit*—And now I have heard him speak, I am extremely glad that I am to profit by his conversation and company, both of which are as much to be desired as talents and politeness can make them. Adieu for to-day—I am sun-burnt, tired, but likewise pleased beyond measure—yes, Sir, pleased to be here, and to call myself by the honoured name of

Your affectionate sister,

E. C——.

---

[1] Kiosk means a summer-house with blinds all round.

From

DR. JOHN MOORE'S

A VIEW OF SOCIETY AND MANNERS IN FRANCE,

SWITZERLAND, AND GERMANY:

With Anecdotes Relating to Some Eminent Characters.

Dr. John Moore was born in 1729: he studied at Glasgow, where he knew Smollett, and became an Army surgeon. Later he took his doctorate at Glasgow, where he practised for some time. The seventh Duke of Hamilton was put under his care, but he died at the age of 15, and Dr. Moore took charge of the eighth Duke, with whom he travelled for five years, making the grand tour. He remained a close friend of the Duke for the rest of his life—a sufficient comment on the excellence of his bear-leading.

Dr. Moore was as much a man of letters as a physician; in 1779 he published his first work, *A View of Society and Manners in France, Switzerland, and Germany: with Anecdotes relating to some Eminent Characters*, from which this extract is taken. It was successful, and he followed it with *A View in Italy;* in 1786 he wrote his curious novel *Zeluco* and a medical treatise.

He was a popular man in society; he knew most people, among them Dr. Johnson, and Sir Thomas Lawrence, who painted his portrait. He corresponded with Burns, and edited Smollett's works.

In 1792 he was in Paris for the bloodier part of the Revolution; he wrote a *Journal during a Residence in France from . . . August to . . . December, 1792*, and later wrote a more considerable work on the Revolution, its causes and progress. There are two other novels of his, *Edward* (1796) and *Mordaunt* (1800): they are said by the D.N.B. to be dull.

Most of Dr. Moore's sons distinguished themselves, but the third, who was the famous Sir John Moore himself, puts the others in the shade.

Dr. Moore died at Richmond in 1802: Dr. Robert Anderson wrote his biography in 1820.

HAVING left Pressburg, we travelled eight posts across a very fertile country to the palace of Estherhasie, the residence of the Prince of that name. He is the first in rank of the Hungarian nobility, and one of the most magnificent subjects in Europe. He has body guards of his own, all genteel-looking men, richly dressed in the Hungarian manner.

The palace is a noble building, lately finished, and situated near a fine lake. The apartments are equally grand and commodious; the furniture more splendid than almost any thing I have seen in royal palaces. In the Prince's own apartment there are some curious musical clocks, and one in the shape of a bird, which whistles a tune every hour.

Just by the palace, there is a theatre for operas, and other dramatic entertainments, and in the gardens, a large room with commodious apartments for masquerades and balls.

At no great distance, there is another theatre expressly built for puppet-shows. This is much larger, and more commodious than most provincial playhouses, and I am bold to assert, is the most splendid that has as yet been reared in Europe for that species of actors. We regretted that we could not have the pleasure of seeing them perform; for they have the reputation of being the best comedians in Hungary.

We had the curiosity to peep behind the curtain, and saw Kings, Emperors, Turks, and Christians, all ranged very sociably together. King Solomon was observed in a corner in a very suspicious tête-à-tête with the Queen of Sheba.

Amongst other curiosities, there is in the garden a wooden house, built upon wheels. It contains a room with a table, chairs, a looking-glass, chimney, and fire-place. There are also closets, with many necessary accommodations. The Prince sometimes entertains twelve people in this vehicle, all of whom may easily sit round the table, and the whole company may thus take an airing together along the walks of the garden, and many parts of the park, which are as level as a bowling-green. The machine, when thus loaded, is easily drawn by six or eight horses.

Prince Estherhasie having heard of M. de Laval's being in the garden, sent us an invitation to the opera, which was to be performed that evening; but as we had brought with us no dress proper for such an occasion, we were forced to decline this obliging invitation. The Prince afterwards sent a carriage, in which we drove round the garden and parks. These are of vast extent, and beautiful beyond description; arbours, fountains, walks, woods, hills, and valleys, being thrown together in a charming confusion. If you will look over Ariosto's description of the gardens in Alcina's enchanted island, you will have an idea of the romantic fields of Estherhasie, which are also inhabited by the same kind of animals.

> *Tra le purpuree rose e i bianchi gigli,*
> *Che tepid aura freschi ognora serba,*
> *Sicuri si vedean lepri e conigli:*
> *E cervi con la fronte alta e superba,*
> *Senza temer che alcun li uccida o pigli,*
> *Pascono, e stansi ruminando l'erba:*
> *E saltan daini e capri snelli e destri,*
> *Che sono in copia in quei luoghi campestri.*

M. de Laval was in raptures with the gardens of Estherhasie. In the height of his admiration, I asked him how they stood in his opinion compared with those of Versailles?

"Ah, Parbleu! Monsieur," answered he, "Versailles étoit fait exprès pour n'être comparé à rien." He acknowledged, however, without difficulty, that, except France, no other country he had seen was so beautiful as this.

Having wandered here many hours, we returned to the inn, where a servant waited with Prince Estherhasie's compliments, and a basket containing two bottles of Tokay, and the same quantity of Champaign and of Old Hock. We lamented very sincerely, that we could not have the honour of waiting on this very magnificent Prince, and thanking him personally for so much politeness.

A company of Italian singers and actors were then at the inn, and preparing for the opera. Great preparations were making for the entertainment of the Empress and all the Court, who are soon to make a visit of several days to Estherhasie. Though the Imperial family, and many of the nobility, are to lodge in the palace, yet every corner of this large and commodious inn is already bespoke for the company which are invited upon that occasion.

Hungary is a very cheap country, the land being infinitely fertile, and in some places producing the most esteemed grape in Europe. It is beautified with lakes, the windings of the Danube, and many streams which flow into that fine river. In the woods of Hungary are bred a race of horses, the most active, hardy, and spirited, for their size, in the world. These have been found very useful in war, and the hussars, or light dragoons of the Austrian army, are mounted on them.

The men in Hungary are remarkably handsome, and well-shaped. Their appearance is improved by their dress, which you know is peculiar, and very becoming.

Lady M. W. Montagu asserts, that the Hungarian women are far more beautiful than the Austrian. For my part, I think of women, as M. de Laval does of Versailles; that they are not to be compared with any thing, not even with one another. And therefore, without presuming to take a comparative view of their beauty, it may be remarked in general, that where the men are handsome and well-made, it is natural to suppose, that the women will possess the same advantages; for parents generally bestow as much attention to the making of their daughters as of their sons. In confirmation of which doctrine, I can assure you, that I have seen as handsome women, as men, in Hungary, and one of the prettiest women, in my opinion, at present at the Court of Vienna, is a Hungarian.

None of the Empress's subjects are taxed so gently, or enjoy so many privileges as the Hungarians. This is partly owing to the grateful remembrance she has of their loyalty and attachment in the days of her distress. But although this sentiment were not so strong in her breast as it really is, there are political reasons for continuing to them the same exemptions and privileges; for nothing can be more dangerous than disobliging the inhabitants of a frontier country, which borders on an inveterate enemy. Nor could any thing please the Turks more, than to find the hearts of the Hungarians alienated from the house of Austria.

I found this country, and the company of M. de Laval, so very agreeable, that I should have been happy to have extended our excursion farther; but he is obliged to set out soon for Chamberry to pay his duty to the Comte d'Artois, who is expected there to wait on his future spouse, the Princess of Savoy. We therefore returned by the direct road from Estherhasie to Vienna.

From

DR. GEMELLI-CARERI'S

TRAVELS THROUGH EUROPE

In Several Letters to the Counsellor Amato Danio.

Dr. Giovanni Francesco Gemelli-Careri was a doctor of civil law, sufficiently rich and leisured. Having travelled through Europe in 1686, he set out on a tour of the entire world, which he accomplished in 1698. He published his *Giro del Mondo* in six volumes octavo in Naples between 1699 and 1700; encouraged by its success, he brought out his *Viaggi per Europa* in two volumes, also at Naples, in 1701–04. In parenthesis, it might be worth observing that the Kingdom of Naples was, at that time, Spanish, which accounts for Dr. Gemelli-Careri's "*our Queen of Spain*".

Both works were popular; in 1719 there was a new edition including both, in Venice, and there were more or less contemporary translations into French, German and English. The tour of the world first appeared in Churchill, vol. IV, and the travels through Europe in Churchill vol. VI (1732); his travels in China (taken out of the *Giro del Mondo*) appeared in Astley's *New General Collection* in 1745. The only comparatively modern books in which he can be found are Macmillan's *The Globe Trotter in India two hundred years ago* . . . (1895), which deals only with the doctor's Indian travels, and A. Magnani's *Il viaggiatore Gemelli-Careri* . . . *e il suo "Giro del Mondo"* (1900).

LETTER II

Of the greatness of Venice, the carnival, the nobility, theatres, etc.

VENICE, JANUARY 29, 1686

PRAY, Sir, observe how punctual I am in keeping my word, since I rather chuse to be troublesome, than to omit acquainting you with all I daily happen to see or hear. I persuade myself, that if you have not read all that epistle, or rather the long story I sent you four days ago, you have at least cast an eye upon the top of it, and consequently are inform'd, that I am in Venice, and, if you please, you may add, in perfect health, and sound as a roach, at your command, which is the main point. As God shall save you, lay aside your gravity, and conform a little to the genius of the carnival season, as I did when I came into this city; for I am not able to forbear being led away, in writing, by the extravagent itch that possesses me, and the Bacchanal fury that runs in my veins. What do you think on't? Don't I write as a pedantick school-master talks? I will now, in the first place, describe to you the city of Venice, such as I have found it in these few days. Venice is a large, magnificent and plentiful city, built for the

49

security, and delightful liberty of all sorts of persons; and govern'd by all the rules of a most excellent, and, by long experience, approv'd policy. Do but observe what I am about to say, and you will plainly perceive the truth of my assertion. As to the first part of it, no man in the world can deny it, if he does but reflect, that it contains three hundred thousand inhabitants, all well to pass, thanks to their great trade, especially into the Levant: besides, there are seventy-two parishes, and fifty-nine monasteries of both sexes, a number not at all contemptible, if we please to call to mind the occasion of the interdict of Paul V.; above fifteen hundred bridges, which join the seventy-two islands; above two hundred stately palaces along the famous canal of Rialto; and lastly, that it is full eight miles in compass. My second article plainly verifies itself, forasmuch as the situation is wonderful strong, and therefore chosen to be the retreat, I know not whether of fishermen, or of noble families, flying from the cruelty of Attila the Hun, about the year 422. As for the charming liberty, it is such as pleases the noblest, and best inform'd nations in Europe; and, tho' it be very chargeable to them, the Germans, Polanders, English and French, never fail coming every year, at this time, to enjoy the excellent opera's, entertainments, balls, and all other sorts of diversions; and the more for that every person is allow'd to go mask'd into all places, concealing both the sex and countenance. Yet I do not think the liberty allow'd the women, in this particular, altogether commendable; and it is certain, that their going about with other masks they meet in the street, at inns, and at the Ridotto, eating sweet-meats, and drinking muskadine wine, is often the occasion of disorders. This very day, a husband had like to have kill'd his wife, they not knowing one another before they came into the inn, had not the good man of the house prevented it. However it is, such accidents daily happen; yet no doubt it is a great matter, that every one may go about where he pleases, without being disturb'd by any body. Since I have mention'd the Ridotto, you must understand, that it is otherwise called the devil's house, being a palace, in the several rooms whereof there are about an hundred tables for gaming, which are worth to the republick at least an hundred thousand crowns a year. So much money is made of the cards and lights paid by the nobility, who alone are allow'd to keep a bank. Hither all the masks retire about the dusk of the evening, for at other times none but noblemen and absolute princes may go in, and they generally play at basset. All is done in silence, laying down the quantity of money every one designs to venture, on what card he pleases, all other particulars being mark'd down with bits of card; and, in the same manner, he that wins is paid without any hesitation or controversy. It is certainly a pleasant sight to behold so many strange fashions of cloaths, and ways of expressing themselves; and that the gamesters should so little value their money, and sometimes their whole estates. I go thither frequently; and am the better pleas'd, because I see their pleasure disturb'd by their losings, and my own satisfaction noway cross'd; forasmuch as I am there only a spectator, without intermedling in what they do: and indeed, were a man to write a play, he could no where make better remarks on the several passions, than at the Ridotto.

Mille hominum species, & rerum discolor usus:
Velle suum cuique est, nec voto vivitur uno.

There are a thousand sorts of men, and as much variety of fashions: Every man has his will, without complying with any one.

As to the point of liberty, it is beyond all credibility; but no man must presume to look into the government of the commonwealth; for it is of the nature of the cancer, which none can handle, without faring the worse. As to other particulars, in the day time, it is frequent to see officers beaten, and their prisoners rescu'd by brothers and sons, with extraordinary impunity and freedom. Tho' the nobility absolutely lord it over the common sort, yet, in outward appearance, they are not very imperious or haughty towards them, but very familiarly permit them to be cover'd in their presence; which, I think, is very requisite in commonwealths, to preserve peace and civil unity. Besides, to avoid being thought proud, which would render them odious to their inferiors, they walk about the streets without any attendance, and sometimes with a small parcel or bundle under their upper garment; and thus, laying aside all ostentation and shew of luxury, they exercise a most absolute sovereignty. They wear a long vest down to their ancles, of black cloth, with great wide sleeves; in winter, lin'd and edg'd with furs, and in summer with some slight silk. On the left shoulder hangs another piece of cloath, about four spans long, and two in breadth, to keep them from the rain. To deal ingenuously with you, I am of opinion, it is the same as the toga among the ancient Romans; as the aforesaid vest, or upper garment tho' long, may be used instead of the senators' *tunica clavata*, or *laticlavium*; for it plainly appears by a certain place in Athenæus, that the toga was once square. Besides that, tho' this sort of garment be also common to lawyers and physicians, however, the nobles do not wear it before they are twenty-five years of age: and whereas the Romans, less discretely, allow'd all men the *toga virilis*, which was the manly habit, at seventeen years of age, the Venetians do not permit it to be worn till twenty-five; excepting those thirty-five youths which are yearly chosen by lot on St. Barbara's day, that they may wear it at eighteen. On their heads they wear a little woollen cap, with a thicker fur about it than the rest. The girdle is of leather, with a buckle, and other ornaments of silver.

I am now well enter'd upon the matter, and have so far play'd the republican and politician, that methinks I have a whole Roman senate in my head, with all the families of the Porcii, Fabricii, Sulpicii, Calpurnii, and Cecilii, but not the Cornificii and Cornelii. It is not at all agreeable to the carnival, especially for one that is at Venice, to enter upon politicks: and I question not but that you think with your self, where is the diversion I promis'd myself, in reading the beginning of this letter? and when will this good man give over his tediousness, and writing long letters? If so, I have done; for I can grow weary of writing; but then you will want the best, that is, what relates to theatres, and is the third part of my description. Then let my importunity prevail upon your patience. There are several theatres in Venice. That of St. Luke, mention'd in my last, contains an hundred and fifty boxes. St. Angelo, where I saw *Jugurtha king of Numidia* excellently acted, has an hundred and thirty-six. In that of Zane, or John of St. Moses, if I mistake not, I counted an hundred and fifteen (small enough), when I was there on Saturday, to see *Clearchus of Negropont*. The following night I saw Dido raving in that of St. John and Paul; and I assure you, it was nothing inferior to any of those we so much applauded there, either for excellent singing, or curious scenes: it contains an hundred and fifty-four boxes. I have not yet seen the theatre of Grimani, but am told, it is finer than all the rest, and has an hundred and sixty-two boxes richly gilt; but there they pay four Italian livres, which is better than three shillings entrance, and thirty-two pence for a seat; whereas, in the others, they give but thirty-two pence entrance, and twenty for a seat, or little more. St. Samuel and St. Cassanus are two other noble theatres, but not for opera's in musick. And, to conclude, the square of St. Mark may be also call'd a theatre; for there are abundance of diversions, volting, dancing on the ropes, and puppet-shews, but, above all, variety of pleasant sights and conversation.

It remains to speak something to the third point, that is, the government; but what shall I do now? my paper will hold no more, and it is too late to scribble another sheet. D'ye think I shall not write to you again the next week? I refer that account till then, when perhaps I may be able to do it better, and upon more solid information than at present. We have here a mighty report of the magnificence of your viceroy, both as to masks and opera's; it would grieve me to be so far from him, were there not so much pleasure in travelling; however, I beg you will give me some account of it, as fully as your important affairs will permit: thus, with my commendations to yourself and friends, I remain, &c.

LETTER III

Of the government of Venice, the great council-chamber, the armory, the Doge's attendance to church, and a notable story.

VENICE, FEBRUARY, 1686

In pursuance of my promise, and at the same time to satisfy you, I have these days apply'd myself, with all possible care, to get some solid information concerning the government of this city; but am of opinion, I have wasted my breath and my time; for their methods are kept wonderful secret, and we can only conjecture at them by the effects: and, in short, all, I believe I have been able to discover, is, that it is this same concert the Venetians are beholden to for the preservation of their state. There is no question to be made, but that Amelot de la Houssaye's relation is very fine and curious, and the contents of it not only likely, but almost palpable demonstration of what he proposes to lay open; yet am I of opinion, that the greatest part of it is rather the product of his own brain, than any information received from others, the men of quality here being always very reserv'd, and upon their guard, tho' others be never so ingenious in diving into them. To confirm the last point relating to the description in my former letter, I must again declare to you, that since we see this republick support itself with so much honour and reputation for so many ages, it must of necessity be allow'd this commendation, of being govern'd by the rules of the most refin'd policy. This is the way men judge, deducing the causes from the effects. And tho' experience shews us, that all things which are excellently contriv'd, do not equally succeed, yet, for the most part, we find, that fortune is the consequence of prudence, and that those which are best order'd, have generally the most prosperous event.

Now, as for the magistrates who govern, I will not pretend to give you any particular or general account of them, because I remember to have often seen the books of Contarini and Giannotti in your hands; so that I might better be inform'd by you in that point, than otherwise. But as to the place where they assemble, I must acquaint you, that the chamber of the great council is all over masterly painted, and will easily hold a thousand men. There are rows of benches about so order'd, that tho' there are seats on both sides, no man turns his back upon another, but they are all face to face. At one end of this hall, where the floor is somewhat raised, is the Doge's seat, fixed in the wall, with benches on both sides. On that which is on his right sit three counsellors, and one of the heads of the *Quarantie*, or council of forty; and on his left, a like number of counsellors, and the other two heads of the *Quarantie*. Opposite to the Doge, that is, at the other end of the hall, sits one of the heads of the council of ten, and at a small distance, one of the advocates of the commons. In the middle are two Censors, some steps above the floor of the hall; and to conclude, in the angles are the old and new auditors.

I have taken great pleasure these days in hearing some trials before the council of twelve, and the *Quarantie*; for the advocates did not talk, but roar; not argue, but scold; and that their way of pleading would make a statue burst with laughing.

On the other hand, they have this very commendable custom, that they only endeavour to gain the judges by proper words, and arguments drawn from natural reason, and well digested, according to the rules of rhetorick, without perplexing themselves with quotations and precedents: the reason whereof perhaps is, because those judges are not always very well read in the civil, and much less in the canon law; and therefore no proofs are at first offer'd, but only a plain bill of what is requir'd, Besides, the most famous advocate, is not allow'd to speak above an hour and an half; a custom, as I take it, observed by the ancients, who measur'd the time allotted for that purpose, by a water hour-glass; whence they said *dare aquam*, and *dicere ad horam*; that is, to allow water, which was the measure of the time, and to speak by the hour: as I think I have read in Quintilian; and once observ'd a curious place of Philostratus, in the life of Apollonius Thyanæus. Those who spoke by this rule, *dicebant ad clepsydram*, talk'd by the water hour-glass; and therefore Martial, scoffing at one Cæcilianus, said,

> *Septem clepsydras magnä tibi voce petenti,*
> *Arbiter invitus, Cæciliane, dedit.*
> *At tu multa diu dicis: vitreisque tepentem*
> *Ampullis potas semisupinus aquam.*
> *Ut tandem saties vocemque, sitimque, rogamus,*
> *Jam de clepsydra, Cæciliane, bibas.*

Which is to this effect. Cæcilianus, the judge, much against his will, allows you to plead whilst seven glasses are running, which you demand with much clamour. You talk much a long while together, and to refresh you, take off several glasses of warm water. That you may at length satiate your voice and your thirst, we intreat you, Cæcilianus, to drink out of the hour-glass.

But methinks, to repeat such things to you, who are so well acquainted with them, by continual reading of good authors, is like carrying of flowers to Flora, and fruit to Alcinous. However it is, the judges give their opinions after this manner: To denote the affirmative judgment, they put a white ball, made of linen, into a vessel of the same colour; for the negative, a green ball into a green vessel; and in a doubtful case, a reddish one, which neither affirms nor denies, into a red vessel; all this in open court, and before the parties themselves. The best custom, in my mind, is, that every one may be there present with his cap or hat on his head, perhaps in token of liberty, or even mask'd, as every one pleases. But what a heinous crime this would be in Naples!

Adjoining to the grand council, is the armory, not furnish'd with any great store of arms, but with the curiousest and rarest armour in Europe; for, besides what the republick itself has bought at several times, and upon sundry occasions, a great quantity has been presented them by the most potent monarchs, very wonderful both for workmánship and value. Among the rest is remarkable, an engine, which at once fires four thousand muskets, and might be of good use upon any mutiny of the people, or such other sudden accident. There are innumerable Turkish colours, tho' there must be more of the Venetians at Constantinople. Among the greatest rarities, is a crystal fountain, and St. Mark's head, drawn with a pen, in which the strokes are not plain lines, but contain the whole gospel of our Saviour's Passion, almost invisible to the eye, so that it cannot be read without a very convex magnifying glass. The provost marshal of Venice, call'd the great captain, has charge of this place, and when I was there I had like to have taken him for a bishop, for he had on a long purple robe, lin'd with crimson damask, and edg'd with furs, and a cap on his head like those the noblemen wear. This post is worth three thousand ducats a year.

On Candlemas Day in the evening, I went to Santa Maria Formosa, because the Doge was to be there, according to antient custom. Touching the original of this practice, it is to be observ'd, that in former ages, the most beautiful maids in Venice, and the adjacent ports on the continent, were given in marriage to those who offer'd most money for them; and then that money was distributed among the ugliest, for them to get husbands by their portions. This good custom having multiply'd the people, another yet better was introduced, which was, that after the betrothing, all the maidens were conducted back to St. Pietro a Castello, call'd Olivole, carrying their portion with them, and there they staid all Candlemas night. The bridegrooms coming in the morning, with all their kindred, they heard the high mass together, and then the nuptial ceremonies being perform'd, they return'd home joyfully with their beloved brides. The Istrians, who were then enemies to the city, knowing this custom, laid hold of the opportunity, and coming over privately by night, in well-rigg'd vessels, carry'd off both the maids and their portions, before any could rescue them. This accident causing a mighty uproar in Venice, abundance of vessels were fitted out in an hour; but particularly by the inhabitants of Santa Maria Formosa's ward, who overtaking the ravishers at Caorle, where they were dividing the booty, made a most bloody slaughter of them, and brought home again the afflicted ladies, with all the rest that had been taken away. These people being order'd by the nobility boldly to ask any reward for their bravery, answer'd, We desire nothing but that you be obliged, in memory of this action, to come once a year, with your prince, to our church. The Doge reply'd, And what if it should happen to rain on that day? Then, said they, we will send you hoods to keep you dry, and if you are thirsty we will also make you drink. In pursuance of which promise, the joyners, and fruiterers, send the prince two hoods on Candlemas day, with two bottles, the one of white the other of red wine, stopp'd with oranges, which are afterwards placed on two stands by the high altar in the said church. Such a sort of ceremony is perform'd by the fathers of mount Olivet towards the patriarch, on Ascension-day, presenting him with a bason full of pick'd chestnuts.

Being come into the church, I saw, in the first place, a canopy of crimson damask set up for the Doge, on the right side of the altar, all the wall being hung with the same.

When it was time to begin the even song, he sat down under it, and the French embassador at a small distance from him. On both sides sat several senators and counsellors, some more some less raised up from the ground, according to their degree and quality. When the Magnificat was begun, he took a lighted candle into his hand, and, the solemnity being over, went away to his boat. The attendance was as follows, first went the clergy of the church with their cross, then follow'd the senators and counsellors, according to their rank, clad in crimson damask, and such of them as had been embassadors, by way of distinction, had an edging of gold-colour cloth embroider'd. Next came two of the Doge's courtiers, he on the right carrying a cushion for him to kneel on, and the other a little folding stool, like those the bishops use upon some occasions. Then the Doge himself had an under garment, or tunick, of a rich white silk, and the upper or vest, crimson lin'd in ermin; his cap was also of white silk, with the usual ducal point, or horn. He is of stature low, but of a good constitution, tho' seventy years of age, very pleasant, well spoken, good, and gracious. After him, besides the person carrying the train, came a nobleman with a naked tuck in his hand, and another courtier carrying the umbrello. The two Gondolas, or boats, which he and all the company went in, were curiously glazed and adorn'd with a beautiful covering of crimson damask, on which were his arms, and those of St. Mark. Each of them was rowed by four men, clad in red. The great captain also appear'd that day in his robes, his very upper garment being of crimson damask, edg'd with furs of the same colour. In short, he looks like something more than a mean provost, in his habit and behaviour.

The next day the Doge went to St. Mark's, with the same attendance but clad in white brocade, the upper garment of gold, and the under of silver. At his entring into the church he had holy water brought him by a canon; and then he went into the choir and sate down before the high altar, on a seat made in the wall like a pulpit, without a canopy. Close by, on a low seat, was the French embassador, and the emperor's, the Spanish never being present, on account of some controversy about precedence; but they had a desk to kneel at without cushions. After the Doge had kiss'd the Gospel, and been thrice incensed, the embassadors kiss'd it, and each was twice incensed: After the consecration, the same was repeated, every senator was once incensed, that is, the censer once wav'd to him, and kiss'd the image of St. Mark, as the others had done before. Four canons came twice and bow'd to the Doge, and he at the offertory gave them a piece of gold. When out of the church, he stopp'd before the giants, and having dismiss'd all those great men, retir'd to his apartment.

I cannot at present acquaint you with any thing else that is curious, except that yesterday the council of ten sate, on account of a barbarous murder, committed on a design of robbing, by one Andino Furno of Torino, on the body of his master, who was a good priest; and this very day he was beheaded between the columns of the Brojo, or the publick place for voting, and his body quarter'd, a great multitude looking on; for no man has been executed these four years. I am sorry this letter should end with a doleful relation; but I ought to be much more concern'd for troubling you so long with my simple tales, so wishing you all happiness, &c.

LETTER IV

Of the arsenal, mint, Jews quarter, churches, &c.

VENICE, FEBRUARY THE 12th, 1686

I have been above this hour puzzling my brain, to begin to write handsomely; and whether it be my misfortune, or my dullness that occasions it, I do not see any likelihood of succeeding; so that this bout, instead of patience, you must afford me your compassion, looking on me as a man quite beside myself among so many opera's, plays, masks, sports, entertainments, and delights; but now give me leave to acquaint you, in short, with what I have seen this week.

The famous arsenal of this city, is a place wall'd in, about three miles in compass. Here about two thousand men are continually at work, upon all things necessary for ships, either of war or merchants. Here are great numbers of galleys, galeasses, transports and other great ships; some of them newly begun, others further advanc'd, and others finished, under very large and spacious arches; besides those taken from the Turks, which lie about in several places, as monuments of the Venetian valour. In one place you may see a numerous train of artillery, with all things belonging to it; in another match, ball, bombs, grenadoes, and all such sorts of inventions. Here are breast-plates, belly-pieces, helmets, and bucklers; there pikes, swords, scymitars, spears, bows, and guns; there sails, rudders, anchors, cables, each of them in a several storehouse. In short, this looks like the palace of Mars, furnish'd both with armour for defence, and weapons for slaughter; so that they can in an hour fit out fifty galleys, and twenty galeasses.

The mint is under the court of the procurators in St. Mark's square, where they coin gold, silver, and brass, not with a mill, but the hammer; and in some rooms there are chests of money, belonging to private citizens, who leave it there for more security, as we use to put it into the banks.

The Jews quarter is a spacious place, and has something in it worth a curious man's observation; as the school where they teach Hebrew, and several synagogues. I went into one call'd the Spanish, because those of that nation meet in it, and saw those wretches sitting on long benches, saying their fruitless prayers, with hoods on their heads, and a white clout on their shoulders, with tassels at the four corners. Their Rabbi sate at one end of the room on a chair, somewhat raised from the ground, who cry'd out like a mad man, the other Jews answering at times. I was full of admiration when I saw five books taken from under the altar, written on vellum, being kept between two tables cover'd with silk, and silver plates. They were carried to the Rabbi for him to read a while, according to their superstitious rites. I was told they were the books of Moses, and that when they were to be copy'd, the transcriber must be a month in purifying himself for that work, nor eat any thing on the days he writes, and make fresh ink in a very clean vessel; adding, that in case one single point were amiss, the whole copy would be look'd upon as erroneous. Next I went up to the galleries where the women meet, where I found a bride, who told me, she had been a month upon her purification, before she could be admitted to that place.

As for the churches I have hitherto seen, the finest in my opinion are, that of the barefoot Carmelites, remarkable for its famous marble frontispiece, and the sixteen statues within it; La Salute, which is oval, and adorn'd both within and without, with incomparable marble statues; that of St. John and Paul, which is spacious enough, and has many chapels, embellish'd with many marble statues, especially that of our lady. In this church-yard, on a large pedestal, stands a brass statue a-horseback, representing Bartholomew Coglione of Bergamo, a renowned soldier in his time, and as such remarkable at the famous battle of Lepanto against the Turks. That of St. George, of the fathers of Cassino, is also rich in statues, both brass and marble, and valuable for its magnificent choir. The library of this place must be allow'd to be one of the best in the city, as well for the number as the variety and choice of books, not to mention the curious binding, the fine cases, all shut up with the clearest glasses, and the noble statues and pictures; for in my opinion, the true ornament of libraries consists in the books themselves, and all the rest is the contrivance of idle persons, who do not much apply themselves to reading. The garden also deserves to be taken notice of for its stately walks, most artfully adorn'd with tall and thick cypress trees, and odoriferous myrtles, and cover'd over with several choice vines.

I shall not say any thing of S. Mark at this time, for fear of growing too tedious; but shall reserve it for the next week. I shall now only add, that the cloaths here are every where excessive costly, and the masks wonderful extravagant, thanks to the vast multitude of strangers resorting hither this year; and many things would have been done, had not the senate forbid all persons wearing gold or silver, much less jewels; as also sitting to talk together under the arches of St. Mark. However, no man forbears diverting himself as he best likes. There is continual revelling and dancing; gaming in all parts; every where comedies and serenades; and to say all in a word, Venice at these times is the habitation of the graces, and of all sorts of delight. Yet amidst these universal pleasures, some things happen which provoke tears, or at least compassion. Yesterday, in the afternoon, a new-marry'd man carry'd his wife mask'd into the aforesaid place of St. Mark, where he stepping a little aside upon some occasion, she was taken away by two masks, who having feasted with her at an inn, vanish'd, and the poor wretch being left by herself, was fain to pawn her bracelets to the host, for the mischievous entertainment. Is not this as pleasant an adventure as any you have heard at home? But if I should tell you that I am myself become a knight-errant, would it not make you laugh? On Saturday, as soon as I got into the street, a mask took me by the hand, having a scarlet coat on his back, with gold lace, a garment much used here, and invited me to go drink some muskadine wine. This he did after such a manner, and as familiarly, as if he had been very long well acquainted with me, so that suspecting nothing, I freely went along with him; but when I came to unmask to see who it was, alas! I found a woman. God knows what art I used to get off clear from her, being well satisfy'd to pay the reckoning and go about my business. Observe how warily a man must walk to avoid being insnar'd. Methinks I have writ enough, or at least laziness persuades me so, and therefore with commendations to my friends, &c.

PHILIP THICKNESSE'S

GENERAL HINTS TO STRANGERS WHO TRAVEL

THROUGH FRANCE

Philip Thicknesse, the seventh son of the Rector of Farthinghoe in Northamptonshire, was born in 1719. After an abortive start as an apothecary he joined the army, and by 1741 he had reached the rank of captain. By 1766 he had married twice, and each lady brought him about £5,000; in that year he bought the post of Lieutenant-Governor of the Landguard Fort in Suffolk. His second wife was Lady Elizabeth Touchet, daughter of the Earl of Castlehaven, from whom his son inherited the barony of Audley.

Governor Thicknesse appears to have quarrelled with everybody worth knowing in his time, and he spent some time in prison for a libel. He was an untiring traveller and a voluminous writer. Much of his work was ephemeral, but his *Bath Guide*, his *Journey through France and Part of Spain* (from which this extract comes), and his *Memoirs and Anecdotes of Philip Thicknesse, late Lieut.-Governor of Landguard Fort, and unfortunately father to George Touchet Baron Audley* are very well worth reading.

I

IF YOU travel post, when you approach the town, or bourg where you intend to lie, ask the post-boy, which house he recommends as the best, and never go to that, if there is any other.—Be previously informed what other inns there are in the same place. If you go according to the post-boy's recommendation, the *aubergiste* gives him two or three livres, which he makes you pay the next morning. I know but one auberge between *Marseilles* and *Paris*, where this is not a constant practice, and that is at *Vermanton*, five leagues from *Auxerre*, where every English traveller will find a decent land-lord, *Monsieur la Brunier, à St. Nicolas*; good entertainment, and no imposition, and consequently an inn where no post-boy will drive, if he can avoid it.

II

If you take your own horses, they must be provided with head-pieces, and halters; the French stables never furnish any such things; and your servant must take care that the *Garçon d'Ecurie* does not buckle them so tight, that the horses cannot take a full bite, this being a common practice, to save hay.

III

If the *Garçon d'Ecurie* does not bring the halters properly rolled up, when he puts your horses to, he ought to have nothing given him, because they are so constantly accustomed to do it, that they cannot forget it, *but in hopes you may too*.

IV

Direct your servant, not only to see your horses watered, and corn given them, but to *stand by* while they eat it: this is often necessary in England, and always in France.

V

If you eat at the *table d'Hôte*, the price is fixed, and you cannot be imposed upon. If you eat in your own chamber, and order your own dinner or supper, it is as necessary to make a previous bargain with your host for it, as it would be to bargain with an itinerant Jew for a gold watch; the *conscience* and *honour* of a *French Aubergiste*, and a travelling Jew, are always to be considered alike; and it is very remarkable, that the *Publicans* in France, are the only people who receive strangers with a cool indifference! and where this indifference is most shown, there is most reason to be cautious.

VI

Be careful that your sheets are well aired, otherwise you will find them often, not only damp, but perfectly wet.—Frenchmen in general do not consider wet or damp sheets as dangerous, at least I am sure French *Aubergistes* do not.

VII

Young men who travel into France, with a view of gaining the language, should always eat at the *table d'Hôte*.—There is generally at these tables an officer, or a priest, and though there may be none but people of a middling degree, they will show every kind of attention and preference to a stranger.

VIII

It is necessary to carry your own pillows with you; in some inns they have them; but in villages, *bourgs*, &c. none are to be had.

IX

In the wine provinces, at all the *table d'Hôtes*, they always provide the common wine, as we do small beer; wine is never paid for separately, unless it is of a quality above the *vin du Païs*; and when you call for better, know the price before you drink it.

X

When fine cambrick handkerchiefs, &c. are given to be washed, take care they are not trimmed round two inches narrower, to make borders to *Madame la Blanchisseuse's* night caps: this is a little *douceur* which they think themselves entitled to, from my lord *Anglois*, who they are sure is *très riche*, and consequently ought to be plundered by the poor.

XI

Whenever you want honest information, get it from a French officer or a priest, provided they are on the *wrong* side of forty; but, in general, avoid all intimacy with either on the *right* side of thirty.

XII

Where you propose to stay any time, be very cautious with whom you make an acquaintance, as there are always a number of officious forward Frenchmen, and English adventurers, ready to offer you their services, from whom you will find it very difficult to disengage yourself, after you have found more agreeable company. Frenchmen of real fashion are very circumspect, and will not *fall in love with you* at first sight; but a designing knave will exercise every species of flattery, in order to fix himself upon you for his dinner, or what else he can get, and will be with you before you are up, and after you are in bed.

XIII

Wherever there is any cabinet of curiosities, medals, pictures, &c. to be seen, never make any scruple to send a card, desiring permission to view them; the request is flattering to a Frenchman, and you will never be refused; and besides this, you will in all probability thereby gain a valuable acquaintance. It is generally men of sense and philosophy, who make such collections, and you will find the collector of them, perhaps, the most pleasing part of the cabinet.

XIV

Take it as a maxim, unalterable as the laws of the Medes and Persians, that whenever you are invited to a supper at *Paris, Lyons*, or any of the great cities, where a *little* trifling play commences before supper, GREAT PLAY is intended after supper; and that you are the marked pigeon to be plucked. Always remember *Lord Chesterfield's* advice to his son: "If you play with men, know with *whom* you play; if with women, for *what*:" and do not think yourself the more secure, because you see at the same table some of your own countrymen, though they are lords or ladies; a *London* gambler would have no chance in a *Parisian* party.

XV

Dress is an essential and most important consideration with every body in France. A Frenchman never appears till his

hair is well combed and powdered, however slovenly he may
be in other respects.—Not being able to submit every day to
this ceremony, the servant to a gentleman of fashion at whose
house I visited in *Marseilles*, having forgot my name, described
me to his master, as the gentleman whose hair was *toujours mal
frisé*.—Dress is a foolish thing, says *Lord Chesterfield*; yet it is a
more foolish thing not to be well dressed.

XVI

You cannot dine, or visit after dinner, in an undress frock,
with or without a bag to your hair: the hair *en queüe*, or a
little cape to your coat, would be considered an unpardonable
liberty. Military men have an advantage above all others in
point of dress, in France. A regimental or military coat carries
a man with a *bonne grace* into all companies, with or without
a bag to his hair: It is of all others the properest dress for a
stranger in France, on many accounts.

XVII

In France it is not customary to drink to persons at table,
nor to drink wine after dinner. When the dessert is taken away,
so is the wine;—an excellent custom, and worthy of being
observed by all nations.

XVIII

It is wrong to be led into any kind of conversation but what
is absolutely necessary, with the common, or indeed the
middling class of people in France. They never fail availing
themselves, of the least condescension in a stranger, to ask a
number of impertinent questions, and to conclude, if you
answer them civilly, that they are your equals.—Sentiment and
bashfulness are not to be met with but among people of rank
in France: to be free and easy is the etiquette of the country;
and some kinds of that free and easy manner are highly
offensive to strangers, and particularly to a shy Englishman.

XIX

When well-bred people flatter strangers, they seldom direct
their flattery to the object they mean to compliment, but to one
of their own country:—As, "What a *bonne grace* the English
have," says one to the other, in a whisper loud enough to be
heard by the whole company, who all give a nod of consent;
yet in their hearts they do not love the English of all other
nations[1], and therefore conclude, that the English in their
hearts do not love them.

XX

No gentleman, priest, or servant, male or female, ever gives
any notice, by knocking, before they enter the bed-chamber, or
apartment of ladies or gentlemen.—The post-man opens it to
bring your letters; the capuchin, to ask alms; and the gentleman, to make his visit. There is no privacy but by securing
your door by a key or a bolt; and when any of the middling
class of people have got possession of your apartment, particularly of a stranger, it is very difficult to get them out.

XXI

There is not on earth, perhaps, so curious and inquisitive
a people as the lower class of French: noise seems to be one of
their greatest delights. If a ragged boy does but beat a drum,
or sound a trumpet, he brings all who hear him about it, with
the utmost speed, and most impatient curiosity.—As my
monkey rode postillion, in a red jacket laced with silver, I was
obliged to make him dismount when I passed through a town
of any size: the people gathered so rapidly round me at *Moret*,
three leagues from *Fontainebleau*, while I stopped only to buy
a loaf, that I verily believe every man, woman, and child,
except the sick and aged, were paying their respects to my little
groom; all infinitely delighted; for none offered the least degree

[1]Nor do they mean in general what they say; for I am persuaded they sneer
so as to be understood by each other, and really mean *mauvaise grace*. There is
nothing so difficult to learn as to sneer in French; I know many gentlemen
perfectly acquainted with every power and use of their language but this.

of rudeness. I fear a Frenchman could not have passed in the same manner, so agreeably, through a country town in England.

XXII

The French never give coffee, tea, or any refreshment, except upon particular occasions, to their morning or evening visitors.

XXIII

When the weather is cold, the fire small, and a large company, some young Frenchman shuts the whole circle from receiving any benefit from it, by placing himself just before it, laying his sword genteelly over his left knee, and flattering himself, while all the company wish him at the devil, that the ladies are admiring his legs. When he has gratified his vanity, or is thoroughly warm, he sits down, or goes, and another takes his place. I have seen this abominable ill-breeding kept up by a set of *accomplished* young fops for two hours together, in exceeding cold weather. This custom has been transplanted lately into England.

XXIV

Jealousy is scarce known in France. By the time the first child is born, an indifference generally takes place: the husband and wife have their separate acquaintance, and pursue their separate *amusements*, undisturbed by domestic squabbles. When they meet in the evening, it is with perfect good humour, and, in general, perfect good breeding.—When an English wife plays truant, she soon becomes abandoned: it is not so with the French; they preserve appearances and proper decorum, because they are seldom attached to any particular man. While they are at their toilet, they receive the visits of their male acquaintance, and he must be a man of uncommon discernment, who finds out who it is she prefers at that time.— In the southern parts of France, the women are in general very *free* and *easy* indeed.

71

XXV

It is seldom that virgins are seduced in France; the married women are the objects of the men of gallantry. The seduction of a young girl is punished with death. . . .

XXVI

Never ask a Frenchman his age; no question whatever can be more offensive to him, nor will he ever give you a direct, though he may a civil answer.—*Lewis* XV was always asking every man about him his age. A king may take that liberty, and even then it always gives pain.—*Louis* XIV said to the *Comte de Grammont*, "*Je sais votre âge, l'Evêque de Senlis qui a* 84 *ans, m'a donné pour époque, que vous avez étudié ensemble dans la même classe.*" "*Cet Evêque, Sire,* (replied the *Comte*), *n'accuse pas juste, car ni lui, ni moi n'avons jamais Etudié.*"—Before I knew how offensive this question was to a Frenchman, I have had many equivocal answers—such as, *O! Mon dieu,* as old as the town, or, I thank God, I am in good health, &c.

XXVII

A modern French author says, that the French language is not capable of the *jeux de mots*. "*Les jeux de mots* are not," says he, "in the genius *de notre langue qui est grave, et sérieuse.*" Perhaps it may be so; but the language and the men are then so different, that I thought quite otherwise—though the following beautiful specimen of the seriousness of the language ought, in some measure, to justify his remark: *Un seul est frappé, & tous sont delivrés, dieu frappe sons fils innocent, pour l'amour des hommes coupables, & pardonne aux hommes coupables, pour l'amour de son fils innocent.*

XXVIII

All English women, as well as women of other nations, prefer France to their own country; because in France there is much less restraint on their actions, than there is (should I not say, than there *was*?) in England. All Englishmen, however, who have young and beautiful wives, should, if they are not indifferent about their conduct, avoid a trip to *Paris*, &c. though it be but for "*a six weeks tour*": she must be good and wise too, if six weeks does not corrupt her mind and debauch her morals, and that too by her own sex, which is infinitely the most dangerous company. A French woman is as great an adept at laughing an English woman into all contempt of fidelity to her husband, as married English women are in general, in preparing them during their first pregnancy, for the touch of a man-midwife—and both from the same motive; *i.e.* to do as they have done, and bring all the sex upon a level.

XXIX

The French will not allow their language to be so difficult to speak properly as the English language; and perhaps they are in the right; for how often do we meet with Englishmen who speak French perfectly? How seldom do we hear a Frenchman speak English, without betraying his country by his pronunciation? It is not so with the Spaniards: I conversed with two Spaniards who were never twenty miles from *Barcelona*, that spoke English perfectly well.—How, for instance, shall a Frenchman who cannot pronounce the English, be able to understand (great as the difference is) what I mean, when I say *the sun is an hour high*? May he not equally suppose that I said *the sun is in our eye*?

XXX

When you make an agreement with an *Aubergiste* where you intend to lie, take care to include beds, rooms, &c. or he will charge separately for these articles.

XXXI

After all, it must be confessed, that *Mons. Dessein's, à l'Hôtel d'Angleterre* at *Calais*, is not only the first inn strangers of fashion generally go to, but that it is also the first and best inn in France. *Dessein* is the decoy-duck, and ought to have a salary from the French government—he is always sure of a good one from the English.

XXXII

In frontier or garrison towns, where they have a right to examine your baggage, a twenty-four *sols* piece, and assuring the officer that you are a gentleman, and not a merchant, will carry you through without delay.

XXXIII

Those who travel post should, before they set out, put up in parcels money for the number of horses they use for one post, two posts, and a post *et demi*, adding to each parcel that which is intended to be given to the driver or drivers, who are intitled by the king's ordonnance to five *sols* a post; and if they behave ill, they should be given no more: when they are civil ten or twelve *sols* a post is sufficient. If these packets are not prepared and properly marked, the traveller, especially if he is not well acquainted with the money, cannot count it out while the horses are changing, from the number of beggars which surround the carriage, and who will take no denial.

XXXIV

People of rank and condition, either going to, or coming from the continent, by writing to PETER FECTOR, Esq; at *Dover*, will find him a man of property and character, on whom they may depend.

XXXV

Never let a Frenchman with whom you live, or with whom you travel, be master. An Englishman cannot possibly live twenty-four hours with a Frenchman who *commands*; he will try for that superiority; but by one single pointed resolution, shew him it must not be so, and he will give it up, and become an useful, and an agreeable companion.

XXXVI

Always carry a machine to secure the bedchamber doors at inns where you sleep, and see that there are no holes behind large pictures in the room, large enough for a man to creep through. Too much caution cannot be taken in a country where murther and robbery are, in a manner, synonimous terms.

LASTLY

Valetudinarians, or men of a certain age, who travel into the southern parts of France, Spain, or Italy, should never omit to wear either a callico or fine flannel waistcoat under their shirts. Strange as it may seem to say so, this precaution is more necessary in the south of France, than in England. In May last it was so hot at *Lyons*, on the side of the streets the sun shone on, and so cold on the shady side, that both were intolerable. The air is much more sharp and penetrating in hot climates than in cold. A dead dog, thrown into the streets of Madrid at night, will not have a bit of flesh upon his bones by eight o'clock the next morning; and that, as I am well assured, from the *vifeness* of the air alone; and if northern people will go thin clad, and contend with the natives, whose long experience ought to be considered, they cannot wonder if they are treated with contempt, especially where the error must be on the safest side; and they must take the consequences.

As to travelling in Spain, little need be said, after what has been inserted in the foregoing sheets; and, therefore, the general account of the country, and character of the people, may be pretty well conceived, by the following account of both:

Spain, then, is at this day a vast desert, inhabited by a grave, steady-appearing race of men, which all their manners and actions, as well as discourse, seem to confirm; but they refuse the bountiful offers of nature, though she stretches out her arms to give it them in the most liberal manner. Perhaps their superstition, and the want of LIBERTY, renders it not worth receiving.

The soil of Spain is in general very fertile, and infinitely variegated, as to heat and cold, by the different aspect of mountains, or in the plains most distant from mountains. Their pastures are excellent, and their sheep numerous. Every climate, and every soil, may be found in this kingdom, and consequently every thing which man can ask of God, might be had there in perfection, were it not for the idle, inactive, slothful disposition of the natives; for they have *in*, and *upon* their soil, the riches of all other nations: but a bag of onions, a piece of bread, and a bunch of grapes, is all that a Spaniard requires for his subsistance in twenty-four hours. There does not live a more abstemious race of men; but their country must, while they remain under their present laws and religion, continue uncultivated, and almost depopulated. They will not labour themselves, nor would they allow Philip III. to bring strangers among them who would! Their HONOUR was too much at stake in that respect, and their pride withholds their own hands. Add to this, their great number of religious houses filled with idle monks, who are of no more use to the public than dead men; for they consume, without adding to the state: had the Spaniards the industry of other nations, what a vast trade might they carry on with their neighbours in Africa! instead of which they hold with them a perpetual war. These considerations, with the multitude of offices; their incredible number of servants, their passion for bull-baiting and intriguing, employ all their attention. They are all, in their own imagination, from the king to the cobbler, men of too high birth to stoop to the earth, but to gather what she offers spontaneously: and the soil is well fitted to the inhabitants, or the inhabitants to the soil; perhaps, too, wisely so ordained by the MAKER OF BOTH. It certainly, however, is fortunate for this country, and perhaps to all their neighbouring nations; and therefore, though as a citizen of the world one cannot behold such a fine country without lamenting its neglected condition; yet, as a native of this, it ought to be a matter of triumph.

UNPLEASANT VOYAGES

The first three voyages are taken from *The Mariner's Chronicle* . . . *a collection* . . . *of Shipwrecks, Fires, Famines, And other Calamities incident to a Life of Maritime Enterprise* . . . *by Archibald Duncan, Esq. Late of the Royal Navy*, published in 1804–05 in four volumes 12mo. There are other accounts of the three voyages, but Mr. Duncan's flat, moralising prose throws the horrors into a sharper contrast than any amount of declamation.

Fra de Carli's travels and May's account of the ship *Terra Nova* come from Churchill, volumes I and VI.

Denis de Carli of Piacenza and Michael Angelo of Gattina were Capuchin friars who went to the Congo as missionaries in 1666. Fra Michael Angelo died there, but his companion returned safely to Italy. Fra de Carli provides his own introduction, so no more is needed here.

Mr. May's account of his dismal passage in the *Terra Nova* contains all that I have been able to find about him. There is an odd thing about the voyage: although the whole ship was on the edge of starvation, the crew never seems to have come into contact with the passengers. Perhaps the prestige of a seventeenth-century duchess was too great to allow any familiarity in any circumstances whatever.

THE DISTRESSES OF THE UNFORTUNATE CREW
OF THE SHIP ANNE AND MARY FROM NORWAY
TO IRELAND IN THE YEAR 1759

THE ship Anne and Mary, of Galway, in Ireland, sailed from Drontheim, in Norway, on the 1st of September, 1759. The crew, consisting of nine persons, after their departure met with a series of contrary winds and bad weather. On the 10th of October, from an observation taken the day before, they computed themselves to be within fifteen leagues of the islands of Arran. As they had been put upon short allowance some time before, the idea of being so near their desired port was highly pleasing; but that very night, the ship oversetting, she was tossed about for the space of five hours. The cabin being soon afterwards entirely carried away, together with their provisions and compass, they were left exposed to the mercy of the seas, and deprived of all means of governing the hull.

Two days passed without their tasting a morsel excepting two rats which they caught. What followed next nothing but devouring famine could have suggested. It was agreed that one should die to support the rest; and they accordingly cast lots. The first fell upon Patrick Lidane, who requested, that, for their immediate subsistence, they would take only the calves of his legs; representing that, perhaps, Providence might do more for them than they expected before they should be necessitated to have farther recourse to him. His request was granted; and after cutting away the flesh of his legs, which they ate raw, and of which he begged a morsel for himself, but was refused, he was permitted to live thirty hours.

The second person who suffered the same fate was James Lee; and the fourth was Bryan Flaherty. On these four bodies, which were eaten raw, and without any kind of drink, but what rain-water they could catch in the skulls of the killed, the rest subsisted from about the 21st October to the 1st of December. In this interval three of them who had escaped the lot, after languishing for a considerable time, expired on the forecastle. On the last mentioned day the vessel was driven into the county of Kerry. The Captain, and Michael M'Daniel, the only survivors, were so worn out with famine and distress, that they were unable to stand, and scarcely shewed any signs of life; and notwithstanding the greatest care, tenderness, and humanity was extended to them by James Crosbie, Esq. of that neighbourhood, and his lady, the Captain died about thirty hours after he was brought on shore. The same charitable attention was continued to M'Daniel, who, as soon as he was in a condition to travel made the best of his way to Galway, to fulfil the dying injunctions of the men who fell by lot, and who severally made it their last and earnest request, that whoever should survive, should repair to that town and relate to their friends their miserable sufferings and sad catastrophe.

CAPTAIN BOYCE'S

NARRATIVE OF THE LOSS OF THE LUXBOROUGH,
AND HIS PROVIDENTIAL ESCAPE AND
SUFFERINGS
IN THE YEAR 1727.

CAPTAIN BOYCE, who for many years enjoyed the highly honorable situation of Lieutenant-Governor of Greenwich Hospital, and died in 1774, was, in the early part of his life, employed in the merchants' service. In the year 1727 he was second mate of the Luxborough, a ship belonging to the South Sea Company. In that year the most terrible of all misfortunes befel the above-mentioned vessel, of which, and the subsequent distresses, we have the following melancholy account from Captain Boyce himself.

On the 23rd of May, 1727, we sailed from Jamaica, and on Sunday, the 25th of June, were in the latitude of 41° 45 N. and in the longitude of 20° E. from Crooked Island, when the galley was perceived to be on fire in the lazaretto. It was occasioned by the fatal curiosity of two black boys, who, willing to know whether some liquor spilt on the deck was rum or water, put the candle to it, which rose into a flame, and immediately communicated itself to the barrel from which the liquor had leaked. It had burned some time before it was perceived, as the boys were too much intimidated to discover it themselves, having tried all means to extinguish the fire in vain. We hoisted out the yawl, which was soon filled with twenty-three men and boys, who jumped into her with the utmost eagerness. The wind now blowing very fresh, and the yawl running seven knots and a half by the log, we expected every moment to perish, as she was loaded within a streak and a half of her gunnel.

We had not a morsel of victuals, nor a drop of water; no mast, no sail, no compass to direct our course, and above one hundred leagues from any land. We left in the ship sixteen men, who all perished with her. They endeavored to hoist out the long boat, but before they could effect it, the flames reaching the powder room she blew up, and we saw her no more. A little before this we could distinguish the first mate and the captain's cook in the mizen-top, every moment expecting the fate that awaited them.

Having thus been eye-witnesses of the miserable fate of our companions, we expected every moment to perish by the waves, or, if not by them, at least by hunger and thirst. On the first two days it blew and rained much, but the weather coming fair the third day, the 28th, as kind Providence had hitherto wonderfully preserved us, we began to contrive the means of making a sail, which we effected in the following manner:— We took to pieces three men's frocks and a shirt, and with a sail needle and twine, which we found in one of the black boy's pockets, we made a shift to sew them together, which answered tolerably well. Finding in the sea a small stick, we woulded it to a piece of a broken blade of an oar we had in the boat, and made a yard of it, which we hoisted on an oar, with our garters for halyards and sheets. A thimble, which the fore-sheet of the boat used to be reeved through, served at the end of the oar or mast to reeve the halyards.

Knowing, from our observations, that Newfoundland bore about north, we steered, as well as we could, to the northward. We judged of our course by taking notice of the sun, and of the time of the day from the captain's watch. In the night, when we could see the north star, or any of the great Bear, we formed a knowledge of our course by them. We were in great hopes of seeing some ship or other to take us up.

The fourth or fifth night a man, Thomas Croniford, and the boy that unhappily set the ship on fire died; and in the afternoon of the next day three more men expired, all raving mad, crying out lamentally for water.

The weather now proved so foggy that it deprived us almost all day of the light of the sun, and of the moon and stars by night. We used frequently to halloo as loud as we could, in hopes of being heard by some ship. In the day time our deluded fancies often imagined ships so plain to us, that we have halloed to them a long time before we have been undeceived; and in the night, by the same delusion, we have thought we heard men talk, bells ringing, cocks crow &c. and have condemned the phantoms of our imagination, believing them to be real ships and men, for not answering and taking us up.

The seventh day our numbers were reduced by death to twelve. The next night the wind being about E.N.E. blew very hard, and the sea running high, we scudded right before it, with our small sail half down, expecting every moment to be swallowed up by the waves.

July the 5th Mr. Guishnot died, and on the 6th died Mr. Steward (son of Dr. Steward, of Spanish Town, in Jamaica) and his servant, both passengers. In the afternoon we found a dead duck, which looked green and not sweet. We ate it, however, very heartily, not without our thanks to the Almighty; and it is impossible for any, not in the like unhappy circumstances, to imagine how pleasant it was to our palate at that time, which at another would have been offensive both to our taste and smell.

On the 7th day of July, at one in the afternoon, we saw land about six leagues off. At four o'clock another man died, whom we threw overboard to lighten the boat. Our number was then reduced to seven. We had often taken thick fog-banks for land, which as often had given us great joy and hopes, that vanished with them at the same time; but when we really saw the land, it appeared so different from what we had so often taken for it, that we wondered how we could be so mistaken; and it is absolutely impossible for any man, not in our circumstances, to form any idea of the joy and pleasure it gave us when we were convinced of its reality. It gave us strength to row, which we had not had for four days before, and most, if not all of us, must infallibly have perished that very night, if we had not reached the land. Our souls exulted with joy and praises to our Almighty Preserver.

About six o'clock we saw several shallops fishing, for which we steered, having a fine gale of wind right on shore. We went, with sail and oars, about three or four knots; when we came so near, that we thought one of the shallops could hear us (being just under sail, and going in with their fish), we hallooed as loud as we could; they at length heard us, and lowered their sail. When we approached pretty near them they hoisted it again, and were going away from us; but we made such a dismal and melancholy noise that they brought to and took us in tow. They told us that our aspect was so dreadful that they were frightened at us. They gave us some bread and water; we chewed the bread small, and then, by mixing it with water, got it down with difficulty.

During our voyage in the boat, our mouths had been so dry, for want of moisture for several days, that we were obliged to wash them with salt water every two or three hours, to prevent our lips glueing together. We always drank our own water; and all the people drank salt water, excepting the captain, the surgeon, and myself. In foggy weather, the sail having imbibed some moisture, we used to wring it into a pewter bason, which we found in the boat. Having wrung it as dry as we could, we sucked it all over, and used to lick one another's clothes with our tongues. At length we were obliged, by inexpressible hunger and thirst, to eat a part of the bodies of six men, and drink the blood of four, for since we left the ship we had saved at one time but about half a pint, and at another a wine glass full of water, each man, in our hats. A little food sufficing us and finding the flesh very disagreeable, we confined ourselves to the hearts only. Finding ourselves now perishing with thirst, we were reduced to the melancholy, distressful, horrid act of cutting the throats of our companions, an hour or two after they were dead, to procure their blood, which we caught in the pewter bason, each man producing about a quart. But let it be remembered in our defence, that, without the assistance this blood afforded to nature, it would not have been possible for us to have survived.

About eight o'clock at night we got on shore in Old St. Lawrence harbor, in Newfoundland, where we were kindly received by Captain Lecrass, of Guernsey or Jersey, then admiral of the harbor. We were cautioned to eat and drink but little at first; which injunction we observed as well as the infirmity of human nature, when so near starving, would allow. We could sleep but little, our transports of joy being too great to admit of it. Our captain, who had been speechless thirty-eight hours, died about five o'clock the next morning, and was buried with all the honors that could be conferred on him, at that place.

Thus, out of the unfortunate crew of the Luxborough, it appears that sixteen perished with the ship, sixteen died of hunger, and only seven lived to get on shore, one of whom, the captain, died a few hours afterwards.

The boat in which the survivors reached Newfoundland, after traversing a distance of above one hundred leagues, was only sixteen feet long, five feet three inches broad, and two feet three inches deep.

It is related of Captain Boyce, that from the year 1727 to his death, he annually observed a strict and solemn fast on the 7th of July, in commemoration of his arrival in Newfoundland, after the dreadful hardships he had endured in consequence of the destruction of the Luxborough. So rigid was he in this act of humiliation, that, when in the decline of life, he became settled at Greenwich, he not only abstained from food, but from day-light, and would not suffer any person whatever to converse with him, lest that time should be unseasonably interrupted, which, with becoming gratitude, he devoted to returning thanks to the Supreme Being, for his wonderful escape. Let those who may be so unhappy as to experience his sufferings, imitate his piety; for signal benefits ought to be repaid by exemplary devotion.

*THE SUFFERINGS OF SIX DESERTERS DURING
THEIR PASSAGE IN A WHALE BOAT FROM THE
ISLAND OF ST. HELENA TO BRAZIL*

THE following extraordinary and affecting narrative relates to six deserters from the artillery of the island of St. Helena, whose singular adventures produced a court of enquiry on the 12th of December 1799, when John Brown, one of the survivors, delivered the following account, upon oath, before Captain Desfountain, president; Lieutenant B. Hodson, and Ensign Young.

"In June, 1799, I belonged to the first company of artillery in the service of this garrison, and on the 10th of that month, about half an hour before parade-time, M'Kinnon, gunner, and orderly of the second company, asked me if I was willing to go with him on board of an American ship, called the Columbia, Captain Henry Lelar, the only ship then in the roads. After some conversation I agreed, and met him, about seven o'clock, at the playhouse, where I found one M'Quin, of Major Seale's company, another man called Brighouse, another called Parr, and the sixth Matthew Conway.

"Parr was a good seaman, and said he would take us to the island of Ascension, or lie off the harbor till the Columbia could weigh anchor and come out.

"We went about eight o'clock to the West Rock, where the American boat, manned with three seamen, was waiting for us, and took us along-side the Columbia. We went aboard; Parr went down to the cabin, and we changed our clothes after having been on board half an hour.

"Brighouse and Conway proposed to cut a whale boat out of the harbor to prevent the Columbia from being suspected. This they accomplished, taking in her a coil of rope, five oars, and a large stone, by which she was moored. This happened about eleven at night.

"We observed lanterns passing on a line towards the sea gate, and hearing a noise, thought we were missed and sought for. We immediately embarked in the whale boat, with about twenty-five pounds of bread in a bag, and a small keg of water supposed to contain about thirteen gallons, one compass, and one quadrant given to us by the commanding officer of the Columbia, but in our hurry the quadrant was either left behind or dropped overboard.

"We then left the ship, pulling with two oars only to get ahead of her: the boat was half full of water, and we had nothing to bale it out; in this condition we rode out to sea, and lay off the island at a great distance, in hourly expectation of the American ship.

"About twelve o'clock, the second day, no ship appearing, by Parr's advice we bore away, steering N. by W. and then N.N.W. for the island of Ascension using our handkerchiefs as substitutes for sail. We met with a gale of wind which continued two days; the weather then became very fine, and we supposed we had run about ten miles an hour. McKinnon kept a reckoning with pen, ink, and paper with which, together with charts and maps, we were supplied by the Columbia.

"We continued our course till about the 18th in the morning, when we saw a number of birds, but no land. About twelve that day Parr said he was sure we must be past the island accounting it to be eight hundred miles from St. Helena. Each of us took off his shirt, and with them we made a small sprit-sail, lacing our jackets and trowsers together at the waist band to keep ourselves warm, and then altered our course to W. by N. thinking to make Rio de Janeiro, on the American coast. Provisions running very short, we allowed ourselves only one ounce of bread and two mouthfuls of water for twenty-four hours.

"On the 26th all our provisions were expended. On the

94

27th M'Quin put a piece of bamboo in his mouth to chew, and we all followed his example. On the night of that day it was my turn to steer the boat, and recollecting to have read of persons in our situation eating their shoes, I cut off a piece of one of mine; but being soaked with the salt water, I was obliged to spit it out, and eat the inside soal, of which I ate a part and distributed to the rest; but we found no benefit from it.

"On the 1st of July Parr caught a dolphin with a gaff that had been left in the boat. We all fell on our knees and thanked God for his goodness to us. We tore up our fish, and hung it to dry; about four we ate part of it, which agreed with us pretty well. On this fish we subsisted till the fourth about eleven o'clock, when finding the whole consumed bones and all, Parr, Brighouse, Conway, and myself, proposed to scuttle the boat and let her go down, to put us out of our misery; the other two objected, observing that God, who had made man, always found him something to eat.

"On the 5th, about eleven, M'Kinnon proposed it would be better to cast lots for one of us to die, in order to save the rest; to which we consented. William Parr, being seized two days before with the spotted fever, was excluded. He wrote the numbers and put them into a hat; we drew them out blindfolded and put them in our pockets. Parr then asked whose lot it was to die; none of us knowing what number we had in our pocket, and each praying to God that it might be his lot; it was agreed that No. 5 should die, and the lots being unfolded, M'Kinnon's was No. 5.

"We had concluded, that he, on whom the lot fell, should bleed himself to death; for which purpose we had provided ourselves with sharpened nails, which we got from the boat. With one of these M'Kinnon cut himself in three places; in his foot, hand, and wrist; and praying God to forgive his sins, he died in about a quarter of an hour.

"Before he was quite cold, Brighouse, with one of the nails, cut a piece of flesh off his thigh, and hung it up, leaving his body in the boat. About three hours afterwards, we all ate of it, but only in very small quantity. This piece lasted us till the 7th. We dipped the body every two hours in the sea to preserve it. Parr having found a piece of slate in the bottom of the boat, he sharpened it on the other large stone, and with it cut another piece off the thigh, which lasted us till the 8th, when it being my watch, and observing the water about break of day, to change color, I called the rest, thinking we were near the shore, but saw no land, it being not quite day-light.

"As soon as day appeared we discovered land right ahead, and steered towards it. About eight in the morning we were close to the shore; there being heavy surf, we endeavoured to turn the boat's head to it, but being very weak we were unable. Soon afterwards the boat upset, Parr, Conway, and myself, got on shore; M'Quin and Brighouse were drowned.

"We discovered a small hut on the beach in which were an Indian and his mother, who spoke Portuguese, and I, understanding that language, learned that there was a village, about three miles distant, called Belmont. The Indian went to the village, with the information that the French had landed, and in about two hours the governor of the village, a clergyman, with several armed men, took Conway and Parr, tied them by their hands and feet, and slinging them on a bamboo stick, conveyed them in that manner to the village. I, being very weak, remained in the hut some time, but was afterwards taken.

"On our telling them that we were English, we were immediately released, and three hammocks provided, in which we were taken to the governor's house, who resigned to us his own bed, and gave us milk and rice to eat; but as we had taken no food for a considerable time we were lock-jawed, and continued so till the 23d. During this time our host wrote to the governor of St. Salvador, who sent a small schooner to Porto Seguto to take us to St. Salvador. We were conducted on horseback to Porto Seguto, passing through Santa Cruz, where we remained about ten days: we afterwards embarked, and on our arrival at St. Salvador, Parr, on being questioned by the governor, told him, that our ship had foundered at sea, and we had saved ourselves in the boat: that the ship's name was the *Sally*, of Liverpool, that she belonged to his father, and was last from Cape Corfe Castle, on the coast of Africa, to touch at Ascension for turtle, and then bound to Jamaica. Parr likewise said he was the captain.

"We remained at St. Salvador about thirteen days, during which time the inhabitants made up a subscription of 200 l. each man. We then embarked in the Maria, a Portuguese ship, for Lisbon; Parr, as mate; Conway, boatswain's mate, and myself, being sickly, as a passenger. In thirteen days we arrived

96

at Rio de Janeiro. Parr and Conway sailed for Lisbon, and I was left in the hospital.

"In about three months, Captain Elphinstone, of the Diamond, pressed me into his Majesty's service, giving me the choice of remaining on that station, or to proceed to the admiral at the Cape. I chose the latter, and was put with seven suspected deserters, on board the Ann, a Botany Bay ship, in irons, with the convicts. When I arrived at the Cape, I was put on board the Lancaster of 64 guns; I never entered, but, at length received my discharge, since which I engaged in the Duke of Clarence as a seaman. I was determined to surrender myself at the first opportunity, in order to relate my sufferings to the men of this garrison, to deter others from attempting so mad a scheme."

In attending to the above narrative, as simple as it is affecting, we cannot help noticing the justice of Providence, so strikingly exemplified in the melancholy fate of M'Kinnon, the deluder of these unhappy men, and the victim of his own disgraceful scheme. May his fate prove a memento to soldiers and sailors, and a useful though awful lesson, to the encouragers and abettors of desertion!

From

FRA DENIS DE CARLI'S

A VOYAGE TO CONGO IN THE YEARS 1666 and 1667

TO satisfy the curiosity of several persons, who press me in such an obliging manner as I cannot easily withstand, to give them an exact account of what I have seen and learned during the long voyage, from which I am lately returned, I will write a relation of the kingdom of Congo and of Africk, where the duty of my mission made me acquainted with strange customs, and go through abundance of hardships, omitting at present to speak of Brasil, and some other parts of America, whither we were first carried, and of which I shall say but very little.

In the year 1666, Alexander the 7th being pope, fifteen Capuchin missioners, of which I was one, were dispatched by the cardinals *de propaganda fide*, and received the commissions or patents at Bononia, where I then resided, at the hands of F. Stephen de Cesa, of the noble family of Clermont, whose virtue has been since rewarded with post of general of the said order. Our patents contained the following privileges: to dispense with any irregularity except incurred by bigamy, or wilful murder: to dispense and commute simple vows even to that of chastity, but not that of religion: to dispense with marriages within the second and third degrees, and for pagans converted to keep one of their wives: to absolve in cases reserved to the pope: to bless church-stuff, churches, and chalices: to give leave to eat flesh and whitemeats, and to say two masses a day in case of necessity: to grant plenary indulgences: to deliver a soul out of purgatory, according to the intention of the priest, in a mass for the dead said on monday and tuesday: to wear secular clothes in case of necessity: to say the rosary for want of a breviary, or any other impediment; to read forbidden books, except Macchiavel. . . .

[The narrative takes them to Africa, describes their work and some of their difficulties.]

The superior finding me in a fever, which increased, thought Providence had sent him to bury us both, and would not go away till he had seen the end of it: however he resolved to try means to cure me, causing me to be blooded twice a day, which I suffered to be done without speaking one word: but in truth that usage in a few days brought me into a desperate condition, having been forty times blooded, and the fever never decreasing. I confessed, and received the holy viaticum, being nothing but skin and bones. The father, but for whose charity I believe I had died like a beast, perceiving the disease was like to be tedious, the fury of the fever abating, gave me to understand, that for the good of the mission he must of necessity be gone. I had scarce strength, bowing myself, to tell him, that since he could not stay longer, he should inform my Blacks how they ought to manage me; and that he would please to send F. Michael de Orvietto to me, with whom I had travelled, and who knew how to look to the sick. He promised to do so, but his orders miscarrying, he came not. I was left in my bed, not able to turn my self; and the worst was, that so much bleeding had almost blinded me. In that condition, half alive and half dead, I was left to the mercy of those Blacks, who stole what they could, and brought me, when they thought of it, a porringer of broth; I being able to swallow nothing of substance, and loathing all sustenance.

One day when I was more cast down with melancholy and sadness than the distemper itself, I received a visit from a Portuguese jesuit, who came from S. Salvador and was returning to the college at Loanda. When he saw me in that miserable condition, How now, father, said he, are you so sick, and yet stay in this desert? I came, said I, very well in health into this country, but after losing my companion, I fell sick, and have been now some months struggling with death; but I perceive it is not God's will it should have the upper hand, though it was one of my wishes. Two days he staid comforting me, and presented me with some pullets, which were more acceptable for coming from his hand, than for their own rarity. We confess'd to one another, he declaring it was a satisfaction to him to be thus provided, being to pass through many places, where the firing of the dry herbage made the wild beasts run about the country. He assured me that as he came, he was forced to get up a tree, tho' there were sixty Blacks with him, to avoid death threatened them by two tigers. Therefore we are not to believe what some authors have writ, that the tigers do not assault Whites, but only Blacks.

After his departure I remained with my continual distemper; but what comforted me was, that every day I baptized ten or twelve children; and not being able to sit up alone in my bed, was held up by two Blacks, another holding the book, and another the bason, receiving what alms they gave me; not for my own sake, for I could eat nothing, but for my family, who would all of them have forsaken me had they wanted meat. I married several of the chief people; one of them gave me a she-goat, whose milk I drank every day, which indeed was little in quantity, but counted a great dainty in that country. This happiness I had in my indisposition, that I slept all night, which is twelve hours long, never varying half an hour all the year round. I would willingly have eaten an egg, but sick people there are forbid eggs, they being looked upon as unwholsom for those that are ill, being too hot in those parts. Whilst I lay thus in bed, several cripples came to beg of me, and I gave them some of those shells that serve instead of money, of which three thousand five hundred make the value of a pistole; so many are given for a pullet, for at Lisbon a pullet is worth a crown, in Brasil a piece of eight, at Angola ten shillings, and at Congo a pistole, which seems to me cheaper than a crown at Lisbon.

My bed was against the wall, which was of fat clay ill put together, and might well be called a nest of rats; for there were so many of them and so large, that they troubled me very much, running over me every night, and biting my toes, which broke my rest very much. To prevent this I caused my bed to be laid in the middle of the room, but to no purpose, for those cursed creatures knew where to find me. I caused mats to be laid all about my bed for my Blacks to lie on, and defend me not only against the rats, but any other wild creatures that might come. This precaution stood me in no stead, for there was no night but the rats disturbed me. Another consideration mov'd me to keep those Blacks in my chamber, which was, that they might see how I lived, and be witnesses of my behaviour, that country being no more free from detraction than others.

I took the freedom to acquaint the great duke [of Bamba] with the trouble I had from the rats, and the stink of my Blacks, who had always some wild and disagreeable smell. He said he would give me an infallible remedy against those two inconveniences, and that had he known it sooner, he would not have failed of sending it: This was a little monkey that would secure me against the rats by blowing on them when he spyed them, and would expel the ill scent by that of his skin, which smelt of musk. I gave him a thousand thanks for his charity towards me, and said I should expect that favour from him. He sent me the tame monkey, whom I laid at the feet of my bed, and who performed his duty exactly; for when the rats came as they were wont, the monkey blew hard at them two or three times, and made them run away; and the scent of musk with which he perfumed the chamber, corrected the ill smell of the Blacks. These monkeys are not the same creatures as the civet cats, for I have seen several of those cats at Loanda, where they keep them shut up in a wooden cage, and fastened with an iron or silver chain, and the owner of them once a week with a spoon takes off the civet, which they call *angeglia*, and which is found in a purse between the hind legs. In short, the little monkey did me extraordinary service, not only for those uses already mentioned, but to keep my head and beard clean and comb'd, better than any of the Blacks would have done: and to say the truth, it is easier to teach those monkeys than the Blacks; for these have enough to do to learn one thing well, but the others do every thing they are put to dexterously.

I just began to mend, tho' the fever had not left me, when one night as I lay asleep, I felt the monkey had leaped upon my head; I thought the rats had frighted him, and made much of him to still him, but at the same time the Blacks arose crying, Out, out father. Being thoroughly awake, I asked them what was the matter? The ants, said they, are broke out, and there is no time to be lost. There being no possibility for me to stir, I bid them carry me into the garden, which they did, four of them lifting me upon my straw bed: Their nimbleness stood me in good stead, for the ants already began to run upon my legs, and get to my body. After shaking them off, they took straw, and fired it on the floor of four rooms, where the ants were already above half a foot thick; and there must needs be a wonderful quantity, for besides the chambers, the porch and walking place were full. They being destroy'd by fire, as I said, I was carried back to my chamber, where the stink was so great that I was forced to hold the monkey close to my face. Having caused the mats to be shaken, we had scarce slept half an hour before I was awakened by the light of a flame of fire at the chamber-door: I called my people to see what it was, they found the fire had taken hold of the thatch of the house, and fearing the fire might increase with the wind, I caused my self to be carried again into the garden. The fire being put out, we endeavour'd to go to sleep again, but all this hurry had discomposed me too much; and before the troublesome night was quite over, I heard a great noise near us: I waked my Blacks that they might be in readiness, in case there was some other army of beasts to engage. One of them laid hold of one of the halberds F. Michael Angelo had caused to be made, and went out to see who made all that hurly-burly. He came back again to tell us, that the pismires having again broke into a neighbouring cottage, they had burnt them as we did; but the hut being all of straw, it was consumed as well as the ants, which made the Blacks get out of their houses for fear the wind should carry about the flame and burn all that quarter. I got off, causing my self to be once more carry'd into the garden giving God thanks that he had delivered me from the pismires; for had I been alone fast in my bed, and unable to stir, as I then was, it is certain they had eaten me up alive. This often happens in the kingdom of Angola, where in the morning there are cows found devoured in the night by ants, and nothing left of them but the bones. It is no small deliverance to escape them, for there are some that fly, and are hard to be removed from the place where they lay hold: but God be praised that my body was not devoured by them alive.

I had a young tiger given me, which I did not care to keep, especially because the monkey would not lie upon the bed with him: I gave it goat's milk to preserve it, but it did not live long, and I was not sorry for it, it being no satisfaction to me to see that fine beast, tho' little, and as yet unfit to do like the old ones. The great duke's visits were a great comfort to me, and when he could not come himself, he sent some of his chief men, who would stay three or four hours sitting about me upon mats; but they always having their pipes in their mouths, and the smoke offended my head, I was forc'd to tell them they would oblige me in coming, but that I beg'd for God's sake not to take tobacco in our house, and that the rather because their pipes which are an ell long have great bowls like a little pot, which are never out. They were so obliging as to comply with me, and when they came left their pipes in the garden. . . .

AN ACCOUNT OF THE WONDERFUL PRESERVA-
TION OF THE SHIP TERRA NOVA *OF LONDON,*
PETER DANIEL COMMANDER, HOMEWARD-
BOUND FROM VIRGINIA.

WRITTEN BY CHARLES MAY, MATE IN THE
SAID SHIP.

THE dangers we ran thro' in this passage, and the distress we were in, were so extraordinary, that they cannot but deserve a place among the many relations the publick has receiv'd, of strange shipwrecks, and unaccountable escapes and deliverances of vessels reduc'd to the utmost extremity.

Tho' here be no new discovery, or description of nations before unknown, but a passage so much frequented, yet the circumstances of it are such, and the providence so singular, as are scarce to be parallel'd in any other voyage. I have been particular in the circumstances, as believing they would be acceptable to all that have any insight in sea-affairs, and represent the whole matter the more lively. As to the truth, I deliver it not upon hearsay, but as an eye-witness, present at every part, and void of any motive to draw me away from it, besides that there are doubtless many still living, who might disprove me should I be any way inclin'd to romance. In fine, this may serve as an encouragement to all that venture upon the sea, ever to hope the best in danger, and to confide in that providence which deliver'd me when all human hopes seem'd to fail.

On the 17th of August 1688, the ship *Terra Nova*, Capt. Daniell commander, arriv'd at Port Royal in Jamaica. His grace the late duke of Albemarle was at that time governor of the island; but whilst we lay there unloading and providing for our return, the duke fell sick and dy'd.

Upon his death, the dutchess resolv'd to return for England with her whole family; and, in order to it, agreed with our commander to take aboard as passengers fifteen of her men-servants, which, with two brothers we had before receiv'd, made seventeen. They laid in a plentiful stock of all manner of provisions, as sheep, hogs, turkies, hens, &c. with a sufficient quantity of Indian wheat, and other sorts of grain to feed them during the passage, according to all probability.

The ship being well fitted, and the provisions and passengers aboard, we sail'd from Port Royal on the 24th of December, being Christmas-eve. We were richly loaden with sugar, logwood, Jamaica pepper, hides, indigo, sarsaparilla, &c. besides my lord duke's costly furniture, such as rich hangings, curious chairs, large looking-glasses, and all other choice goods. But above all, in the great cabbin, was a large chest, so heavy, that five or six men could but just draw it along the deck, full of pigs of silver, bags of pieces of eight, and some gold.

This treasure brought us into some danger; for the night after our departure, a sloop came up with us, and bearing along our side, after haling us, pretended to be sent on purpose with some letters from the then deputy-governor, and desir'd we would send our boat aboard for them, they having no boat, or else they would lay us aboard on our larboard quarter, and deliver the packet. Our commander suspecting some knavery, commanded them to keep off till day, and then they might deliver their message, our guns and small-arms being all ready to fire upon them if they offer'd to come near us. However, they ventur'd sometimes to make up towards us, but our commander threatening them hard, they fell astern of us again; and at last, seeing us so resolute in keeping them off, they durst not attempt us, but made away, firing two guns with shot at us, which we return'd in like manner with interest.

Being rid of them, we pass'd by the islands of Caimanes, and that of Pinos, so round the west cape of Cuba, call'd St. Antonio, in 21° 52′ N. lat. and then enter'd the gulph of Florida, which we pass'd in a few days with safety; and being got into the open sea, we ply'd to the northward till we got to the westward islands, of which Corvo is the most northerly in lat. of 40° 9′ N. Our commander fearing the north winds, stood on, still plying to the northward, till we got into the latitude of 45° N. It was then the beginning of February, at which time we met with very hard winds, for the most part east southerly; and being got so far northerly, we design'd not to raise our lat. any more as yet, but were forc'd by the violence of the said winds to ply with our three courses, for about seven days, our topmasts struck and lower'd snug down.

On the 8th of February 1688/9 the time when the sun enters Pisces, the storm ceas'd, and it prov'd a pleasant morning, with a fine easy gale, tho' in the same corner still, which made us all fall to work with willing minds; so we sway'd up our topmasts, set our topsails, and let out all our reefs. But at noon, when we expected a good observation, having had none for some days, we found the weather thickened again, and look'd foul, the wind at the same time shifting to S.E. and beginning to blow hard. We reef'd our topsails again, then handed them, lower'd our topmasts snug down, as before, and lay some short time under three courses. Towards night, perceiving the weather grew still worse, and the wind stronger, we handed our foresail, and lower'd the yard close down a portlongs; then did the same by our mizen, and before night reef'd our mainsail; but at last finding the wind too fierce for us to hold that sail, we lower'd our main-yard snug down a portlongs, and furl'd the sail. Having then but one mizen-sail, which was to the yard, our commander was loth to venture it in the force of the wind, and therefore order'd a main-bonnet should be spread on our weather quarter; which done, and our helm clap'd aport, being then our lee-side, the ship answer'd our expectations, and lay very well, looking upon the sea all night.

About four in the morning, the commander consulted with us all what was best to be done, the wind raging, and the sea running very high; and it was agreed to let her lie as she had done all the night, not daring to scud, lest the sea should overtake us, or for fear of broaching to, and so foundering the ship. This was the 9th of February 1688/9 when about six of the clock in the morning, day appearing, as I stood at the steerage door, a violent sea fell in upon our deck, and floated our deal yawl, which was then stow'd in our long-boat on the deck, clear over our lee-gunnel; but her painter being made fast to the ring of our long-boat's bow, she tow'd by it under our lee, till we presently cut her loose, and never saw her more. Next our sprit-sail broke loose, and in a moment was gone clear out of the boltrope. No sooner was this past, but a second violent sea broke in upon us, and carry'd away our two bowers and stream-anchor clear out of the lashings, and they were quite lost; but the same sea wash'd our sheet-anchor off the lee-gunnel, where she was stow'd; however, the stopper to which the stock was lash'd, holding, and the bill of the anchor lighting upon the upper channel-wale, there she remained, tho' without board. Fearing lest the past unhappy accidents should be follow'd by a worse, our men went forward upon the fore-castle to overhawl our runner and tackle, whilst I stood in the lee-scuppers with a pair of slings to fling the anchor that lay quite without board. We were at least half an hour slinging and hooking the tackles, all which time I was, without any intermission, beaten by the sea continually breaking in; yet we compass'd our design, and lash'd the anchor, with a rope thro' the scuppers, to the gunnel.

This done, and having try'd the pump, and found the ship tight, we went in to refresh us, it being about eight of the clock in the morning, our passengers all abed as if they had been ashore; but our commander bearing an equal share in our labour, and endeavouring to secure all things. When we had set all to rights, and provided the best we could for other accidents, I brought some bread, and every one having taken what he thought fit, for we had plenty enough of that and other provisions for a long West-India voyage, yet, as it happened, little enough, tho' it had been much more, as will appear hereafter, I went to the leeward, and stood looking forward out at the steerage door, when on a sudden a pro-digious wave broke to the windward of our ship, and fell with such violence upon us, that it set us all a-swimming, scarce knowing whether we were within or without the ship, but that on me roul'd the men, chests, handspikes, shot, and whatever lay to windward. The same sea broke away our starboard gallery, in which were all our compasses but two that stood in the bittacle in the steerage, and stav'd all the great cabbin windows, so that it was like the rest, full of water; and the chest of drawers, cabbin table, chairs, and what else lay to windward, fell all upon the captain, keeping him striving for life under water. The passengers far'd no better; for being in close low cabbins, they were almost smother'd before they could get out.

The violence of this sea had quite overset our ship, so that the coamings of the main-hatches lay under water, and a man might have walk'd upon her starboard side without-board, as he could before upon the main deck. We could not have lain long in this condition, without perishing, and therefore it pleas'd God, that the same sea which overset us, raking us along on our weather quarter with so much violence, hove our ship quite round against the sea, so that, tho' thus overset, being so violently toss'd round, she brought the sea under our lee bow, and that side of the ship which before was the weather side, became the lee side. Having now the sea under our lar-board bow, it gave her such a second toss, as set her upright again; and being at a stand, the water fell from off the deck.

Tho' this disaster all together was not the work of a minute, yet the damage our ship sustained by it was incredible. It carry'd away her head and cut-water, broke the boltsprit within a foot and an half of the stem, bore away the foremast close by the forecastle, the main-mast within five foot and an half of the deck, and the mizen-mast, which was stept in the gun-room, close to the quarter-deck. It wash'd away seven powder chests plated fast to the deck with winding plate, off the fore-castle and quarter-deck, stav'd the long-boat in her lashings all to bits, and in her drown'd and wash'd overboard six hogs, as many sheep, and some goats, besides six hen-coops full of hens it carry'd away; and in one hen-coop left on the quarter-deck with about two dozen of hens, there was not one alive. Thirteen turkies were drowned in the forecastle, standing on the guns, two tire of watercasks wash'd off the main-deck, and a spare topmast which was broke into three pieces, two minion guns, carriages and all, were lost from off the main-deck, on each side the bulkhead of the steerage, tho' well lash'd with new britchings and tackles; two falconets and a paterero were taken off the quarter-deck, and both the bulk-heads of steerage and great cabbin stav'd to bits, so that there was not the bigness of a trencher to be found of them. But the worst of all was, that it carry'd away our starboard-side, fore and aft, from the steerage to the cook-room, as if it had been saw'd close by the deck, and at the same time stav'd our bittacle to mash, with one of the compasses that were in it. The dish of the other compass, by great providence, rouling about among the other broken things, was taken up by the duke's first gentleman, who threw it carelessly into his cabbin, without considering of what value and use it was like to be to us, but the box of it was lost.

When our captain had, with much difficulty, clear'd himself of all the things that fell upon him, he call'd to me to know how things stood, who soon acquainted him how all our masts were gone, and we lay like a wreck. Here-upon we run to clap our helm a-weather; and coming to lay hold of the whipstaff, I found it was fallen into the gun-room; and going down to see the cause of it, was almost up to the knees in water upon our lower deck, which, with the beating of the ship, wash'd from side to side in such manner, that I had much ado to scramble in to feel for the tiller. Having at length waded thro', I found the tiller lying in the gun-room on the deck, broke off short at the rudder head. Whilst I was thus groveling in the dark, I felt my body all over cover'd with rats, as thick as they could stand upon me, on my coat, arms, neck, and my very head, so that I was forc'd to make my escape into the light to get rid of those vermin. Going up to see if we could by any means get the stump of the tiller from the rudder head, we perceiv'd our rudder hanging only by the upper gudgin, and floating in the sea across our counter; and in less than a glass's time it broke clear away.

All this while our gunnel lay open, the water continually pouring down into the hold, and we could not tell which way to remedy it to prevent foundering. Our masts and yards lay still under our lee; and the ship driving in the trough of the sea upon them, it was hard to get rid of them, and it was altogether impossible to save any, because of the violence of the wind and sea, and the rouling of the ship. All our main chain-plates, both of shrouds and back-stays, both to leeward and windward, broke off short as if they had been glass, and not one of them held: so did all the chain-plates before, excepting the two aftermost plates of our larboard shrouds, which alone held, and kept the wreck under our lee, till at last our boatswain cut them away with a hatchet, and then they drove away a-head of us. Our mizen chain-plates broke all to windward, but those to leeward held; by which means we sav'd our mizen shrouds, which, with one half of our cross-jack yard, and a piece of our ensign-staff, was all we could save of our wreck. Besides, we found our grindstone at the end of our windlass, in the corner of our starboard gunnel; which was very strange, considering that before we lost our mast, the stone lay in its trough, and that nail'd down to the deck, between the guns by the steerage door; yet the trough was wash'd overboard, and the stone roul'd so far forwards, and lodg'd in that unlikely place very unaccountably, considering the rouling of the ship; and we should have had a great miss of it, had it been lost. Nor was it a less providence, that our main-mast and all the rigging falling overboard, did no harm to neither of our pumps; for had they been spoil'd, we could never have out-liv'd the next day.

Next we must contrive to secure our broken side, and keep the water from running down into the hold; for our ship, by the shuffling of the wind, lay again with her broken side to windward, and the weather continuing tempestuous, we were afraid the sea would drive away our other gunnel, by beating upon it continually; besides that, the water which broke in upon our deck was constantly running down into the hold betwixt the side and the ceiling. The first thing we did was to stretch a coil of two inch rope from the timbers of the fore-castle to those of the quarter-deck, fore and aft, in the nature of a rope-maker's walk when their tenterhooks are all full of cable yarns. This we did to lay hold of as we walk'd along the deck, because, having nothing to steady our hull, she roul'd intolerably, and it was almost impossible for a man to keep his feet on the deck, without holding. This done, the boatswain and I having a bolt of Holland's duck deliver'd us by the captain, and our pockets full of nails, we stretch'd the said duck from the top of our broken gunnel, afore all along the deck, tacking it down with here and there a nail, both within and without the deck; and, to keep it the closer, our commander bored some hoops taken off an old cask, and drawing them out strait, we nail'd them upon it. It had been impossible for the boatswain and myself to have done this, had we not had two long pieces of new rope about our middles, which were made fast at the other end to the rings on the deck, and two men attending us, they were let loose or shorten'd as we had occasion. With all this precaution and care the work took us up about two hours; during all which time, the sea continually beating in over us, we could scarce keep our eyes open to see what we were doing, or have full time to breath for fear of the water, which never ceas'd falling upon us.

By that time we had done, it was near night, and our commander had made two long hoses of canvas, and nail'd them to the pumps to convey the water we pumped out of the hold, over-board; and whilst the pumps were fixing, we tack'd up a main-topgallant-sail for a bulk-head to our steerage, rather to keep out the wind than the sea. Then our captain encourag'd the men the best he could to stand by one another in their distress, which they promising to perform, he sat him down on the steerage with an half-hour glass, the only one that had escaped breaking, betwixt his legs, and four men were set to pump, being reliev'd every half-hour by four others; which was continu'd for eighteen hours incessantly; at the end whereof, to our unspeakable joy, we found the pumps did suck.

What water was betwixt decks we were forc'd to cut holes to let out, the scupper holes being all stopp'd, except what was let down into our run, at the powder-room scuttle; which was done by our boatswain, who seeing so much water between decks, took up the said scuttle, thinking it might have drain'd down there to come to the pump; but we paid dear for this his indiscretion; for the water gushing down there, fell into our bread-room, and damnify'd half our bread. Thus ended the 9th of February.

The next morning after our pump had suck'd, we found several great leaks in the run of our ship, which were occasion'd by the breaking loose of the rudder-bands, and the leaks were in such places that there was no coming to stop them; only the upper gudgin being nail'd to the rudder, was hung upon an iron hook drove thro' the stern-post; which drawing, and the whole being left open, I stripp'd an ear of Indian wheat, and thrust the husk of it strongly into the hole, where it remain'd till the ship got a new rudder. The other leaks were a continual trouble to us; for besides them our ship was as tight as a drum, notwithstanding all the damage receiv'd.

About eight of the clock in the morning, this 10th of February, to lighten the ship, our commander caus'd six minion guns to be hove over-board, which was done by giving them a run out at the port-holes, on the lee side, where they stood in the steerage. Then we got up several West-India hogsheads of Jamaica pepper in baskets, and threw it over-board, with several casks of indigo, and the duke's curious chairs, and rich hangings as also abundance of logwood and other goods: but the indigo scattering about the decks, spoil'd all our beds and cloathes, so that not one man had a dry or clean rag to put on. Still the storm continued, and the pump was ply'd day and night.

We were now tired, and, what was worse, must think of retrenching our allowance, for we had fed two days on the hens and turkies that were drowned, which was dainty fare; but no more being left, and we not knowing how long we might remain in that condition, judg'd it convenient to begin in time, and reduce ourselves to short allowance that it might last the longer, about half of our bread being damag'd by the salt-water. The cook had every day a pail full of it deliver'd to him, which he heat'd in the furnace, and then every six men had a mess bowl of it full: this we eat with sugar, having cut a hole thro' the bulkhead of our bread-room, to come at a hogshead, which prov'd very good, and was a great help to get down that wet bisket. This choice fare last'd us about ten or twelve days, and agreed with us well; but after that, the wet bread grew perfectly rotten, mouldy, and of several colours, so that we could eat no more of it, but hove what was left overboard in ballast baskets, and our allowance still grew harder. I had hitherto kept the key of the bread, but now observing that some men mutter'd as believing I could go to it when I would, and so fare better than they; therefore to satisfy all, I deliver'd up the key to the captain. From this time our allowance was settl'd all alike for men and boys, our commander himself not except'd. When we were rid of our rotten bread, we liv'd for some days upon the provisions that were laid in for the sheep and hogs, being Indian wheat, which lay about the gun-room damnified by the sea water: this we boil'd sometimes whole, and sometimes, when we could, would beat it in a piece of canvas, and eat sugar with it to get it down. When the Indian wheat was done, then every six men had two pounds of bread for a week; four times a-week stockfish was boil'd, and then every six men had a pound and a half; and three times a-week beef, each time a small piece between six; also puddings three times a-week, each time a pound and a half of flour between six. The meat was water'd, and puddings made with salt-water, and boil'd in the same, as were the stockfish, and eaten without any oyl, butter, or other thing whatsoever. Our allowance of drink was a small cocoa-nut-shell a-man, being about half a pint, or little more, deliver'd every night by the captain himself, or his steward, and then the spike cut off close till next night. The carpenter and I had a thirteen gallon cask of lime-juice, after all the rum was gone, which we broach'd, and when we could come at it without being seen, drank it with melasses, or sugar spoil'd by the sea water; but it lasted not long. We always drank it in private, because if any man saw another eat or drink, he would beg most earnestly, tho' he knew not what it was; for our short allowance pinch'd hard.

I was often commanded to go help stow the dry provisions with the steward, they being apt to shake loose in the lazaretto under the cook-room, which was a very agreeable employment, because I always found some scatter'd pease lying about in the scuppers, which I put in my pocket; and tho' they were swollen and ready to burst with salt-water, I eat them very greedily in some corner, not daring to be seen to eat upon the deck. Other times going to scuttle a cask of beef, and giving out the allowance to be put into water, I put into my pocket all the loose bits I found in the pickle, or could pick off the pieces, and would afterwards privately eat them raw without bread. But when the steward went down for sugar or bread, I had always some pretence, as looking to the powder, or the like, to go down with him; and when his head was thrust thro' the hole in the bulk-head of the bread-room to come at the sugar which was in the hold, then would I stuff a pair of Turkish boots I wore, as full of bread as I could, so as not to be discovered, and getting up into the gun-room where my chest lay, put out my cargo there in the dark; which done, I got again into the bread-room, and waited till the steward came out, begging a bit of bread of him, which he seldom refused me. This lasted not long, for at last the steward found the bread in my boots; and tho' he said nothing to any body but myself, yet I lost the favourable opportunity, and was forc'd for the future to fare as my brethren did. When we could gather rain-water on the quarter-deck, we boil'd pease, and not else; and tho' they were, when boil'd, as hard as swan-shot, and as bitter as gall, yet they went down pleasantly enough without butter. Very often when the beef was laid in water, it would be slic'd away, and half of it eaten raw, and yet we never knew who did it. The manner of dividing our victuals was thus. When six men had their allowance given them, it was laid down fairly betwixt them, and divided as equal as possible; then one man stood aside so that he could not see it; and another pointing to a piece, ask'd who should have it? and he that was nam'd by the other that did not see, took it; by which means we had no dispute about victuals. There were abundance of parrots aboard, and almost starv'd for want, and the duke's servants would commonly sell a parrot for a bisket to any man that could pinch one out of his belly, which several seamen did, and brought some of them home, tho' many dy'd by the way. I brought a delicate bird to Plymouth, which cost me five dollars in the West Indies, and thought it harder to maintain that poor creature aboard than I have since done a wife and two children. Rain water sav'd in a blanket was often sold by the men for a royal plate, or sixpence a pint to the passengers.

But to come now to the manner of building our bulk-heads, we had, as I said before, sav'd half our cross-jack, and a piece of our ensign-staff; with these two we made a pair of shoves, and fixing them on the deck over our starboard pump, lifted it clear off our lower deck. Then I went down into the hold, or well, and having made way by removing some sticks of logwood, I got at our dry oxe-hides, and rouling them close together, made a shift to hand up sixteen of them through the hole of the pump. Then the pump was again lower'd down into its place, we struck our shoves, and with the hydes we made up our bulk-heads, which when dry did very well, but as soon as wet they flopped like a piece of tripe.

All this while the weather was no way favourable, and we were spent with labour, and had not a dry thread to put on, and for about a week the boatswain's eyes and mine were so sore with the great cold we had taken, that we were not able to do any thing, but sit all day in a dark hole; but with our surgeon's assistance we soon recover'd of that distemper. However the blisters we had on our knees by nailing Holland's duck on the side of our ship troubled us long after. The foul weather held us full twenty days without any abatement, and all this time we drove in the trough of the sea, the same side still to windward. However by the dish of our compass we always observ'd her drift according to judgment, and now and then took a bad observation, and every day at noon lay flat on the deck to write down our past four and twenty hours work.

On the 21st day it prov'd fair weather, and being on the deck we spy'd a sail to windward of us standing to the eastward with his larboard tack aboard, the wind being now westerly; whereupon we fir'd four or five guns out of our forecastle on the starboard side, and at last perceiv'd the ship bear down upon us, to our great joy, as hoping for some relief. When she was within a bowshot to windward and a head of us, discovering us to be a wreck, she hoisted out a small boat; and in her sent four men, two of whom were Dutch and Portuguese. I was the only man that could speak to them, having learnt some Dutch in my youth, when I lived two years in the city Zutphen. The Dutchman told me the ship was a Portuguese homeward bound from Brazil, of about 5 or 600 tuns, as I remember. A Portuguese and a Dutchman were left aboard our ship, and the captain and I went aboard the Portuguese. The Dutchman interpreted betwixt the Portuguese captain and me, and I told our commander what the Dutchman said: we told the Portuguese the condition we were in, and heartily begg'd of him to afford us a spare yard or top-mast to make us a jury-mast. He had three or four of each sort lash'd along his gunnels and upon deck. Our commander offer'd him goods or money for them, and desir'd he would spare us a compass. The proud fellow stood on the deck with his hands in the sleeves of his watch-coat, and without returning any answer to our request, ask'd, How far we thought the rock of Lisbon distant from us? we answer'd, about 160 leagues eastward; then the Portuguese, shrugging his shoulders, told us, that he could not spare us so much as a compass, for fear the same accident should befall him in sailing those 160 leagues, as had happened to us. But in case we were willing to quit our ship and bring our provisions and water with us, he would receive us aboard, and carry us to Lisbon. Hereupon our captain resolving to stay by his ship, left him, and the unnatural monster never so much as ask'd him to sit down, or to drink a draught of water; so we went into the boat again, and return'd to our own ship. As we put from his side, he order'd some of his men to throw us a piece of wood, which was so rotten that it did us no service. Our commander made their men drink some rum, and then sent them back to their own ship, which then hoisted sail, and in three hours time was out of sight. But before the boat went off, our commander call'd all the seamen and passengers together, and told them, if any had a mind to go aboard the Portuguese whilst the boat was there, he would send them away with a competent allowance of provision, he being resolv'd to stay by his ship. To which the duke's chief gentleman made answer, he would stay and share his fortune, and all the company resolv'd the same; whereupon the boat was dismiss'd. Within half an hour after the boat was gone, the boat-swain began to revile me, as if I had been the cause, that he and all the ship's crew were not taken aboard the Portuguese, but our captain hearing it, took him up severely, and never lik'd him well after.

The weather now growing fair, and the water smooth, a black we had aboard, and I, were let down in ropes out at our great cabbin ports, with each a pocket full of spikes and a hammer, to try if we could stop the leaks made by the tearing of the rudder bands; which with great trouble we perform'd, driving in two and thirty spikes between us, about a foot and a half under water: which made our hull so tight in the run, that she made not a drop of water there all the voyage after; so that we had no more trouble of the pump. The same black that afternoon going up on the poop, happen'd to drop the piece of our ensign-staff over-board, and knowing we should be at a mighty loss for want of it, he boldly leap'd into the sea, and brought it to us again, which after serv'd us for a mizen-mast. Being now somewhat favour'd by the weather, as hath been said, we began to consult how to get new masts and yards. In order to it, with the help of our former shores, *viz.* the piece cross-jack yard, and the piece of our ensign-staff, we got up the stump of our mizen-mast, which was about seven foot long serviceable, and no more. Our carpenter proving a meer bungler, and unfit to do any thing, the captain himself made a pair of cross-trees on one end of the aforesaid stump; then I saw'd away all the splinter'd part of our main-mast down to the sound wood, and about two foot and a half lower down I saw'd the remaining stump one third part through, and with a coopers-ads I hollow'd a place in the said stump of the main-mast, large enough to contain the stump of the mizen-mast when plac'd in it. These two stumps we spik'd and woulded together, and, with wedges drove within the woulding with a maul, secur'd them. Then taking out the stump of the bolt-sprit, whose serviceable timber was not above three foot and a half, we fix'd that to the lower part of our main-mast in the well, which, with the help of another man, I plac'd in the step, and spik'd them together, then woulded and wedg'd them securely. So that when we had done, our main-mast was about seventeen foot high above our upper-deck. The piece of bolt-sprit was lower'd down to me through the hole of the pump into the well. Whilst I was in the well, I knock'd down two boards at the bottom of it to get at the ground tire of sugar, and beating in the head of a hogshead, found all the said ground tire was quite out, and pumpt over-board. The piece of our cross-jack yard made us a main-topmast. A main-yard we made with a spare tiller we had in the ship, and the tiller that broke in the rudder head. The top-sail yard was a main-top gallant yard that lay between decks. Our mizen-shrouds made us main-shrouds, and for the top-mast we made shrouds of two inch rope. Our main-top gallant sail was a main-top-sail, and we made a main-sail out of an old fore-sail. Thus the main-masts, yards and sails were fix'd.

What to do for a fore-mast we knew not, but being one day in the gun-room, I perceiv'd a beam under the great cabbin, which was loose upon the ceiling, not bolted nor kneed. Having acquainted the captain with it, he view'd it and had it cut down at both ends, and carrying it on the deck, he himself lin'd it all round with three-inch plank, after which we clapt eleven wouldings on it, and having fix'd on a cap and cross-trees, we stept it in the stump of our fore-mast, and made shrouds of two inch and a half rope; so was our fore-mast fix'd. For a top-mast to it, we took our whip-staff, and to strengthen it with a small gouge, on that side we design'd to stand aft, we goug'd a score, into which we put a long piece of a spare iron-bolt of about two inches and a half in size, and having woulded it securely with seven yarn sidnet, we got it over head, and it prov'd serviceable all the voyage. Our boltsprit was the long-boat's davit, lash'd to the stump of the cut-water, and spik'd. It was lash'd with our two main-top gallant clunings, and our fore-stay, being a two inch and a half rope, came over the roule, and then reev'd upwards through the hole, where the lanier of the davit was wont to be reev'd, so with three or four round turns about the davit, we hitch'd the end on the standing part, and belay'd it. Our fore-top sail was the fore-top gallant sail, and the yard belonging to the same for a fore-top sail yard, which went as a down-hall top-sail. Our fore-yard was made of pieces of three-inch plank nail'd together, and then woulded. We made a sail to it of our sprit-sail top-sail, adding two cloths to it in the middle of the sail. The mizen-mast was made of the piece of our ensign-staff, on which we carry'd our long-boat's main-sail with a reef in it. We also made a stay-sail, which was hoisted up to the head of our main-mast, and belaying the tack forward, we hawl'd aft the sheet.

This was the best shift we could make, and had then about 260 leagues to the lands-end of England. It pleas'd God the wind from this time always continu'd westerly, and yet the greatest of our run with all our sails drawing, was scarce a knot and a half, that is a mile and a half an hour, so that we could scarce perceive the ship's motion through the water. Our lame side we had made up by clenching a piece of our main-sheet we had sav'd about a timber on the quarter deck, which with a small gun-tackle we brought taught forwards upon the fore-castle, and belay'd the fall. Then we sew'd the wet hides round this rope with some marline and a boltrope needle, and then nail'd them without board with small battens to the side, which serv'd to keep off the spray of the sea. We endeavour'd to steer with our head sails, but they not being enough to command her, it was an unspeakable trouble; for when our course was to be north-east, she would take a fling and look south-west. Then the way to pull her about was thus: we had lash'd two of our burton clocks forward, one at each cat-head to a timber of the gunnel, and having aboard two small warps of about 120, or 130 fathom long each, one of these warps being reev'd in a block to the uttermost end of it, we did bend a grapnel, which had a cross made of three-inch plank slipt over the ring down the shank, and a coil of old rope coil'd round the said cross, which was of two pieces, each five foot and a half long; this rope was seiz'd securely fast to make it hold water taught, and on the fluke of the iron grapnel was a nun-buoy made fast, to keep it from sinking. Then veering this out to the better end of our warp, all our people, being 31, would turn violently to, and by meer strength pull her about the right way again. It would sometimes take up two or three hours to get her about, and in five or six minutes she would look again as she did before. Thus were we continually plagu'd till our commander found out another way to steer, which was very ingenious; but it somewhat hindred the ship's way.

The thing was this; we took the end of our stream cable, about five inches and a half in size, and veer'd out at the larboard stern port in the great cabbin about five or six fathom, and bringing the end upon our poop or quarter-deck, there we had a cross made of three-inch and half elm plank, about five foot and a half in length, bolted in the center with a short pump bolt, and having a small ring over the small end of it, we forelock'd it, and then drove two spikes in each quarter; then clench'd them securely; and in each end of the cross we bor'd with a large auger two holes, into which we drove two trennels; then we coil'd an old rope about the cross, and between the two trennels, and bor'd other small holes in each end of the cross, and through them seiz'd this rope very fast, and on one end of the cross we bor'd a hole, and there splic'd in a wooden buoy, to keep the cross from sinking. Then we took a round turn about the cross with the end of the stream cable, and clench'd it round the standing part of it; which done, we hove the cross, thus fix'd to the cable, over-board, and veer'd it astern about twelve fathom; next we took one of our small warps, and reev'd one end of it through the block at our cat-head on the starboard, and the other on the larboard side, and passing the ends of the hauser or warp round our quarters, we brought them into our great cabbin stern-port, and clapping both ends on the stream-cable with rowling hitches, and seizing them fast, veer'd the cross in all about sixteen fathom astern. Then we belay'd the cable to our main-mast, and with good caskets seiz'd it securely to the rings of our ports, along the larboard side within board, in the great cabbin and steerage, and with a piece of two inch and a half rope, we made two small sarvices splicing in each an iron thimble. These sarvices we clapt upon each part of the warp within board, abaft the windlass on deck, and hook'd therein two small tackles. They being hook'd in the eye-bolt, where our top tackle was wont to be hook'd at the bulk-head of our steerage, and a man standing on the main-hatches with a tackle-fall in each hand, when he saw the ship fall off, he slack'd the lee-tackle, and hawl'd lightly the weather-tackle, and the ship answer'd immediately. And if the ship came too near the wind, he slack'd the weather-tackle, and gently hawl'd the lee-tackle, and so she fell off without any trouble. So that in short one man could steer the ship, and she answer'd as well as she would before the rudder. All the harm was, that the draught of water of the cross, did hinder our way.

By these contrivances we were fitted for sailing, and had a little ease from labour; but our fare was still very hard. And therefore for fear we should be drove to greater distress, we made tryal of eating hides, both by boiling and broiling, but still found them not eatable, for the first way they were but meer thong, and the latter no better than a burnt sole of a shoe. Some days after we had fix'd our new rudder, we met with another storm, which lasted a few days, and one night we shipt a sea, which falling upon the bunt of our main-sail, tore it to rags, and carry'd our main-top mast by the board. The mast we soon got up again, tho' about two foot shorter than before. We cut up an old top-sail to make a main-sail, and for want of twine to fix it, we cut a piece of a white steering hauser, which we open'd and made hemp, and holding one end in our teeth, with our hands made small threads, and the captain and boatswain sewed them up. Thus we made the sail, and quilted it all over, and it prov'd serviceable. When it blew so hard, that we were fain to lie try, we would bowse our stream-cable up to the cat-head, with that part of the hauser or warp that lay to windward, by which means, and the help of our main-sail, she always tended the sea well. A great dog we had, who before was as fat as bacon, was now grown as lean as a rake, and so ravenous, that he was ready to seize upon the men; him we now threw over-board. We had contriv'd to make a box to our only compass left us, which the captain had one day upon deck, and coming down, left it wrapt up in his watch-gown. Our black going up, put the gown about his shoulders; but being still very cold, left it again carelessly with the compass upon deck; and soon after he was gone, we heard a rumbling above, a man ran up, and found the dish of the compass standing fast on the top of our lee gunnel, but the box it hung in before was fallen over-board. This was the stranger, because our ship being but 130 ton burthen, the gunnel was very low on the quarter-deck; and had this compass been lost, we had been in a miserable condition, being still many leagues from land. The storm continu'd about 48 hours; and tho' the wind was fair, we could carry no sail to it, which made us lie a-try.

When the weather broke up, we out with all the sail we

could make, and crouded on to the eastward, with the wind sometimes upon our quarter, a brisk gale, yet she seldom ran above a knot and half, or six miles in four hours; but if ever she happen'd to run two knots, or eight miles in four hours, we were all over-joy'd, and presently began to reckon how long we should be getting into the soundings. At length, when by our reckoning we judg'd we could strike ground, our deep-sea lead and line were brought out, and having hove it over-board, we struck ground the first cast at 100 fathom water. But when I drew up the lead, I perceiv'd two of the strands of the deep-sea line quite broke asunder just above the eye of the line, so that only one strand brought up the weight. Then going to hang it on a cleat at the main-mast, the strap was so rotten, that it broke from the lead, so that it had a double escape in the sea, being so near failing in two places; and if that had been lost, we had none left aboard. For joy of striking ground and preserving our lead, the captain made a half powder barrel of punch, and gave every man a large cocoa-nut shell full, which was about a pint. By our soundings we guess'd our selves to be upon one of the outward banks coming into the channel from the westward, so we held on our course with very brisk westerly winds, and a day's good observation, often heaving our lead.

At length, by our account, observations, and soundings, we judg'd our selves very near the channel, and expected by the next day at noon, to fall in about six leagues to the south-ward of Scilly. That night I was upon deck from twelve till four in the morning, and, according to my commander's order, carefully steer'd E.N.E. it being a clear moonlight night. This was the 11th day of April, 1689. and at 4 in the morning I went off, leaving the boatswain upon deck, and my orders. When day appear'd, one of our passengers coming upon the deck, and looking forward over our larboard bow, the weather being foggy, he thought he discover'd a parcel of rocks; and acquainting the captain with it, he was of the same opinion, and took them to be the rocks by Scilly, call'd the bishop and his clerks. Hereupon he calls for me up, and asking what course I had steer'd, all I could say did not perswade him that I had steer'd E.N.E. according to his orders, but was positive I had fallen asleep, and not minded which way we were, concluding we were lost, as not able to avoid being upon the island of Scilly: however, he order'd in a hurry, the ship to be brought to, with our larboard tack aboard, to stand for Milford haven. I us'd all possible means to convince the captain, that I had punctually fulfill'd his orders, yet we could not guess what those we took for rocks should be. We held our course for Milford haven; but the fog clearing up in half an hour, we discover'd those we had taken for rocks, to be sixteen men of war, with some yachts, and other tenders in their company, which proved to be admiral Herbert, or lord Torrington, bound for Bantry bay, where, on the first day of May, he engag'd the French fleet.

The fleet discovering us, and judging we were in distress, the *Ruby* man of war stood with us; and being come alongside of us, hois'd out her boat and came aboard. They told us, King James had left the kingdom, that the prince of Orange was proclaim'd king, and war declar'd against France, which was all news to us. They took a particular account of all our damages, and then return'd to their ship, and made sail to the fleet, our commander having desir'd them to acquaint the admiral with our condition, and beg the assistance of some ship to tow us into any harbour of England, for fear the wind should come about easterly, and drive us out to sea again, where we must all perish. The commander of the *Ruby* went and acquainted the admiral with our distress; and captain Greenville, commander of the *Advice*, and youngest son to the earl of Bath, whom the voyage before we had carry'd from Smyrna to Constantinople, being there present, and hearing the ship's and commander's name, acquainted the admiral with it, and had orders to sail after us, and tow us into Plymouth. We were now in despair of any help, the fleet being almost sail'd out of sight, when at last we discover'd a great ship making all the sail she could after us. She came up with us, and prov'd to be the *Advice* aforesaid. The lieutenant came aboard, and acquainted us his captain had orders to tow us into Plymouth: then our commander order'd the tarpaulins to be taken off our hatches, and the hatches unlaid. By the by I must observe, that these tarpaulins were no other but some of the duke of Albemarle's rich hangings curiously painted in oyl colours, which had lain there ever since our misfortune, and kept out the wet to admiration. When our hatches were open, we rous'd up the end of our best bower-cable, and brought it to the windlass; and then passing the end of it out at the hawse, we bent it to a warp we had on board from the man of war; then we veer'd the cable out, and their men rouz'd the end of it on board their ship, where making it fast on one quarter with a spring from the other quarter, they tow'd us after the rate of eight knots a glass, that is, eight miles an hour, or, ten leagues and two miles a watch, which is four hours.

When we were fast to the man of war, our commander gave up the keys of the bread-room and lazaretto, and order'd we should all have what bread, meat, and drink we would, which we were very greedy of; and yet when it was dress'd, we had very little stomach to it. The *Advice* tow'd us in as far as the buoy in Plymouth sound, where she cast us off; then we rouz'd in our cable, and by the help of their pinnace and our sails, we ran our ship fast a-ground at low-water mark, under the Lammey, and against the Barbican at Plymouth; then running our stream-anchor and cable out to windward upon the flood, we veer'd her into the harbour between the old causey and the Barbican, and warp'd her up to Smart's key, thousands of people flocking on shore to see us. This was on the 11th of April, 1689. Abundance of people came from all parts of the country to see the wreck ship, by which name she is call'd at Plymouth to this day. Here we entred a solemn protestation against the sea, drawn by Mr. Samuel Eastlick, notary-publick of that town, and sign'd by our commander, the boatswain, and myself; but nevertheless the *Cambridge* man of war press'd eight of our men the next day; and had I not by chance made my escape down thro' the hole of our pump, into the well, they had carry'd me away too. The next morning their press-gang came to beset me before day, but I kept close in my hole till they were gone; then I made my escape in a small boat to one Madam Spark's at the Friery, where I was known, and the lady kept me above a week in her house, till having an opportunity to ride out as far as a place call'd St. Austin, where my parents dwelt, I had the satisfaction of seeing them again, and they new rigg'd me. When my commander sent me word that the press ship was gone, I return'd to Plymouth, and by that time he had got our boatswain clear. Here we new rigg'd, got new masts and yards, boltsprit, sails, and rudder, but did not repair our sides or bulk-heads till she came to London, where, I suppose, our masts may now be seen lying at our captain's house near Rotherhith church. From Plymouth we went in company with the fleet that came from Bantry engagement, to Spithead, where I and all the ship's crew, except the commander, his servant, and the black, were press'd to sail in his majesty's ship the *Old Lion*, Capt. Charles Skelton commander; from aboard whom I was one of the 106 men put ashore sick at Godsport, upon the king's account. Our ship went away to Chatham, and I left my chest with our old boatswain, who being careless, consum'd and lost all my books, instruments, and cloaths, and among the rest, the journal I kept of this voyage.

Thus have I given an exact account, to the best of my knowledge, of all our proceedings, without deviating the least from the truth, which whoever is pleas'd to read this relation, I hope, will give credit to, and not think it too tedious. Written on board his majesty's ship the *Resolution*, at Spithead, the 2nd of February 1698/9.

CHARLES MAY

EDWARD PELLHAM'S

VOYAGE TO GREENLAND

This account of an involuntary wintering in the Arctic comes from a pamphlet entitled *God's Power and Providence: Shewed, In the Miraculous Preservation and Deliverance of eight Englishmen, left by mischance in Green-land Anno 1630, nine moneths and twelve dayes. With a true Relation of all their miseries, their shifts and hardship they were put to, their food, &c., such as neither Heathen nor Christian men ever before endured. With a Description of the chiefe Places and Rarities of that barren and cold countrey. Faithfully reported by Edward Pellham, one of the eight men aforesaid. As also with a Map of Green-land.*

> They that goe downe into the Sea in ships; that doe businesse in great
>   waters:
> These see the workes of the Lord, and his wonders in the deepe.
>
> Psal. 107. 23, 24.

London. Printed by R. Y. for John Partridge, and are to be sold at the Signe of the Sunne in Pauls Church-yard. 1631.

Pellham's narrative has been reprinted several times, nearly always in a mangled condition, but it has not appeared since 1855, when it was edited by the Hakluyt Society. The text I have used is that of the exceedingly scarce 1631 edition.

Despite the "Greenland" of the title, the place in which Pellham spent his long winter was Spitsbergen: it appears that the names were often confused or held to be synonymous in the sixteenth and seventeenth centuries.

TO THE right Worshipfull Sir John Merick Knight, Governour of the worshipfull Company of Muscovie Merchants; Sir Hugh Hamersly Knight, and Alderman of the Citie of London: And to the Worshipfull, Mr. Alderman Freeman, Captaine William Goodler; And to all the rest of the Worshipfull Assistants and Adventurers in the said famous Company. Edward Pellham dedicateth both this and his future Labours.

Right Worshipfull and most famous Merchants:

The hard adventure my poore selfe and fellowes underwent in your Worships service, is a great deale pleasanter for others to reade, than it was for us to endure. However hard, wee have now endured it; and if ever after-ages shall speake of it, (as the world still doth of the Dutch-mens hard Winter in Nova Zembla:) thus much of the Voyage shall redound to your honours, that it was done by your Servants. This may also returne to our Countreys good; that if the first inhabiting of a Country by a Princes Subjects (which is the King of Spaine's best title to his Indyes) doth take possession of it for their Soveraigne: Then is Green-land by a second right taken livery and Seisin of, for his Majesties use; his Subjects being the first

133

that ever did (and I believe the last that ever will) inhabite there. Many a rich returne may your Worships in generall, and the brave Adventurers in particular receive from this and all other places: and may your Servants be ever hereafter, warned to take heede by our harmes. God send your Worships long life, and much honour, and sufficient wealth, to maintaine both. This is the hearty prayer of your Worships poor servant

EDWARD PELLHAM.

To the Reader.

Courteous Reader: That God may have the only glory of this our deliverance, give mee leave to looke backe into that voyage, which the Dutch-men made into Nova Zembla, in the yeare 1596. In which place, they having beene (like our selves) overtaken with the Winter, were there forced to stay it out as we were. Which being an Action so famous all the world over, encouraged mee both to publish this of ours, as also now to draw out some comparisons with them: that so our deliverance, and Gods glory may appeare both the more gracious and the greater.

This Nova Zembla stands in the Degree 76. North latitude: our wintering place is in 77. Degrees and 40. minutes, that is, almost two Degrees neerer the North Pole than they were; and so much therefore the colder. The Dutch were furnished with all things necessary both for life and health; had no want of any thing: Bread, Beere, and Wine, they had good, and good store. Victuals they had Gods plenty; and Apparell both for present clothing, and for shift too: and all this they brought with them in their Ship. We (God knowes) wanted all these. Bread, Beere, and Wine we had none. As for meate, our greatest and chiefest feeding was the Whale Frittars, and those mouldie too; the loathsomest meate in the world. For our Venison, 'twas hard to finde, but a great deale harder to get: and for our third sort of provision the Beares; 'twas a measuring cast which should be eaten first, Wee or the Beares, when wee first saw one another: and we perceived by them, that they had as good hopes to devoure us, as wee to kill them. The Dutch kill'd Beares, 'tis true; but it was for their skinnes, not for their flesh. The Dutch had a Surgeon in their companie; wee none but the great Physician to take care and cure of us. They had the benefite of Bathing and Purging: we of neither. They had their Ship at hand to be-friend them; wee had here perished, had not other Ships fetcht us off. They had Card and Compasse, wee no direction.

If the Dutch complained therefore of the extremity of the cold, (as well they might) and that when in building their house, they (as Carpenters use to doe) put the iron nayles into their mouthes, they there froze, and stuck so fast, that they brought off the skinne and forced blood: how cold, thinke you, were we, that we faine to maintaine two fires, to keepe our very mortar from freezing.

The Dutch complain'd, that their walls were frozen two inches thicke on the inside for all their fire: and if ours were not so, 'twas our paines and industry at first in building. The Dutch-mens clothes froze upon their backes, and their shooes were like hornes upon their feete: but that was their owne ignorance, for they had Sea-coles enough with them, if they had knowne how to use them. If their drinke and Sacke were so hard frozen into lumps of yce, that they were faine to cut it out; how much harder was it for us, that were forced to make hot irons our best toasts to warme the snow withall, for our morning's draughts? They used heated stones and billets to their feete and bodies, to warme them: which, though an hard shift, yet was it better than we had any.

Lay now, all these together, the distance of place, wee being many miles more into the cold than they: the want both of meate and clothes; and that the house wee lived in, wee had but three dayes respite to build for nine months to come; and then may the world see, that the Dutch had the better provisions, and wee the abler bodies. If therefore the Dutch-mens deliverance were worthily accounted a wonder, ours can amount to little lesse than a miracle. The greater glory therefore our deliverance, the greater must be Gods glory. And that's the Authors purpose in publishing of it. God keepe the Readers from the like dangers. So prays he that endured what he here writes of

Edw. Pellham.

The names of the Men thus staying in GREEN-LAND for nine moneths and twelve dayes.

William Fakely, Gunner. Edward Pellham, Gunners mate, the Author of this Relation. John Wise, and Robert Good-fellow, Sea-men. Thomas Ayers, Whale-cutter. Henry Bett, Cooper. John Dawes, and Richard Kellet, Land-men.

GODS POWER AND PROVIDENCE
IN THE PRESERVATION OF EIGHT MEN IN GREENLAND, NINE MONETHS AND TWELVE DAYES

But wee had the sentence of death in our selves, that wee should not trust in our selves, but in God which raiseth the dead.

Who delivered us from so great a death, and doth deliver: in whom wee trust that hee will yet deliver us.

2 Cor. 1. ver. 9, 10.

GREENLAND is a countrey very farre Northward, situated in 77. degrees, and 40. minutes, that is, within 12. degrees and 20. minutes of the very North Pole it selfe. The Land is wonderfull mountainous; the Mountaines all the year long full of yce and snow: the Plaines in part bare in Summer time. There growes neither tree nor hearbe in it, except Scurvey-grasse and Sorrell. The Sea is as barren as the Land, affording no fish but Whales, Sea-horses, Seales, & another small fish. And hither there is a yearely Fleet of English sent. Wee eight men therefore being employed in the service of the Right Worshipfull Company of Muscovie Merchants, in the good ship called the *Salutation* of London, were bound for this Green-land aforesaid, to make a voyage upon Whales or Sea-horse, for the advantage of the Merchants, and for the good of the Common-wealth. Wee set sayle from London the first day of May, 1630, and having a faire gale, wee quickly left the fertile bankes of Englands pleasant shoares behind us. After which, setting our comely sayles to this supposed prosperous gale, and ranging through the boysterous billowes of the rugged Seas, by the helpe and gracious assistance of Almighty God, we safely arrived at our desired Port, in Greenland, the eleventh of June following. Whereupon having moored our ships, and carryed our caske ashoare, wee, with all expedition, fell to the fitting up of our Shallops, with all things necessarie for our intended voyage. Wee were in companie three Ships; all which were then appointed by the order of our Captaine, Captaine William Goodler, to stay at the Foreland, untill the fifteenth of July; with resolution, that if we could not by that time make a voyage according to our expectation, then, to send one ship to the Eastward, unto a fishing place some fourscore leagues from thence; whither at the latter end of the yeare, the Whales use more frequently to resort. A second of the three ships was designed for Green-Harbour, (a place some fifteen leagues distant to the Southward) there to trie her skill and fortune, if it were possible there to make a voyage. The third ship (which was the same wherein wee were) was appointed to stay at the Fore-land, untill the twentieth of August. But the Captaine having made a great voyage at Bell Sownd, dispatches a Shallop towards our ship, with a command unto us to come to him at Bell Sownd aforesaid: his purpose being, to have us take in some of his Trane Oyle, as also by joyning our forces together, to make the Fleete so much the stronger for the defence of the Merchants goods homeward bound, the Dunkirkers being very strong and rife at sea in those dayes. Upon the eighth day of August (thereupon) leaving the Foreland, we directed our course to the Southward, towards Green-Harbour, there to take in twenty of our men, which had out of our ships company beene sent into the lesser ship, for the furtherance of her voyage.

But the winde being now contrary, our ship could no way lye our course. The fifteenth day, being calme and cleare, and our ship now in the Offing, some four leagues from Blacke-Point, and about five from the Maydens pappes (which is a place famous, both for very good, and for great store of Venison,) our Master sent us eight men here named, altogether in a shallop for the hunting and killing of some Venison, for the ships provision. Wee thus leaving the ship, and having taken a brace of dogs along with us, and furnisht our selves with a snap-hance, two lances, and a tinder-box; wee directed our course towards the shoare, where in foure houres we arrived, the weather being at that time faire and cleare, and every way seasonable for the performance of our present intentions. That day we laid fourteene tall and nimble Deere along; and being very weary and thoroughly tyred, first with rowing, and now with hunting, wee fell to eate such victuals as we had brought along, agreeing to take our rest for that night, and the next day to make an end of our hunting, and so fairely to returne to our ship againe. But the next day, as it pleased God, the weather falling out something thicke, and much yce in the

Offing betwixt the shoare and the ship (by reason of a Southerly winde driving alongst the coast) our ship was forced so farre to stand off into the Sea, to be cleare of the yce, that we had quite lost the sight of her: neither could we assure our selves, whether she were inclosed in the drift yce, or not: and the weather still growing thicker and thicker, we thought it our best course to hunt alongst the shoare, and so to goe for Greene-harbour there to stay aboard the ship with the rest of our men, untill our own ship should come into the Port.

Coasting thus along towards Greene-Harbour, wee kill'd eight Deere more; and so at last having well loaden our Shallop with Venison, wee still kept on our course towards Green-Harbour: where arriving upon the seventeenth day, we found (to our great wonderment) that the ship was departed thence, together with our twenty men aforesaid. That which increased our admiration was, for that wee knew they had not victuals sufficient aboard, to serve them (by proportion) homewards bound: which made us againe to wonder what should be the reason of their so sudden departure.

Perceiving our selves thus frustrated of our expectation, and having now but bare three dayes (according to appointment) to the uttermost expiration of our limited time for our departure out of the Country; we thought it our best course to make all possible speed to get to Bell Sownd, unto our Captaine, fearing that a little delay might bring a great deale of danger. For the lightening therefore of our Shallop, that she might make the better way through the waters, wee heaved our Venison over-board, and cast it all into the Sea. Having thus forsaken Green-Harbour, with a longing desire to recover Bell Sownd (from thence distant some sixteene leagues to the Southward) that night wee got halfe way about the point of the Nesse, or point of land, called Low-Nesse: But the darknesse or mistie fogge increasing so fast upon us, that it was impossible for us to get further; even there betweene two rocks we coved from the seventeenth day at night, untill the eighteenth day at noone. At which time the weather being somewhat clearer (though very thicke still) wee left the Nesse behinde us, still desirous to recover Bell Sownd: but having never a Compasse to direct our course by, nor any of our company that was Pilot sufficient to know the land when he saw it, we were faine to grabble in the darke (as it were) like a blinde man for his way, and so over-shot Bell point at least tenne leagues to the Southward towards Horne Sownd.

Some of us in the meane time knowing that it was impossible to bee so long a rowing and sayling of eight leagues (for wee did both row and sayle) made enquirie, How the harbour lay in? whereunto there was a ready answer made, That it lay East in. Taking the matter therefore into our better consideration, some of us judged, that it could not possibly be further to the Southward (our reason being, our observation of the lands rounding away and trenting towards the Eastward) and resolved thereupon to row no further on that Course, for the finding of Bell Sownd. And though wee were againe perswaded by William Fakely our Gunner, (a proper Sea-man, though no skilfull Mariner, who had been in the Country five or sixe times before, which none of our Sea-men had beene) that it was further to the Southwards: yet we, trusting better to our own reasons than unto his perswasions, againe returned towards the Northward: which was our best and directest Course indeed, for the finding of Bell Sownd. Steering of which Course, wee were now come within two miles of Bell Point; & the weather being faire and cleare, wee presently descryed the tops of the loftie mountaines. William Fakely thereupon looking about him, presently cries out unto us, *That wee were all this while upon a wrong Course*: upon hearing of which words, some of our companie (yea the most) were perswaded, to wend about the Boates head the second time, unto the Southwards: which one action was the maine and onely cause of our too late repentance, though for mine owne part (as it is well knowne) I never gave consent unto their counsell.

And thus upon the fatall twentieth day of August (which was the utmost day of our limited time for staying in the Country) wee againe returned the quite contrary way, namely to the Southward. Thus utterly uncertaine when and where to finde the Sownd; a thousand sadde imaginations overtooke our perplexed minds, all of us assuredly knowing, that a million of miseries would of necessitie ensue, if wee found not the ships, whereby to save our passage. In this distracted time of our thoughts, wee were now againe the second time runne as farre to the Southward as at the first: and finding by all reason thereupon, how that there was no likelihood at all of finding any such place further to the Southward, we wended the Shallop the second time unto the Northward. William Fakely hereupon, being unwilling to condescend unto our agreement, still perswaded us, that *That could not possibly bee our Course*: but we not trusting any longer unto his unskilfull perswasions, (though all in him was out of good will, and strong conceit of his being in the rights) bent our Course to the Northward; and hee not consenting to steere any longer, I tooke the Oare out of his hand to steere the Boate withall. The weather all this while continued faire and cleare, and it pleased God at the very instant time, to send the winde Easterly: which advantage wee thankfully apprehending, presently set sayle. The winde increased fresh and large, and our Shallop swiftly running, we arrived the one and twentieth day at Bell point, where wee found the winde right out of the Sownd at East Northeast so fiercely blowing, that we could not possibly row to Windwards; but being forced to take in our sayle, we were faine to betake ourselves unto our Oares, by helpe of which wee recovered some two miles within the shoare, where we were constrained for that time to Cove, or else to drive to Lee-wards.

Thus finding this to be the very place we had all this while sought for, (he now also agreeing thereunto) we forthwith sought out and found an harbor for our Shallop: and having brought her thereinto, two of our men were presently dispatched over land unto the Tent at Bell Sownd, to see if the Ships were still there; of which, by reason of the times being expired, and the opportunitie of the present faire winde, wee were much afraid. The Tent being distant ten miles at the least from our Shallop, our men at their comming thither finding the ships to be departed out of the Roade, and not being certaine, whether or not they might be at Bottle Cove, (three leagues distant on the other side of the Sownd) riding there under the Loome of the land; againe returne unto us with this sadde newes. The storme of winde hitherto continuing, about mid-night fell starke calme: whereupon we, unwilling to lose our first opportunity, departed towards Bottle Cove; betwixt hope and feare of finding the ships there: whither comming the two & twentieth, and finding the ships departed, we, having neither Pilot, Plat, nor Compasse for our directors to the Eastward, found our selves (God he knoweth) to have little hope of any delivery out of that apparent danger. Our feares increased upon us, even whilst we consulted whether it were safest for us either to goe or stay. If goe, then thought wee upon the dangers in sayling, by reason of the much yce in the way; as also of the difficultie in finding the place, when wee should come thereabouts. If we resolved stille to remaine at Bell Sownd, then wee thought that no other thing could be looked for, but a miserable and a pining death, seeing there appeared no possibility of inhabiting there, or to endure so long, so darksome, and so bitter a winter.

And thus were our thoughts at that time distracted, thus were our feares increased; nor were they causelesse feares altogether. Well, we knew that neither Christian or Heathen people, had ever before inhabited those desolate and untemperate Clymates. This also, to increase our feares, had wee certainly heard; how that the Merchants having in former times much desired, and that with proffer of great rewards for the hazarding of their lives, and of sufficient furniture and provision of all things that might bee thought necessary for such an undertaking, to any that would adventure to winter in those parts; could never yet finde any so hardy, as to expose their lives unto so hazardous an undertaking: yea notwithstanding those proffers had beene made both unto Mariners of good experience, and of noble resolutions, and also unto divers other bold spirits; yet had the action of wintering in those parts, never by any beene hitherto undertaken. This also had we heard, how that the company of Muscovie Merchants, having once procured the reprive of some malefactors, that had here at home beene convicted by Law for some haynous crimes committed; and that both with promise of pardon for their faults, and with addition of rewards also, if so be they would undertake to remaine in Green-Land but one whole yeare, and that every way provided for too, both of Clothes, Victuals, and all things else, that might any way be needfull for their preservation: These poore wretches hearing of this large proffer, & fearing present execution at home, resolved to make tryall of the adventure. The time of yeare being come, and the ships ready to depart, these con-demned creatures are imbarked, who after a certaine space there arriving, and taking a view of the desolatenesse of the place; they conceived such a horrour and inward feare in their hearts, as that they resolved rather to returne for England to make satisfaction with their lives for their former faults committed, than there to remaine, though with assured hope of gaining their pardon. Insomuch as the time of the yeare being come, that the ships were to depart from these barren shoares, they made knowne their full intent unto the Captaine: who being a pittifull and a mercifull Gentleman, would not by force constraine them to stay in that place, which was so contrary to their minds; but having made his voyage by the time expired; hee againe imbarked and brought them over with him into England; where, through the intercession and meanes of the Worshipfull Companie of Muscovie Merchants, they escaped that death, which they had before beene condemned unto. The remembrance of these two former stories, as also of a third (more terrible than both the former, for that it was likely to be our own case) more miserably now affrighted us: and that was the lamentable and unmanly ends of nine good and able men, left in the same place heretofore by the selfe same Master that now left us behinde: who all dyed miserably upon the place, being cruelly disfigured after their deaths by the savage Beares and hungry Foxes, which are not onely the civilest, but also the onely inhabitants of that comfortlesse Countrey: the lamentable ends and miscarriage of which men had beene enough indeed to have daunted the spirits of the most noble resolution.

All these fearefull examples presenting themselves before our eyes, at this place of Bottle Cove aforesaid, made us, like amazed men, to stand looking one upon another, all of us, as it were, beholding in the present, the future calamities both of himselfe and of his fellowes. And thus, like men already metamorphosed into the yce of the Country, and already past both our sense and reason; stood wee with the eyes of pittie beholding one another.

Nor was it other mens examples and miscarriages and feares alone, that made us amazed, but it was the consideration of our want of all necessary provision for the life of man, that already strooke us to the heart: For we were not only unprovided, both of clothes to keepe us warme, and of foode to prevent the wrath of cruell famine: but utterly destitute also wee were of a sufficient house, wherein to shrowd and shelter our selves from the chilling cold. Thus for a space standing all mute and silent, weighing with our selves the miserie wee were already fallen into, and knowing delay in these extremities to be the mother of all dangers, we began to conceive hope, even out of the depth of despaire. Rowsing up our benummed senses therefore, wee now lay our heads and counsels together, to bethinke our selves of the likeliest course for our preservation in that place; seeing that all hopes of gaining our passage into England, were then quite frustrate. Shaking off therefore all childish and effeminate feares, it pleased God to give us hearts like men, to arme our selves with a resolution to doe our best for the resisting of that monster of Desperation. An agreement thereupon by a generall consent of the whole Companie we then entred into, to take the opportunity of the next faire weather, and goe for Green-harbour, to hunt and kill Venison for part of our winter provision.

Having thus agreed amongst our selves, the five and twentieth day of August, the weather and wind being both faire, wee direct our course towards Green-harbour, some sixteene leagues (as I before told you) distant from Bell Sownd: and the winde being fresh and faire, within the space of twelve houres we there arrived. Upon which place being now landed, the first thing we did, was to make us a Tent with the sayle of our Shallop, pitcht up and spread upon our Oares; a sorry one (God knowes) though it were, yet under it we resolved to rest our selves that night, to refresh our bodies with such food as wee there had, and the next day to returne againe unto our hunting. The weather that night proving faire and cleare, wee made our sleepe the shorter: (and alas what men could sleepe in such an extremitie!) and fitting our selves and Shallop the best we might, to Coles Parke we went, a place some two leagues distant from us, and well knowne unto Thomas Ayers, that was one of our Companie, to be well stored with Venison. Comming a shoare at which place, though we found not so many Deere as we indeed expected, yet seven we killed the same day, and foure Beares to boote; which wee also intended to eate.

But the weather beginning now to overcast, and not likely to continue good for hunting; wee that night returned againe unto Green-Harbour; where making us a Tent of our Sayle and Oares (as is before described) we fell to eate of such meate as God had sent us, and betooke our selves to our rest upon it. Having rested our selves a while, and now finding the weather to cleare up, we broke off our sleepe for that time, fitting our selves and two dogges againe to goe a hunting; leaving William

143

Fakely and John Dawes behinde us in the Tent at Green-harbour, as our Cookes (for the time) to dresse some meate that wee had, for our refreshment at our returne.

Departing thus from the Tent, wee rowed towards Coles Parke; in the way whither, upon the side of a hill, by the Sea side, wee espyed seven Deere feeding, whereupon presently a shoare we went, and with our Dogs kill'd sixe of them, after which, the weather againe overcasting, wee thought it to little purpose to goe any further at that time, but resolved to hunt all along the side of that hill, and so at night to returne unto our Tent. Going thus along, wee kill'd sixe Deere more; which wee had no sooner done, but it began to blow and raine, and to be very darke: whereupon wee hasted towards the Tent, there intending to refresh our selves with victuals and with rest for that night, and the next day to returne againe unto our hunting. This purpose of ours was by the foule weather the next day hindered: for it fell so blacke, so cold, and so windy, that we found it no way fitting for our purpose. Lading therefore our owne Shallop with Beares and Venison; and another Shallop which we there found haled up, and left by the Ships Companie, as every yeare they use to doe: lading this other Shallop, I say, with the Graves of the Whales that had beene there boyled this present yeare, (which wee there found in heapes flung upon the ground) wee, dividing our selves into two equall companies, that is to say, William Fakely with one Sea-man and two Land-men with him, betaking themselves unto one Shallop; and Edward Pellham with another Sea-man and two Land-men more with him, going into the other Shallop; wee all committed our selves unto the Sea, intending with the next faire weather to goe to Bell Sownd unto our Tent: which was the place wee set up our Rest upon, to remaine at all the Winter.

Towards Bell Sownd therefore we went, with a purpose there to lay up our Store of what victuals wee had already gotten together; and with the next faire winde to come hither againe, to trie if it were possible for us there to provide our selves of some more Venison for our Winter provision.

Having thus laden both our Shallops, appointed our Companie, and all ready now for our departure; wee were overtaken with the night, and there forced to stay upon the place. The next day was Sunday; wherefore wee thought it fit to sanctifie the Rest of it, and to stay our selves there untill Munday, and to make the best use we could of that good day, taking the best course wee could for the serving of God Almighty; although we had not so much as a Booke amongst us all, the whole time that wee staid in that Country.

The Sabbath day being shut up by the approaching night, we betooke our selves to our Rest: sleeping untill the Sunne awakened us by his beginning to shew himselfe upon the Munday morning. The day was no sooner peept, but up we got, fitting our selves and businesse for our departure. The weather was faire and cleere at the first; but after some foure houres rowing, the skie began so to overcast, and the winde to blow so hard, that we could not possibly get to Bell Sownd that night, but Coved halfe way, untill the next morning; at which time we recovered Bottle Cove. To which place when wee were once come, we found the winde (then at Southwest) to blow so hard, that it was impossible for us to reach Bell Sownd, but were forced to stay at Bottle Cove for that night. Our Shallops we made fast one unto another, with a Rope fastning the head of the one unto the sterne of the other; and so casting our Grabnell or Anchor over-board, we left them riding in the Cove.

But see now what a mischance, for the tryall of our patience, and for the making of us to relye more upon his providence, than upon any outward meanes of our owne; God now suffered to befall us: We being now all a-shore, the Southwest winde blew so hard and right into the Cove, that it made the Sea go high; our Anchor also comming home at the same time, both our Shallops casting alongside the shoare, sunke presently in the Sea: wetting by this meanes our whole provision, the weather with-all beating some of it out of the Boates, which wee found swimming up and downe the shoare. For, comming out of our Tent in the meantime, judge you what a sight this was unto us, to see by mischance, the best part of our provision (the onely hope of our lives) to be in danger utterly to be lost, (or at least spoyled with the Sea-water,) for which we had taken such paines, and run such adventures in the getting. In this our miserie wee saw no way but one (and that a very desperate one) namely, to runne presently into the high-wrought Sea, getting by that meanes into our Shallops to save the remainder of our provisions, ready now to be washt quite

145

away by the billowes. A Halser thereupon we got, which fastening unto our Shallops, wee, with a Crabbe or Capstang, by maine force of hand heaved them out of the water upon the shoare. This done, all along the Sea side we goe; seeking there and taking up such of our provisions, as were swumme away from our Shallops. Having by this meanes gleaned up all that could be gotten together, we resolved from thenceforth to let our Boates lye upon the shoare, till such time as the weather should prove faire and better; and then to goe over unto Bell Sownd.

The third of September the weather proving faire and good, we forthwith launched our Shallops into the water, and in them wee that day got into Bell Sownd. Thither so soone as we were come, our first businesse was, to take our provision out of our Shallops into the Tent: our next, to take a particular view of the place, and of the great Tent especially; as being the place of our habitation for the ensuing Winter. This which we call the Tent, was a kinde of house (indeed) built of Timber and Boards very substantially, and covered with Flemish Tyles: by the men of which nation it had in the time of their trading thither, beene builded. Fourescore foot long it is, and in breadth fiftie. The use of it was for the Coopers, employed for the service of the Company, to worke, lodge, and live in, all the while they make caske for the putting up of the Trane Oyle. Our view being taken, we found the weather beginning to alter so strangely, and the nights and frosts so to grow upon us, that wee durst not adventure upon another hunting voyage unto Green-harbour; fearing the Sownd would be so frozen, that wee should never be able to get backe to our Tent againe. By land it was (we knew) in vaine for us to thinke of returning: for the land is so mountainous, that there is no travelling that way.

Things being at this passe with us, we bethought our selves of building another smaller Tent with all expedition: the place must of necessity be within the greater Tent. With our best wits therefore taking a view of the place, we resolved upon the South side. Taking downe another lesser Tent therefore, (built for the Land-men hard by the other, wherein in time of yeare they lay whilest they made their Oyle) from thence we fetcht our materials. That Tent furnisht us with 150 Deale-boards, besides Posts or Stancheons, and Rafters. From three

Chimneys of the Furnaces wherein they used to boyle their Oyles, we brought a thousand Bricks: there also found wee three Hogsheads of very fine Lyme, of which stuffe wee also fetcht another Hogshead from Bottle Cove, on the other side of the Sownd, some three leagues distant. Mingling this Lyme with the Sand of the Sea shore, we made very excellent good morter for the laying of our Bricks: falling to worke whereupon, the weather was so extreame cold, as that we were faine to make two fires to keepe our morter from freezing. William Fakely and my selfe undertaking the Masonrie, began to raise a wall of one bricke thicknesse, against the inner planks of the side of the Tent. Whilest we were laying of these Bricks, the rest of our Companie were otherwise employed every one of them: some in taking them downe, others in making of them cleane, and in bringing them in baskets into the Tent: Some in making morter, and hewing of boards to build the other side withall: and two others all the while, in flaying of our Venison. And thus having built the two outermost sides of the Tent with Bricks and Morter, and our Bricks now almost spent, wee were enforc't to build the other two sides with Boards; and that in this manner. First, we nayl'd our Deale boards on one side of the Post or Stancheon, to the thicknesse of one foot; and on the other side in like manner: and so filling up the hollow place betweene with sand, it became so tight and warme, as not the least breath of ayre could possibly annoy us: Our Chimneys vent was into the greater Tent, being the breadth of one deale board, and foure foot long. The length of this our Tent was twenty foot, and the breadth sixteene; the heighth tenne: our seeling being Deale boards five or sixe times double, the middle of one, joyning so close to the shut of the other, that no winde could possibly get betweene. As for our doore, besides our making it so close as possibly it could shut; we lined it more-over with a bed that we found lying there, which came over both the opening and the shutting of it. As for windowes, we made none at all: so that our light wee brought in through the greater Tent, by removing two or three tyles in the eaves, which light came to us through the vent of our Chimney. Our next worke was, to set up foure Cabbins, billetting our selves two and two in a Cabbine. Our beds were the Deeres skinnes dryed, which wee found to be extraordinary warme, and a very comfortable kinde of lodging to us in our distresse.

Our next care then was for firing to dresse our meate withall, and for keeping away the cold. Examining therefore all the Shallops that had beene left-ashoare there by the Ships, we found seven of them very crazie, and not serviceable for the next yeare. Those wee made bold withall; brake them up, and carried them into our house, stowing them over the beames in manner of a floore; intending also to stow the rest of our firing over them, so as to make the outer Tent the warmer, and to keepe withall the snow from dryving through the tyles into the Tent: which snow would otherwise have covered every thing, and have hindered us in comming at what wee wanted. When the weather was now growne cold, and the dayes short, (or rather no dayes at all) wee made bold to stave some emptie Caske that were there left the yeare before: to the quantitie of 100 Tunne at least. We also made use of some planks, and of two old Coolers (wherein they cool'd their Oyle) and of whatsoever might well be spared, without damnifying of the voyage the next yeare. Thus having gotten together all the firing that wee could possibly make, except we would make spoyle of the Shallops and Coolers that were there, which might easily have overthrowne the next yeares voyage, to the great hinderance of the Worshipfull Companie, whose servants we being, were every way carefull of their profite. Comparing therefore the small quantitie of our wood, together with the coldnesse of the weather, and the length of time that there wee were likely to abide; wee cast about to husband our stocke as thriftily as wee could, devising to trie a new conclusion: Our tryall was this. When wee rak't up our fire at night, with a good quantitie of ashes and of embers, wee put into the midd'st of it a piece of Elmen wood: where after it had laine sixteene hours, we at our opening of it found great store of fire upon it; whereupon wee made a common practice of it ever after. It never went out in eight moneths together or thereabouts.

Having thus provided both our house and firing; upon the twelfth of September a small quantity of drift yce, came driving to and fro in the Sownd. Early in the morning therefore wee arose, and looking every where abroad, we at last espyed two Sea-horses lying a-sleepe upon a piece of yce: presently thereupon taking up an old Harping Iron that there lay in the Tent, & fastening a Grapnell Roape unto it, out lanch't wee our Boate to row towards them. Comming something neere them, wee perceived them to be fast a-sleepe: which my selfe, then steering the Boate, first perceiving, spake to the rowers to hold still their Oares, for feare of awaking them with the crashing of the yce; and I, skulling the Boate easily along, came so neere at length unto them, that the Shallops even touch't one of them. At which instant William Fakely being ready with his Harping Iron, heav'd it so strongly into the old one, that hee quite disturbed her of her rest: after which shee receiving five or sixe thrusts with our lances, fell into a sounder sleepe of death. Thus having dispatch't the old one, the younger being loath to leave her damme, continued swimming so long about our Boate, that with our lances wee kill'd her also. Haling them both after this into the Boate, we rowed a-shoare, flayed our Sea-horses, cut them in pieces, to roast and eate them. The nineteenth of the same moneth we saw other Sea-horses, sleeping also in like manner upon severall pieces of yce: but the weather being cold, they desired not to sleepe so much as before; and therefore could wee kill but one of them: of which one being right glad, we returned againe into our Tent.

The nights at this time, and the cold weather increased so fast upon us, that wee were out of all hopes of getting any more foode before the next Spring: our onely hopes were, to kill a Beare now and then, that might by chance wander that way. The next day therefore taking an exacter survey of all our victuals, and finding our proportion too small by halfe, for our time and companie; wee agreed among our selves to come to Allowance, that is, to stint our selves to one reasonable meale a day, and to keepe Wednesdayes and Fridayes Fasting dayes; excepting from the Frittars[1] or Graves of the Whale (a very loathsome meate) of which we allowed our selves sufficient to suffice our present hunger: and at this dyet we continued some three moneths or thereabouts.

Having by this time finished what ever we possibly could invent, for our preservations in that desolate desert; our clothes & Shooes also were so worne and torne (all to pieces almost) that wee must of necessity invent some new device for their reparations. Of Roape-yarne therefore, we made us thread, & of Whale-bones needles to sew our clothes withall. The nights were wax't very long, and by the tenth of October

[1] These be the Scraps of the Fat of the Whale, which are flung away after the Oyle is gotten out of it.

the cold so violent, that the Sea was frozen over: which had beene enough to have daunted the most assured resolutions. At which time our businesse being over, and nothing now to exercise our mindes upon; our heads began then to be troubled with a thousand sorts of imaginations. Then had wee leisure (more than enough) to complaine our selves of our present and most miserable conditions. Then had wee time to bewaile our wives and children at home; and to imagine what newes our unfortunate miscarriages must needes be unto them. Then thought wee of our parents also, and what a cutting Corasive it would be to them, to heare of the untimely deaths of their children. Otherwhiles againe, wee revive our selves with some comfort, that our friends might take, in hoping that it might please God to preserve us (even in this poore estate) untill the next yeare. Sometimes did we varie our griefes; complaining one while of the cruelty of our Master, that would offer to leave us to these distresses: and then presently againe fell wee, not onely to excuse him, but to lament both him and his companie, fearing they had beene overtaken by the yce, and miserably that way perished.

Thus tormented in mind with our doubts, our feares, and our griefes; and in our bodies with hunger, cold and wants; that hideous monster of desperation, began now to present his ugliest shape unto us: he now pursued us, hee now laboured to seize us. Thus finding our selves in a Labyrinth, as it were, of a perpetuall miserie, wee thought it not best to give too much way unto our griefes; fearing, they also would most of all have wrought upon our weakenesse. Our prayers we now redoubled unto the Almighty, for strength and patience, in these our miseries: and the Lord graciously listned unto us, and granted these our petitions. By his assistance therefore, wee shooke off these thoughts, and cheer'd up our selves againe, to use the best meanes for our preservations.

Now therefore began we to thinke upon our Venison, and the preserving of that; and how to order our firing in this cold weather. For feare therefore our firing should faile us at the end of the yeare, we thought best to roast every day halfe a Deere, and to stow it in hogsheads. Which wee putting now in practice, wee forthwith filled three Hogsheads and an halfe; leaving so much raw, as would serve to roast every Sabbath day a quarter and so for Christmas day, and the like.

This conclusion being made amongst us; then fell wee againe to bethinke us of our miseries, both passed and to come: and how, (though if it pleased God to give us life, yet should) we live as banished men, not onely from our friends, but all other companie. Then thought we of the pinching cold, and of the pining hunger: these were our thoughts, this our discourse to passe away the time withall. But as if all this miserie had beene too little, we presently found another increase of it: For, examining our provisions once more, wee found that all our Frittars of the Whale were almost spoyled with the wet that they had taken: after which by lying so close together, they were now growne mouldie. And our Beare and Venison we perceived againe not to amount to such a quantity, as to allow us five meales a weeke: whereupon we were faine to shorten our stomacks of one meale more: so that for the space of three moneths after that, we for foure dayes in the weeke fed upon the unsavory and mouldie Frittars, and the other three, we feasted it with Beare and Venison. But as if it were not enough for us to want meate, we now began to want light also: all our meales proved suppers now; for little light could we see; even the glorious Sunne (as if unwilling to behold our miseries) masking his lovely face from us, under the sable vaile of cole-blacke night. Thus from the fourteenth of October, till the third of February, we never saw the Sunne; nor did hee all that time, ever so much as peepe above the Horizon. But the Moone we saw at all times, day and night (when the cloudes obscured her not) shining as bright as shee doth in England. The Skie, 'tis true, is very much troubled with thicke and blacke weather all the Winter time: so that then, we could not see the Moone, nor could discerne what point of the Compasse shee bore upon us. A kinde of daylight wee had indeed, which glimmer'd some eight houres a day unto us; in October time I meane: for from thence unto the first of December, even that light was shortened tenne or twelve minutes a day constantly: so that from the first of December till the twentieth, there appeared no light at all; but all was one continued night. All that wee could perceive was, that in a cleare season now and then, there appeared a little glare of white, like some show of day towards the South: but no light at all. And this continued till the first of Ianuary, by which time wee might perceive the day a little to increase. All this darkesome time, no certainety could wee have when it should be day, or when night: onely my selfe out of mine owne little judgement, kept the observation of it thus. First bearing in minde the number of the Epact, I made my addition by a day supposed, (though not absolutely to be known, by reason of the darkenesse) by which I judged of the age of the Moone: and this gave me my rule of the passing of the time; so that at the comming of the Ships into the Port, I told them the very day of the moneth, as directly as they themselves could tell mee.

At the beginning of this darkesome, irkesome time, wee sought some meanes of preserving light amongst us: finding therefore a piece of Sheete-lead over a seame of one of the Coolers; that we ript off, and made three Lampes of it: which maintaining with Oyle that wee found in the Coopers Tent, and Roape-yarne serving us in steed of Candle-Weekes, wee kept them continually burning. And this was a great comfort to us in our extremity. Thus did we our best to preserve our selves; but all this could not secure us: for wee in our owne thoughts, accounted our selves but dead men; and that our Tent was then our darkesome dungeon, and we did but waite our day of tryall by our judge, to know whether wee should live or dye. Our extremities being so many, made us sometimes in impatient speeches to breake forth against the causers of our miseries: but then againe, our consciences telling us of our owne evill deservings; we tooke it either for a punishment upon us for our former wicked lives; or else for an example of Gods mercie, in our wonderfull deliverance. Humbling our selves therefore under the mighty hand of God, wee cast downe our selves before him in prayer, two or three times a day, which course we constantly held all the time of our misery.

The new yeare now begun, *as the dayes began to lengthen, so the cold began to strengthen*: which cold came at last to that extremitie, as that it would raise blisters in our flesh, as if wee had beene burnt with fire: and if wee touch't iron at any time, it would sticke to our fingers like Bird-lime. Sometimes if we went but out a-doores to fetch in a little water, the cold would nip us in such sort, that it made us as sore as if wee had beene beaten in some cruell manner. All the first part of the Winter, we found water under the yce, that lay upon the Bache on the Sea-shoare. Which water issued out of an high Bay or Cliffe of yce, and ranne into the hollow of the Bache, there remaining with a thicke yce over it: which yce, wee at one certaine place daily digging through with pick-axes, tooke so much water as served for our drinking.

This continued with us untill the tenth of Ianuarie: and then were wee faine to make shift with snow-water; which we melted by putting hot Irons into it. And this was our drinke untill the twentieth of May following.

By the last of Ianuarie, were the dayes growne to some seven or eight houres long; and then we again tooke another view of our victuals: which we now found to grow so short, that it could no wayes last us above sixe weekes longer. And this bred a further feare of famine amongst us. But our recourse was in this, as in other our extremities, unto Almighty God; who had helps, we knew, though wee saw no hopes. And thus spent wee our time untill the third of Februarie. This proved a marvellous cold day; yet a faire and cleare one: about the middle whereof, all cloudes now quite dispersed, and nights sable curtaine drawne; Aurora with her golden face smiled once againe upon us, at her rising out of her bed: for now the glorious Sunne with his glittering beames, began to guild the highest tops of the loftie mountaines. The brightnesse of the Sunne, and the whitenesse of the snow, both together was such, as that it was able to have revived even a dying spirit. But to make a new addition to our new joy, we might perceive two Beares, (a shee one with her Cubbe) now comming towards our Tent: whereupon wee straight arming our selves with our lances, issued out of the Tent to await her comming. Shee soone cast her greedy eyes upon us; and with full hope of devouring us, shee made the more haste unto us: but with our hearty lances we gave her such a welcome, as that shee fell downe upon the ground, tumbling up and downe, and biting the very snow for anger. Her Cubbe seeing this, by flight escaped us. The weather now was so cold, that longer wee were not able to stay abroad: retiring therefore into our Tent, wee first warmed our selves; and then out againe to draw the dead Beare in unto us. We flaied her, cut her into pieces of a Stone weight or thereabouts, which serv'd us for our dinners. And upon this Beare we fed some twenty dayes; for shee was very good flesh, and better than our Venison. This onely mischance wee had with her: that upon the eating of her Liver, our very skinnes peeled off: for mine owne part, I being sicke before, by eating of that Liver, though I lost my skinne, yet recovered I my health upon it. Shee being spent, either wee must seeke some other meate, or else fall aboard with our roast Venison in the Caske, which we were very loath to doe for feare of famishing, if so be that should be thus spent, before the Fleete came out of England. Amid'st these our feares, it pleased God to send divers Beares unto our Tent; some fortie at least, as we accounted. Of which number we kill'd seven: That is to say, the second of March one; the fourth, another; and the tenth, a wonderfull great Beare, sixe foote high at least. All which we flayed and roasted upon woodden spits, (having no better kitchen-furniture than that, and a frying-pan which we found in the Tent.) They were as good savory meate, as any beefe could be. Having thus gotten good store of such foode, wee kept not our selves now to such straight allowance as before; but eate frequently two or three meales a-day: which began to increase strength and abilitie of body in us.

By this, the cheerfull dayes so fast increased, that the severall sorts of Fowles, which had all the Winter-time avoyded those quarters, began now againe to resort thither, unto their Summer-abiding. The sixteenth of March, one of our two Mastive Dogges went out of the Tent from us in the morning: but from that day to this he never more returned to us, nor could wee ever heare what was become of him. The Fowles that I before spake of, constantly use every Spring time to resort unto that Coast, being used to breede there most abundantly. Their foode is a certaine kinde of small fishes. Yearely upon the abundant comming of these Fowles, the Foxes which had all this Winter kept their Burrowes under the Rockes, began now to come abroad, and seeke for their livings. For them wee set up three Trappes like Rat-trappes, and bayted them with the skinnes of these Fowles, which wee had found upon the snow; they falling there in their flight from the hill whereupon they bred, towards the Sea. For this Fowle, being about the bignesse of a Ducke, hath her legs placed so close unto her rumpe, as that when they alight once upon the land, they are very hardly (if ever) able to get up againe, by reason of the misplacing of their legs, and the weight of their bodies; but being in the water, they raise themselves with their pinions well enough. After wee had made These Trappes, and set them apart one from another in the snow, we caught fiftie Foxes in them: all which wee roasted, and found very good meate of them. Then tooke we a Beares skinne, and laying the flesh side upward, wee made Springes of Whales bone, wherewith wee caught about 60. of these Fowles, about the bignesse of a pigeon.

Thus continued wee untill the first of May; and the weather then growing warme; wee were now pretty able to goe abroad to seeke for more provision. Every day therefore abroad we went; but nothing could we encounter withall, untill the 24. of May: when espying a Bucke, wee thought to have kill'd him with our Dogge: but he was growne so fat and lazie, that hee could not pull downe the Deere. Seeking further out therefore, we found abundance of Willocks egges; (which is a Fowle about the bignesse of a Ducke) of which egges though there were great store, yet wee being but two of us together, brought but thirty of them to the Tent that day; thinking the next day to fetch a thousand more of them: but the day proved so cold, with so much Easterly winde, that wee could not stirre out of our Tent.

Staying at home therefore upon the 25. of May, we for that day omitted our ordinary custome. Our order of late (since the faire weather) was, every day, or every second day, to goe up to the top of a mountaine, to spie if wee could discerne the water in the Sea; which untill the day before we had not seene. At which time, a storme of winde comming out of the Sea, brake the maine yce within the Sownd: after which, the vvinde comming Easterly, carried all the yce into the Sea, and cleared the Sownd a great way, although not neere the shoare at first, seeing the cleare water came not neere our Tent by three miles at least.

This 25. of May therefore, wee all day staying in the Tent, there came two Ships of Hull into the Sownd: who knowing that there had been men left there the yeare before; the Master (full of desire to know wether we were alive or dead) man'd out a Shallop from the Ship; with orders to row as farre up the Sownd as they could, and then to hale up their Shallop, and travell over-land upon the snow unto the Tent. These men at their comming ashore, found the Shallop which we had haled from our Tent into the water, with a purpose to goe seeke some Sea-horses the next faire weather: the Shallop being then already fitted with all necessaries for that enterprize. This sight brought them into a quandary; and although this encounter made them hope, yet their admiration made them doubt, that it was not possible for us still to remaine alive. Taking therefore our lances out of the Boate, towards the Tent they come; wee never so much as perceiving of them: for wee were all gathered together, now about to goe to prayers in the inner Tent; onely Thomas Ayers was not yet come in to us out of the greater Tent. The Hull men now comming neere our Tent, haled it with the usuall word of the Sea crying *Hey*, he answered againe with *Ho*, which sudden answer almost amazed them all, causing them to stand still, halfe afraid at the matter. But we within hearing of them, joyfully came out of the Tent; all blacke as we were with the smoake, and with our clothes all tattered with wearing. This uncouth sight made them further amazed at us: but perceiving us to be the very men left there all the yeare; with joyfull hearts embracing us, and wee them againe, they came with us into our Tent. Comming thus in to us, wee shewed them the courtesie of the house, and gave them such Victuals as we had; which was Venison roasted foure moneths before, and a Cuppe of cold water; which for noveltie sake they kindly accepted of us.

Then fell we to aske them what newes? and of the state of the Land at home: and when the London Fleete would come? to all which, they returned us the best answers they could. Agreeing then to leave the Tent; with them wee went to their Shallop, and so a-board the Ship, where we were welcomed after the heartiest and kindest English manner; and there we stayed ourselves untill the comming of the London Fleete, which we much longed for: hoping by them to heare from our friends in England. Wee were told that they would be there the next day; but it was full three dayes ere they came, which seemed to us as tedious a three dayes as any we had yet endured: so much we now desired to heare from our friends, our wives and children.

The 28. of May, the London Fleete came into the Port to our great comfort. A-board the Admirall we went, unto the right noble Captaine, Captaine William Goodler, who is worthy to be honoured by all Sea-men for his courtesie and bounty. This is the Gentleman that is every yeare chiefe Commander of this Fleete; and right worthy he is so to be, being a very wise man, and an expert Mariner as most be in England, none dispraised. Unto this Gentleman right welcome we were; and joyfully by him received: hee giving order, that we should have any thing that was in the Ship, that might doe us good, and increase our strength; of his owne charges giving us apparell also, to the value of twenty pounds worth.

Thus after fourteene dayes of refreshment, wee grew perfectly well all of us: whereupon the noble Captaine sent William Fakely, and Iohn Wyse (Masons own Apprentice) and Thomas Ayers the Whale-Cutter, with Robert Good Fellow, unto Master Masons Ship, according as themselves desired. But thinking there to be as kindly welcomed, as the lost Prodigall; these poore men after their enduring of so much misery, which through his meanes partly they had undergone: no sooner came they a-board his ship, but he most unkindly call'd them Run-awayes, with other harsh and unchristian termes, farre enough from the civility of an honest man. Noble Captaine Goodler understanding all these passages, was right sorie for them, resolving to send for them againe, but that the weather proved so bad and uncertaine. I for mine owne part, remained with the Captaine still at Bottle Cove according to mine owne desire: as for the rest of us that staid with him, hee preferr'd the Land-men to row in the Shallops for the killing of the Whales; freeing them thereby from their toylesome labour a-shoare; bettering their Meanes besides. And all these favours did this worthy Gentleman for us.

Thus were wee well contented now to stay there till the twentieth of August; hoping then to returne into our native Countrey: which day of departure being come, and we im-barked, with joyfull hearts we set sayle through the foaming Ocean, and though cross'd sometimes with contrary windes homeward bound; yet our proper ships at last came safely to an Anchor in the River of Thames: to our great joy and comfort, and the Merchants benefite. And thus by the blessing of God came wee all eight of us well home, safe and sound: where the Worshipfull Companie our Masters, the Muscovie Merchants, have since dealt wonderfully well by us. For all which most mercifull Preservation, and most wonderfully powerfull Deliverance, all honour, praise and glory be unto the great God, the sole Author of it. He grant us to make the right use of it, Amen.

ORIENTAL SPLENDOUR

THE MOGUL'S BIRTHDAY

from

THE JOURNAL OF SIR THOMAS ROE

Thomas Roe went to Magdalen, where he was a commoner at about the age of twelve. He was Esquire of the Body during the last years of Queen Elizabeth, and he was knighted in 1605. In 1615 he was chosen to go as ambassador to Jehangir, the Great Mogul: by this time he had distinguished himself in the fighting against the Spaniards in the Low Countries, and in Parliament, where he represented Tamworth; he had also made voyages to the West Indies and the Spanish Main in search of gold.

His account of his journey and embassy (from which the first extract is taken) gives a striking picture of the endless delays, intrigues, changes of mind and inefficient splendour so characteristic of Eastern courts. By unremitting perseverance and judicious bribery Sir Thomas managed to conclude a commercial treaty with the Mogul, and so founded the prosperity of the East India Company. After this success he spent most of the rest of his life as an ambassador, although for a time he represented Oxford University in Parliament; he was also chancellor of the Order of the Garter and a privy councillor.

THE second of September [1616] was the king's birth-
day, and kept with great solemnity. On this day the
king is weigh'd against some jewels, gold, silver, stuffs of
gold, silver, and silk, butter, rice, fruit, and many other things,
of every sort a little, which is all given to the Bramas or
Bramans. The king commanded Asaph Chan to send for me
to this solemnity; who appointed me to come to the place
where the king sits at Durbar, and I should be sent for in:
but the messenger mistaking, I went not till Durbar time, and
so miss'd the sight; but being there before the king came out,
as soon as he spy'd me, he sent to know the reason why I came
not in, since he had order'd it. I answer'd according to the
mistake, yet he was very angry, and chid Asaph Chan publickly.
He was so rich in jewels, that I own in my life I never saw such
inestimable wealth together.

The time was spent in bringing his greatest elephants before
him; some of which being lord elephants, had their chains,
bells and furniture of gold and silver, and many gilt banners
and flags carried about them, and eight or ten elephants
waiting on each of them, clothed in gold, silk, and silver. In
this manner about twelve companies passed by most richly
adorned, the first having all the plates on his head and breast

set with rubies and emeralds, being a beast of wonderful bulk and beauty. They all bow'd down before the king, making their reverence very handsomly; this was the finest show of beasts I ever saw. The keepers of every chief elephant gave a present. Then having made me some favourable compliments he rose up and went in.

At night at about ten of the clock he sent for me. I was then abed. The message was, that he heard I had a picture which I had not shew'd him, desiring me to come to him and bring it; and if I would not give it him, he would order copies of it to be taken for his women. I got up, and carried it with me. When I came in, I found him sitting cross-leg'd on a little throne, all covered with diamonds, pearls, and rubies. Before him a table of gold, and on it about fifty pieces of gold plate, all set with jewels, some very great and extremely rich, but all of them almost cover'd with small stones. His nobility about him in their best equipage, whom he commanded to drink merrily, several sorts of wine standing by in great flagons. When I drew near, he asked for the picture. I shew'd him two; he seem'd astonish'd at one of them, and ask'd whose it was. I told him a friend of mine that was dead. He asked if I would give it him. I answered I valued it above all things, but if his majesty would pardon me, and accept of the other, which was an excellent piece, I would willingly bestow it on his majesty. He thank'd me, and said he desir'd none but that picture, and if I would give it him, he should prize it above the richest jewel in his house. I replied, I was not so fond of any thing, but I would part with it to please his majesty, with other expressions of respect. He bow'd to me, and said it was enough, I had given it him; that he own'd he had never seen so much art, so much beauty, and conjur'd me to tell him truly, whether ever such a woman liv'd. I assured him there did, but she was now dead. He said he would shew it his women, and take five copies, and if I knew my own I should have it again. Other compliments pass'd, but he would restore it, his painters being excellent at copying in water colours. The other picture being in oil, he did not like. Then he sent me word that it was his birth-day, and all men made merry, and ask'd whether I would drink with them. I answer'd, I would do whatsoever his majesty commanded, and wished him many happy days, and that the ceremony might be renewed an hundred years.

He asked me whether I would drink wine of the grape, or made, whether strong or small. I reply'd, what he commanded, but hoped it would not be too much, nor too strong. Then he called for a gold cup full of mixed wine, half of the grape and half artificial, and drank; causing it to be filled again, and then sent it by one of the nobles to me with this message, that I should drink it off twice, thrice, four, or five times for his sake, and accept of the cup and appurtenances as a present. I drank a little, but it was stronger than any I ever tasted; insomuch that it made me sneeze, which made him laugh; and he called for raisins, almonds, and sliced lemons, which were brought me on a gold plate, bidding me eat and drink what I would and no more. I made reverence for my present after my own manner, tho' Asaph Chan would have had me kneel, and knock my head against the ground; but his majesty accepted of what I did.

The cup was of gold, set all about with small rubies and Turky stones, the cover with large rubies, emeralds, and Turky stones in curious works, and a dish suitable to set the cup on. The value I know not, because the stones are many of them small; and the greater, which are many, not all clean, but they are in number about two thousand, and the gold about twenty ounces.

Thus he made merry, and sent me word, he esteemed me more than ever he had done, and asked whether I was merry at eating the wild boar sent me a few days before; how I dress'd it, what I drank, assuring me I should want for nothing in his country: the effects of all which his publick favours I presently found in the behaviour of all his nobility. Then he threw about to those that stood below two chargers of new roupies, and among us two chargers of hollow almonds of gold and silver mixed; but I would not scramble, as his great men did, for I saw his son take up none. Then he gave sashes of gold, and girdles to all the musicians and waiters, and to many others. So drinking, and commanding the others to do the same, his majesty and all his lords became the finest men I ever saw, of a thousand several humours. But his son, Asaph Chan, two old men, the late king of Candahar, and my self forbore. When he could hold up his head no longer, he lay down to sleep, and we all departed.

THE MOGUL'S PEACOCK THRONE

from

JEAN-BAPTISTE TAVERNIER'S

TRAVELS THROUGH TURKEY AND PERSIA TO THE INDIES

Jean-Baptiste Tavernier was born in Paris in 1605; he was the son of a Belgian dealer in maps. By the age of 22 Tavernier, having seen most of Europe, began to travel in the East, where he traded profitably in precious stones.

Louis XIV, for whom Tavernier bought some magnificent diamonds, ennobled him, and in 1668 Tavernier bought the barony of Aubonne on the shores of Lake Geneva. He settled down on his estate and, with the help of a man of letters, wrote an account of his voyages, which appeared in 1679 in two quarto volumes. The book was widely read and went through several editions: the English translation by J. Phillips (Milton's nephew) appeared under the title of *The Six Travels of Jean-Baptiste Tavernier, Baron of Aubonne, through Turkey and Persia, to the Indies, during the space of Forty Years . . . made English by J.P. 1684.*

Tavernier continued to occupy himself with commerce, and he entrusted a nephew with a venture to the Levant from which he hoped for a profit of a million *livres*. The nephew deceived him, and he was obliged to sell his lands. Tavernier started on another voyage, hoping to recover his fortune, but he died on reaching Moscow, being then 84.

THE Great Mogul has seven Thrones, some set all over with Diamonds; others with Rubies, Emraulds, and Pearls.

The largest Throne, which is set up in the Hall of the first Court, is in form like one of our Field-Beds, six foot long, and four broad. The Cushion at the back is round like a Bolster: the Cushions on the sides are flat.

I counted about a hundred and eight pale Rubies in Collets, about this Throne, the least whereof weigh'd a hundred Carats, but there are some that weigh'd two hundred. Emraulds I counted about a hundred and sixty that weigh'd some three-score, some thirty Carats.

The under-part of the Canopy is all embroider'd with Pearls and Diamonds, with a Fringe of Pearls round about. Upon the top of the Canopy, which is made like an Arch with four Panes, stands a Peacock, with his Tail spread, consisting all of Saphirs, and other proper colour'd Stones; the Body is of beaten Gold, enchas'd with several jewels; and a great Ruby upon his Breast, at which hangs a Pearl, that weighs fifty Carats.

On each side of the Peacock stand two Nose-gays, as high as the Bird, consisting of several sorts of Flowers, all of beaten Gold enamel'd. When the King seats himself upon the Throne there is a transparent Jewel, with a Diamond Appendant, of eighty or ninety Carats, encompass'd with Rubies and Emraulds, so hung that it is always in his Eye. The twelve pillars also that uphold the Canopy, are set with rows of fair Pearl, round, and of an excellent Water, that weigh from six to ten Carats a piece. At the distance of four feet, upon each side of the Throne, are plac'd two Parasols, or Umbrello's, the handles whereof are about eight food high, cover'd with Diamonds; the Parasols themselves are of crimson Velvet, embroider'd and fring'd with Pearls.

This is the famous Throne which Tamerlane began, and Cha-Jehan finish'd; which is really reported to have cost a hundred and sixty Millions, and five hundred thousand *livres* of our Money.

Behind this stately and magnificent Throne there is another less, in the form of a Tub, where the King bathes himself; it is an Oval, seven foot long, and five broad. The outside whereof shines all over with Diamonds and Pearls; but there is no canopy over it.

HUNTING WITH THE EMPEROR K'ANG HSI

from

JOHN BELL'S

TRAVELS FROM ST. PETERSBURG IN RUSSIA

TO DIVERSE PARTS OF ASIA.

Mr. Bell of Antermony was born in 1691; he went to Russia in his twenties, while Peter the Great was Czar. There he joined the Russian embassy to the Emperor K'ang Hsi, and it is possible that he acted as doctor to the expedition, for the Dictionary of National Biography says that he may have had the degree of M.D.

K'ang Hsi (the Kamhi of the narrative) was, in his old age, the most amiable of the Manchu emperors. He was the third of his line, and he retained the Manchurian way of life in spite of ruling over China for close on seventy years. He died in 1723.

Mr. Bell accompanied another Russian embassy to China later, and several to Turkey; he settled for a while in Constantinople, but returned to spend the rest of his life in Scotland, where he died in 1780.

When he came to write his book he thought he needed the help of a literary man (I take this from the D.N.B.) and applied to Mr. Robertson, the historian. Robertson advised the style of Gulliver's Travels, but did not meddle with the book. The *Travels from St. Petersburg in Russia to Diverse Parts of Asia* was published first in Glasgow, where it was beautifully printed by the Foulis brothers in 1763, and then in London, by W. Homer, in two volumes 12mo., in 1764. The *Travels* were well received and went through several editions, including one in Dublin; they last appeared in 1811 as part of Pinkerton's collection.

THE 11th [of February, 1721], several officers came
from the court, with presents to the ambassador, and
every person of the retinue, corresponding to their
different stations and characters, and, so minutely and exactly
was the matter managed, that even the meanest of our servants
was not neglected. The presents, consisting of a complete
Chinese dress, some pieces of damasks, and other stuffs, were,
indeed, of no great value. They were, however, carried along
the streets, wrapped up in yellow silk, with the usual parade
of things belonging to the court; a circumstance which is
reckoned one of the greatest honours that can be conferred on a
foreign Minister.

Next day, the Emperor sent to ask the ambassador, whether
he inclined to accompany him to a hunting-match, in a forest
not far distant from Pekin; to which his excellency readily
agreed.

The 13th, I dined with one of my Chinese friends, called
Fangfung. . . .

The 17th, being now on the point of our departure, in
order to make the most of the short time we had to stay, I
rode about twelve miles eastward from Pekin, accompanied
with a Chinese friend, to the banks of the river; which I found
crowded with a number of barques, of different sizes, which

are constantly employed in carrying provisions, and other stores, to the city, from distant parts of the country. I saw many vessels sailing down the stream, towards the south-east. And I was informed, there are nine thousand nine hundred and ninety nine vessels constantly employed on this river; but why confined to such an odd number I could neither learn, nor comprehend.

On this occasion also I revisited the China-manufactory, in order to try whether I could learn any thing of that curious art. But, though the people were very complaisant, and showed me every thing I desired them, I returned as ignorant as I went thither; and, I am persuaded, that, before a person can get any knowledge of the affair, he must be bred a potter, and have time to inspect its whole progress; of which these people seem to make no secret. . . .

On the 18th, all our gentlemen dined with my Chinese friend, named Siasiey, where we met with a friendly reception and a sumptuous feast. After dinner our hospitable landlord put about his cups very freely. At last, he took me by the hand, and desired I would let the ambassador return and remain with him, and he would give me the choice of which of his wives or daughters I liked best. I could not but return my friend hearty thanks for his obliging offer; which, however, I thought it not proper to accept.

Next day, I went to see the market where provisions were sold. It was a spacious oblong, spread with gravel, very neat and clean. The butchers had their shops in a shed, running quite round the place. I saw little beef, but a great deal of mutton. In the middle, was great store of poultry, wild-fowl, and venison; but, what surprised me not a little, was, to find about a dozen dead badgers exposed for sale. The Chinese, it seems, are very fond of these animals; which are accounted unclean in other parts of the world. All the Chinese merchants have the art of exposing their goods to sale dressed up in the most advantageous manner; and, even in purchasing any trifling thing, whatever the case be that holds it, it is half the cost, and often exceeds it in value.

The 21st, being the day appointed for hunting with the Emperor, at one of the clock in the morning, horses were brought to our lodgings, for the ambassador and those who attended him. We immediately mounted, and, after riding about six miles, to the south-west of the city, at break of day, we reached the gates of the park called Chay-Za; where we were received by an officer, and conducted, through the forest, to a summer-house, about a mile from the gate, in which the Emperor had slept the preceding night. This was a small but neat building, having a double row of galleries, open to the forest, on all sides, and an avenue leading to it from the gate, planted with several rows of trees. At some distance from the house, we dismounted, and were met by the master of the ceremonies, who conducted us into a gallery. As soon as we entered, the good old Emperor, who had risen long before our arrival, sent one of his eunuchs to salute the ambassador, and ordered us tea and other victuals. On the south side of the house is a canal, filled with clear water, and several large fish-ponds, which make a great addition to the beauties of this charming place. At a convenient distance from the house, stood about a thousand tents, where the courtiers and grandees had lodged the night before.

Breakfast being over, the Emperor, who was very fond of arms, sent to desire a sight of the ambassador's fowling-piece. He returned it, with several of his own to be shown us. They had all match-locks. The Chinese are possessed with a notion, that flints, in their climate, acquire a moisture which hinders their firing. But, as far as I could perceive, the air had little effect upon our flints.

A signal was then given that the Emperor was coming; upon which all the great men drew up in lines, from the bottom of the stairs to the road leading to the forest, all on foot, dressed in their hunting habits, the same with those used by the officers and cavalry of the army, when in the field, and armed with bows and arrows. We had a proper place assigned us, and made our bows to his Majesty, who returned a gracious smile, with signs to follow him. He was seated, cross-legged, in an open machine, carried by four men, with long poles rested on their shoulders. Before him lay a fowling-piece, a bow, and a sheaf of arrows. This has been his hunting equipage for some years, since he left off riding; but, in his youth, he went usually every summer, several days' journey without the long wall, and carried along with him all the Princes his sons, and many persons of distinction, to the number frequently of some thousands, in order to hunt in the woods and deserts; where he continued for the space of two or three months. Their provisions were restricted to bare necessities, and often to what they caught in the woods of Tartary. This piece of policy he practised chiefly with a view to hardening the officers of his army, and prevent their falling into idleness and effeminacy among the Chinese; and at the same time, to set a good example of the austerities he recommended, by living on the same hard fare he prescribed to others.

As soon as the Emperor had passed, the company mounted and followed him, at some distance, till we came into the open forest, where all formed into a semi-circle, in the centre of which was the Emperor, having on his left hand about eight or ten of his sons and grandsons, and the ambassador on his right, about fifty paces distant; close by him, were the master of the chase, with some grey-hounds, and the grand falconer with his hawks. I could not but admire the beauty of these fine birds. Many of them were as white as doves; having one or two black feathers in their wings or tails. They are brought from Siberia, or places to the north of the river Amoor.

Our wings being extended, there were many hares started, which the company endeavoured to drive towards the Emperor, who killed many of them with arrows as they passed; those he missed, he made a sign to some of the Princes to pursue, who also killed several of them with arrows; but no other person was permitted to draw a bow or stir from the line. The same rules of hunting, I formerly observed, are practised by the Mongalls.

From the open field, we continued our route westward, to a place among thickets, and tall reeds, where we sprung a number of pheasants, partridges, and quails. His Majesty then laid aside his bow and arrows and carried a hawk on his hand; which he flew as occasion offered. The hawks generally raked in the pheasants while flying; but, if they took the reeds or bushes, they soon caught them.

After proceeding about two or three miles farther into the forest, we came to a tall wood, where we found several sorts of deer. The young men went and beat the woods, whilst the rest of the company remained without. We saw much game pass us, but nobody drew a bow, till the Emperor had killed a stag, which he did very dexterously, with a broad-headed arrow; after which the Princes had leave to kill several bucks; among which was one of that species, that bears the musk, called *kaberda* in Siberia, of which I have formerly given a description. The Chinese musk is stronger, and therefore preferable to that from northern parts.

We had now been six hours on horse-back, and, I reckon, had travelled about fifteen English miles, but no end of the forest yet appeared. We turned short from this wood southwards, till, coming to some marshes, overgrown with tall reeds, we roused a great many wild boars; but, as it was not the season for killing them, they all escaped. The hunting these fierce animals is reckoned the most dangerous of all kinds of sport, except the chase of lions and tigers. Every one endeavoured to avoid them, and several of them ran furiously through the thickest troops of horse. The Emperor was so cautious as to have a company of men, armed with lances, to guard his machine.

We continued the sport till about four o'clock, when we came to a high artificial mount, of a square figure, raised in the middle of a plain, on the top of which were pitched about ten or twelve tents, for the imperial family. This mount had several winding paths leading to the top, planted, on each side, with rows of trees, in imitation of nature. To the south was a large bason of water, with a boat upon it; from whence, I suppose, the earth had been taken that formed this mount. At some distance from the mount, tents were erected for the people of distinction, and officers of the court. About two hundred yards from it, we were lodged in some clean huts, covered with reeds. The Emperor, from his situation, had a view of all the tents, and a great way farther into the forest. The whole scene made a very pretty appearance.

As soon as we alighted, the master of the ceremonies was sent, by the Emperor, to ask the ambassador how he liked their manner of hunting. He made a suitable return, acknowledging, at the same time, the great honour done him on this occasion. The Emperor then sent us great plenty of dressed provisions of all kinds; and the officers, who brought them, pointed out several dishes, which his Majesty sent from his own table, consisting of mutton, venison, pheasants, and other sorts of wild fowl.

After dinner, the Emperor sent two of his chief eunuchs to compliment the ambassador; and inform him, that he intended to entertain him with the baiting of three tigers, which had been kept for some time, cooped up in a strong grate-work, for that purpose.

The hill, where the Emperor's tent stood, was surrounded with several ranks of guards, armed with long spears. A guard, also, was placed before the ambassador's, and the rest of the tents, to secure the whole encampment from the fury of these fierce animals. The first was let out by a person mounted on a fleet horse, who opened the door of the coop by means of a rope tied to it. The tiger immediately left his cage, and seemed much pleased at finding himself at liberty. The horseman rode off at full speed; while the tiger was rolling himself upon the grass. At last he rose, and growled, and walked about. The Emperor fired twice at him with bullets; but the distance being considerable, missed him, though the pieces were well pointed. Upon which his Majesty sent to the ambassador, to try his piece upon him; which being charged with a single ball, he walked towards the animal, accompanied by ten men, armed with spears, in case of accidents; till, being at a convenient distance, he took his aim, and killed him on the spot.

The second was let out in the same manner. The horseman, retiring a little, left the creature rolling on the grass, like the first. He then returned, and shot at him with a blunted arrow; which roused the animal, to such a pitch, and made him pursue so closely, that the horseman narrowly escaped within the ranks, where the furious tiger, endeavouring to leap over the men's heads, was killed at the foot of the mount.

The third, as soon as he was set at liberty, ran directly towards the Emperor's tent; and was, in like manner, killed with the spears. A man must be well mounted and armed, who hunts this kind of animals in the woods; where they must be much stronger and swifter than those we saw, which had been confined for many months, and whose limbs, for want of exercise, were become stiff and unwieldy; but, notwithstanding this advantage, the courage and nimbleness even of these animals was very surprising. I have seen four sorts of them, the tiger, panther, leopard, and lynx, which are all very fierce; but the first is the largest and strongest.

The Emperor, in his youth, was very fond of hunting these creatures in the woods of Tartary; but, now, he confines himself within the limits of the forest, where there is game sufficient to gratify any sportsman.

The killing of the tigers finished the diversion of the day; after which we retired to our huts, where we were entertained with a plentiful supper, sent us by the Emperor. After supper, an officer was sent by his Majesty to the ambassador, who brought the tiger's skin he had shot; telling him, that, by the laws of hunting, he had a right to it.

Next morning, the sport was resumed, and varied little from that of the preceding day. About three o'clock, afternoon, we came to another summer-house in the middle of the forest, where the Emperor lodged the following night; while we lay in a small neat temple in the neighbourhood; and were entertained, by his Majesty, in the same manner as before.

The 23rd, about eight of the clock in the morning the master of the ceremonies waited on the ambassador, in order to conduct him into his Majesty's presence, to receive his audience of leave. The Emperor received him, in a most friendly manner, in his bed-chamber. He repeated his assurances of the great friendship he entertained for his Czarish Majesty; and expressed great respect for the personal merit of the ambassador. After which the ambassador took leave; and we returned to our lodgings in the city.

I shall only observe further, that this forest is really a most delightful place; is well stored with variety of game; and is of great extent, as will easily be conceived from the account I have given of our two days hunting. It is all inclosed with a high wall of brick. The value of the park, so near the capital, shews the magnificence of this powerful monarch.

THE NABOB'S LADY

from

THE GENTLEMAN'S MAGAZINE FOR JANUARY 1745

Mr. Urban,

The agreeable entertainment, which your Magazine affords at our factories in the East-Indies, where it is as eagerly sought after as any part of the lading of an European ship, entitles you to some return from thence. I have therefore sent you the following little piece, in part, and doubt not of its meeting a favourable reception, from your fair readers especially, as it must shew them that their free condition is abundantly preferable to the state, magnificence, and splendour of the highest princesses of the most opulent kingdom in the world.

Part of a letter from a lady at Fort St. George, in the East-Indies, To Mrs. B——.

WE have had a great man called the Nabob, (who is the next person in dignity to the Great Mogul) to visit the governour[1] (Benyon) who with the council and all the head gentlemen of Madrass went in great state to meet him; his lady with all her women attendance came the night before him; all the guns were fired round the fort upon her

[1] Lately come home.

arrival, as well as his. He and she are Moors, whose women are never seen by any men upon earth except their own husbands. He staid here about a fortnight, but his lady remained in the black town; his attendance consisted of many thousands of people. The governor waited upon him at his house in the black town, and he returned to visit the governor; all the ladies went to see him go: it was a fine procession of palanquens, and he a fine man in person; the richness of his dress with pearls and diamonds is beyond description; he sent the governour a rich present, which was put in a large philligree silver box, placed upon the back of a beautiful Moor's horse, which are fine large creatures; it was adorn'd with all manner of rich gold and velvet trappings, I believe there were a thousand horse and foot people to attend it. After he left Madrass, Mrs. Benyon went to visit his lady. The governor was so obliging to write me a letter over night, to invite my self and your sister to go with Mrs. Benyon the next morning to visit this great lady; we drest ourselves in the very best of things we had, and went to the governor's, where we breakfasted, and found Mrs. Benyon[1] as fine as a queen; the governor made tea for us that we might not put our dress out of form; Mrs. Beard, who is the governor's sister in law, and her eldest daughter, made up the rest of the company; we had all the governor's attendance as well as his lady, and the musick playing before us all the way, and thousands of people looking at us; we had about a mile to go. When we arrived, Mrs. Benyon was handed by a lady who was to introduce her through two halls, which brought us into a large garden with a pavilion at the end of it, where the Nabob's lady was seated. A grand Moor lady of her attendance came to receive Mrs. Benyon in the middle of the garden, and presented her to the Nabob's lady, who was seated in the middle of the pavilion upon a settee cover'd with embroidery on crimson velvet, and embroider'd carpets hung over it. She received our governess with the utmost gentility and good breeding, and paid her proper compliments to us.

I must now give you a description of her person and dress; her person was thin, genteel, and middle-sized, her complexion was tawney, as the Moors are, her eyes as black as possible, large and fine, and painted at the edges of them black, which is what most of the Moors do, her lips painted red, and between

[1]Since dead. January 1745.

184

every tooth painted black, to look like ebony. All her attendance, which were about thirty ladies, were the same: her face was done over like frosted work with leaf gold, the nails of her fingers and toes were painted red, and likewise the middle of her hands. You will perhaps think this a strange description, but I assure you it is literally true. And now for her dress; her hair was as black as jett, very long and thick, which was combed neatly back, and then braided; it hung a great deal below her waist. She had a fillet of diamonds round her head, edged with pearls of a large size, her ear-rings were as broad as my hand, made of diamonds and pearls, so that they almost covered each side of her face; then she had a nose jewel that went thro' her left nostril; round her neck she had twenty rows of pearls, none smaller than a pea, but a great number of them as large as the end of my little finger. From her necklace there hung a great number of rows of large pearls, which came down below her waist, at the end of which hung a large emerald as large as my hand, and as thick, her coat which she had on was made of fine gold muslin, made close to her, and a slash'd sleeve, a gold vail which she hung loosely over her head and the rest, went carelessly over her body, all the front part of it was trimm'd with one row of large pearls. She had a girdle, or rather hoop, of diamonds, which went round the bottom of her waist, it was above an inch broad, several strings of large pearls round her waist, and ten rows round her arms a little above her elbow, and her fingers every one of them adorn'd with rich rings of all sorts and sizes, her foot and ancles adorn'd with much finer than her hands and arms. In short, Mrs. Beard and myself computed she had many more pearls and diamonds about her than would fill a peck measure. Some of the ladies that attended her were near as fine as herself.

She had a little son brought in to see us, the richness of whose dress was I to describe, you would imagine I was telling you some fairy story; but, in short, he was loaded with gold, pearls and diamonds; the fan which was carried to keep the sun off him (made like a fire-screen, but four times as large) was crimson velvet all set in figures with diamonds and pearls. I own I thought myself in a dream all the time I was there. I must not omit giving you a description of the pavilion; it was very large, and all the bottom cover'd with fine carpets, and entirely hung round with muslin valens; on one end stood the bed, or cott, as we call it, the frame work and pillars were of solid gold, and gold gause curtains, and a rich counterpane; there were several fine dressing tables with large gold filligree candlesticks upon them. At the entrance of the pavilion there was a long embroider'd velvet carpet, with a pillar of the same work at each end, which was opposite to the settee which the lady sat upon, for us to walk over; there was something like an awning made of crimson silk, which went all on the outside of the pavilion, and was supported by pillars of gold; we had two gold censors of incense and sandal wood, which almost suffocated us with its perfumes. Our entertainment was tea, which seemed to be made with rose-water and cinnamon; every thing was served in plate. Then we had beatle, brought us in filligree boxes made of gold, upon large scollop'd silver waiters, which we lik'd better than what was in them; for the beatle is a large green leaf which the Indians chew, of an intoxicating nature, and very disagreeable to the English, but we were forced to comply with that out of compliment. After all this was over, we saw a large silver board brought, cover'd with a work'd carpet, which was presented to Mrs. Benyon; when uncovered there appeared a fine Moor's coat, and a couple of rich gold vails, then a present to each of us a Moor's coat and one gold vail. The Nabob's lady put Mrs. Benyon's vail upon her, so we in compliment put on ours, which she was pleased with. Then we came back to the governor's in form, where we dined, and spent the evening. The Nabob's lady sent an entertainment after us, which consisted of sixty dishes, all under silver covers, and put into scarlet cloth bags, made for that purpose:—The governor's lady made a present of a hundred pagodas to all her attendance.—The Nabob's lady and her attendance admired us all, but thought our dress very odd; two of the ladies examined our dress till they came to our hoop petticoat, which they were much astonished at; they admired my tweeser, and the trinkets in it. To end all, we were the first English women they had ever seen, and I doubt not we appeared as odd to them as they did to us. Their numerous riches are all the enjoyment they have, for the lady is not suffered to go out the year round, and if obliged to travel, she is cover'd up in her palanquen, in such a manner that no mortal can see her, and it would be death to any man to attempt to see a Moor's lady.

THE INDEFATIGABLE TOURIST

from

PHILIP SKIPPON'S

ACCOUNT OF A JOURNEY MADE THRO' PART

OF THE LOW-COUNTRIES, GERMANY, ITALY

AND FRANCE, 1663

Philip Skippon was the son of Major-General Skippon, a prominent Roundhead and a vigorous pamphleteer.

Skippon made his breakneck tour in company with Ray the botanist and Willughby the ornithologist; they both wrote accounts of the journey, rather after the same style as Skippon's but with very much more about their own subjects. Both Ray and Willughby are published separately and in Harris' *Iterinarium Bibliotheca* of 1705, but Skippon only appears in Churchill, where he occupies a great deal of space, being no less than 350,000 words long.

Skippon's parentage was not held against him, for King Charles II knighted him, possibly in recognition of his scientific attainments.

APRIL 17. 1663. St. Vet. being Friday, Mr. Ray and my self took horse at Leeds in Kent, and rode to Canterbury 20 miles, and 15 miles further we arrived at Dover, where we stay'd all night, and met the rest of our company, *viz.* Mr. Willughby and Mr. Bacon, with two servants, who came post from Gravesend.

April 18. In the morning we went up to the castle, seated on a high hill, garisoned by 150 soldiers, and governed by C. Stroud; without the walls is a deep trench, and within nigh 30 acres of ground; here stand the ruins of a church, and the palace, a compact building, now somewhat defaced; a broad pair of stairs make the ascent into two or three large rooms; some small impressions were made by cannon bullets in the siege 1648. Within the castle walls are three wells, one in the outward space about 60 fathoms deep; a stone let down perpendicularly into it, strikes against the sides many times. Another well at the palace in the inner space about 80 fathoms deep; it has a little house over it, where they put two asses into a great wheel which being mov'd round by them, brings up the bucket of water: the third well is near the broad stairs of the palace. In a little vault where beer is sold, we saw the brass horn call'd Julius Cæsar's, the sound whereof gave notice to the workmen to begin and leave off their days work, when they were building this castle. Below the cliff, and under the castle, is a platform, with guns that command the sea near the shore. On the walls of the castle are many platforms, having great guns mounted, among which one we observ'd about 23 foot long, made in Flanders, 1544; the bore of it is small. In this castle we saw a Turky ram with four horns, two of the horns recurved like a goat's, the other two hanging down by his ears, which were much larger than our ordinary sheep's; his snout was arched, and his tail cut off because it trail'd upon the ground; the body seem'd not much bigger than our common sheep; the wooll was coarser.

The town of Dover is large and long, situated under the cliffs; it is a corporation, and sends two parliament-men to the house of commons. The haven has a peer of wood, and not far off is a ware-house of an indifferent bigness.

Before we entred the packet-boat, we pay'd to the clerk of the passage four-pence custom for a trunk, and two-pence a portmanteau, four shillings and ten-pence for transcribing a pass for four persons, and three shillings and six-pence for transcribing a pass for two persons. To the water-bailiff one shilling; to the master of the ferry one shilling and six-pence a man; *i.e.* one shilling town-custom, and six-pence for himself. To the searcher, six-pence a man for writing down our names, and we gave him two shillings and six-pence because he did not search us.

April 18. About two in the afternoon we went aboard the packet boat; about eight in the evening we were becalm'd, and were forced to lie two leagues short of Calais till the morning, and then about five o'clock we arriv'd at Calais-shore, having sail'd eight leagues from Dover. We gave five shillings a man for our passage, and five shillings for the use of the master's cabbin. Two French boats met us off at sea, and boarded us, and paying three-pence a-head to the master of the ferry, we enter'd one of the boats in the haven; but before they would set us ashore, after much wrangling with those brawling shark- ing fellows, we were forced to give them six-pence apiece. When we came to the town gate, the searchers opened our portmanteaus: they can demand nothing for searching, except any new things are found, as silk stockens, laced bands, &c. for which there a considerable custom must be paid. When we came to our inn, we repos'd our selves till noon, and then walk'd over a large square market-place, where there is a market twice a week, *viz.* on Tuesdays and Saturdays. The town-house (*maison de la Ville*) hath a fair tower; the hall for lawyers courts was burnt down 1659. We view'd Nostre Dame church, and saw many altars dress'd with pictures, &c. The high altar is curious wood-work, adorned on one side with the statue of Charlemagne, on the other side with the statue of St. Louis, and on the top the virgin Mary. To this church belong 20 priests, the chief of which is *Le Doyen.* On the north side of the church is a monument erected to Sir Andrew Young, an Englishman, Baron de Baume, who dy'd 1637. In the church-yard the tombs are set up on the wall, as in Scotland. While they are at their devotions, the poor will beg of strangers and others in the church. We visited the nuns of the Dominican order, they were 28 in number; their chapel is a plain building without and within; none of the nuns appear in the chapel, but their singing may be heard thro' the wooden grates in the wall. We were brought into a little parlour, and discoursed through a wooden grate with two of them, (one could speak a little English). They sold us several things made of straw, and saints bones wrought up in wax, and made at Rome, which were impress'd with the saint's effigies; they did not give them immediately to us with their own hands, but put the lesser thro' the grate, and the bigger things into a cylindrical box, which having a hole in one side, they turn'd the box, and then we took the things out of it. They would not shew us their faces. Besides the grate they have a curtain within, and they have a maid that stands nigh the altar to put out some of the candles when service is done. They chuse their abbess once in three years. Another nunnery call'd the Hospital.

At the convent of the Minnums who are of the order of St. Francis de Paolo, we saw a poor maid in the church, who (they say) was three years before miraculously cured of a palsy and asthma in a quarter of an hour's time, by praying before St. Francis his picture, she herself telling us that she was thus suddenly restor'd to her health and use of her limbs, after she had been four years distemper'd; her picture hangs up there, praying to that saint, and underneath are her crutches. And we also observ'd a great many legs, arms, hearts, &c. of wax, being resemblances of such parts as were cur'd. The friars brought us into their parlour, where the story of St.

Francis is painted in several pictures, and we were in one of their cells, where they shew'd us a piece of our Saviour's cross brought out of England, and a piece of the spunge us'd at the passion. They have a small library, and garden; 20 monks did belong to this place, but now they are reduc'd to 12. Their cells are mark'd 1, 2, 3, &c.

April 20. being Rogation week, we saw their procession.

We went to the Capuchins chapel, but saw nothing there remarkable.

Calais is populous, it hath two gates, one at the haven, and the other very handsome, call'd *la Porte Royalle*. The houses are much after the Scotch fashion, built of brick, and tyl'd; their windows are half glass, and the lower half is a wooden casement. The great church (Nostre Dame) and a large square stone building, were built by the English. Many of the women wear green rugs in cold weather about their heads and shoulders, like the Scotch plads; they call'd this rug *une mante*.

A strong old wall made by the English encompasses the town, and a deep trench full of water round about it, and without this trench is a new wall, built about 35 years ago, with two trenches of water about it. They would not suffer us to go up any steeple to view the town, nor permit us to go into the citadel, which is large, and within the walls of Calais; two forts besides and bulwarks without the walls. The number of the soldiers in garison is sometimes 2000, sometimes 3000, more or less. The present governor's name is Mons. Le Conte de Chano, one of the four captains of the king's guard, *mareschal de Camp*, counsellor to the king, governor of Calais and *le pais Conquis*. Soon after we came to Calais we sent our names to him; drums and trumpets gave us their salutes. Old Calais is not far distant. Hereabouts and in the town are 22 windmills.

The government of Calais is by a mayor and four eschevins chosen by the freemen every year; the eldest eschevin is deputy mayor. None can be mayor except he hath first been treasurer and four times eschevin. There is a court of justice to decide controversies between merchants.

The Hugonots or Protestants that are freemen, are not capable of the aforesaid honours; the governor can arbitrarily dispose of the town offices.

On the sands near Calais we found growing *Rhamnus Ius Diosc.* and *Cochlearia minor rotundifolia.*

April 21. paying first to the searchers at the gate five-pence a portmanteau, and five-pence a trunk, and five-pence for a pass through the Gate, and eleven-pence for a pass to Greveling and Dunkirk, we went into our waggon, and travelled by Oye in a fenny level. Some distance before we came to Greveling, our portmanteaus were visited by a troublesome searcher, notwithstanding the pass we procur'd in the morning; then we ferry'd over the river Aa in a boat, which was pull'd over by a rope that cross'd the water. Four leagues from Calais we arriv'd at Greveling, passing first over five draw-bridges. Many trenches, strong bulwarks, and a firm wall about this place. The houses are poorly built, being a frontier of Flanders which is divided from France by the Aa; the streets are broad and well paved; we saw Nôtre Dame church, and gave a visit to the English nuns of the order of St. Clare; the name of the abbess was Taylor; she spake very civilly to us, and told us they were in number 44. They live very strictly, and never see the face of any man; the bars were of iron that we discours'd through. They have a large house and garden. About eight years ago part of their chapel was blown up with the magazine of the town. The abbess is chosen for life by the major vote.

Another nunnery of 14 black nuns. And a monastery for 14 recollets.

A large market-place, where are markets on Wednesdays and Fridays.

He that is governor of Dunkirk is governor of this place. They would not permit us to walk the fortifications.

After dinner we pass'd in sight of Borborgh steeple, and riding a sandy way by little hills, we saw the ruins of Mardyck fort. The country hereabouts is much spoil'd by wars.

In the evening we entred Dunkirk, and the next morning, April 22. we had drums beating at our chamber door. About five or six months before, the town was garisoned by 5000 English soldiers, but now sold to the French king for 5.000.000 livres; the governor is monsieur le Strade ambassador at the Hague, and his deputy-governor is the marquis Monpessant; there are about 3000 in garison. The soldiers have two or three streets of uniform lodgings, two stories high, three beds in the lower room and two above, and three soldiers lie in a bed. We went in a boat to the fort built lately by the English; it is on the sand, which by some winds is so driven, that you may walk over the walls. The English made two firm bulwarks which command the sea, and under them is a broad platform, and then a thick wall (not yet finish'd) and within the wall is a passage for soldiers to stand in, and shoot through; a trench round besides; beyond the fort, towards the sea, is another sand. There are three gates besides the watergate; the town is not so populous as Calais. Most of the dead are buried in a church without the suburbs, and a little chapel called St. Louis. The *Stadthuys* is a good stone-building; there are three market-places, one for corn, another for fish, and a third for herbs, called the green-market.

There are three gilds of fraternities, first, of the cross bow; second, the hand-bow; third, the musket. St. George is patron to the first, St. Sebastian to the second, and St. Barbara patroness to the last.

Dunkirk town is govern'd by 16 magistrates, who out of their own number make a yearly choice of two bailiffs and a burgomaster. The freemen elect the 16.

The buildings are fair and uniform, and the streets broad and handsomely pav'd. St. Peter's street is so called from his statue erected there.

[They visit several nunneries and churches. Having viewed Nieuport they come to Ostend.]

Having passed over three draw-bridges, we came into a neat square market-place, where one of our company went to the captain of the guard to be examined whence we came, &c. At night we sent our names to the governor's deputy, there being no governor at present; but Don Pedro Cheval is expected; there were not above 500 or 600 soldiers that garison'd this exactly fortify'd place, and the curious bulwarks. The town is indifferently full of inhabitants, who are under the government of eight magistrates, one bailiff, and one burgomaster, who are chosen every year, two years, or three years, as the commissaries of the country please.

There is a little square market-place for cattel. The key is handsome and broad, and the haven is large.

The great church is indifferent; but having no chapels, the altars are set against the pillars. At the high altar is a fair picture of St. Peter fishing. At the west end hangs this inscription.

Ab insidijs Gallorum liberavit nos Dominus. Anno 1648. 15. *Jun.*

Two monuments, one of the last governor.

The prison is well built, and hath a beautiful tower, with many chiming bells in it. The king of Spain hath granted many immunities to this town. There are but two gates, and but two monasteries, one of Capuchins, the other of Jacobin or Dominican nuns.

April 24. we took our places in a boat that went a league, being a fourth part of the way to Bruges; and then we came to Sluces, and entred another boat, which brought us betimes in the afternoon to Bruges. In our passages the boatman pay'd something at two bridges, which were remov'd aside, to let the boats pass.

The city of Bruges hath very fair streets, well pav'd, strait and broad, the citizens houses are handsome, five or six stories high; in the market-place, a spacious square, we saw a multitude of people about a stage, where actors entertained the company with dancing, &c. this week being a time of jollity, there being a kermes or fair. The gentlewomen in their coaches rode through the principal streets, and observe a tour as our English gallants do in Hyde-Park, and the ladies are treated with sweet-meats, &c. And yet it is reputed a great absurdity to eat apples or any thing else as one walks in the streets.

We saw a very tall man, 27 years old, born at Schoonhoven in Holland, his name is Jeanne Taeks; I stood under his armpits with my hat on, which was two yards; from his middle finger's end to his elbow, 25 inches and a half; the length of his hand from the tip of his finger 11 inches. His finger was as long as my hand, eight inches. He spoke English, having some years since been in England. . . .

In this city are five gilds or fraternities; 1. of the fences; 2, 3. Two of the cross-bows; 4. The musket; 5. The hand-bow; this last we saw, and went into a garden, where, in a long gallery, the spectators stand to see the shooting: here a high pole stands with a wooden parrot on the top, which is shot at every last Sunday in April; he that shoots it off is chosen master with a great deal of triumph; the late duke of Gloucester took it down, and under his picture in the great hall is inscrib'd.

Henrico *D. G. Duci* Glocestriæ *Sodalitij Sti.* Sebastiani Mœcenati *et Sodali.*

Our king Charles the second's picture is in white marble with his arms.

In the garden lies a whale's throat-bone.

We saw one of the cross-bow gilds. In the garden are long bowling alleys (made like Pall-malls) where they play with sphærical bowls; a chapel at this gild. . . .

[Having toured Bruges and Ghent with wonderful thoroughness and rapidity, they go on their way.]

In the afternoon we rode bad way mended with wood, the country shaded with trees. Two Spanish soldiers on horseback begg'd of us. At night we reach'd Brussels; where, on the 30th of April, we walk'd to the warrande or park, which is a pleasant place planted with many high beeches, &c. This park is between the two walls of the city; a pall-mall, many deer kept here; three fountains. We saw three gardens; in the first a *corona* of dancers mov'd by water; in the second garden we saw a comical cap of copper kept up by a stream of water; out of the garden knots the water sprung up in several places, and a ball playing on the top of a stream; in the third garden we saw a Cupid shooting water, and a goose putting water out of its mouth; a summer-house supported by pillars over the water, and a water-work in the midst of a labyrinth of arbors. Near the palace lies a good statue of Mary Magdalen, the statue of Charles V. and a Hercules standing against a pillar, and another of Hercules struggling with Anteus. The riding place is just by, and a gallery where we heard our voices eccho'd ten times distinctly; the wind hindered, else we were assur'd we might have heard the eccho 15 times. Organs are here mov'd by water. We saw at this place two eagles, two white Moscovy ducks, and an ostrich which was about an ell high, the feathers of the body black, except the tail and the wings, which were white and little; great eyes and large ears, a long neck, being most of it covered with a whitish down; large nostrils, a broad head and bill; it had short thin blackish hairs on the head, long legs, both legs and thighs naked. It had two toes, and no heel or posticus.

The palace is a stately building. In a gallery there are standing the statues of 13 emperors [follows a list].

In the royal chapel, over the altar is written on a picture of the wisemen offering,

Aurum, Myrrham, Thus Regique, Hominique Deoque dona ferunt.

At the west end of the chapel is this inscription.

Anno Domini 1553. *sexto nonas Julias, Nos Hieronymus Dandinus Cæsenus titulis Mathæi S.R.E. Pbr. Cardinalis cognomento Imolensis Julii 3. Pont. Max. & sanctæ Apost. sedis ad gloriosiss. & invictiss. Principem Carolum Roman. Imp. semper Aug. universamque Germaniam Superiorem & Inferiorem, reliquasque illius ditiones Legatus à Latere. Piissis. votis desiderioque ipsius Caroli, & utriusque ejus sororis Helleonoræ Galliarum & Mariæ Hungariæ Reginarum, hoc sacellum, & summam in eo aram, Divo Philippo Apostolo, & Divo Joanni Baptistæ, consecravimus, ac omnibus Christi fidelibus, qui hodie eodemve per singulos annos die facellum hoc religionis adorationisque causâ adierent, Veniæ absolutionisque annos 7 in morem Ecclesiæ solitum condonavimus.*

One side of the court of the palace hath cloisters, and in the middle is a fountain.

The exchange or hall is a large and high roof'd place, where are many little shops. Before the entrance into the palace is a piazza environed with stone pillars, whereon are placed but five statues yet.

We endeavoured to see the galleries of pictures in the palace; but meeting with the marquis Carraceni (the king of Spain's governor of the Low-Countries) he commanded us away, and in French bid us go out.

We saw the stable, and therein six mules, and two English horses much valued. The manger is of free-stone. One of the grooms wip'd our shoes; which ceremony was requited with a piece of money. Here we took notice of a sheep brought either out of Armenia or Africa; it was of a good stature; the tail was as broad as the buttocks, and hung divided, the weight whereof was between 15 and 20 *lib.*

Over the stable is an armory, where we saw Charles V. his armour inlaid with gold, his baston, sword wherewith he used to knight men, coat of mail, gun with seven barrels in it, his shield which he used when he visited his mistress in the night; a spear came out of the side of it, besides that in the middle; if any thrust were made at the shield, the sword's point was catch'd in it and broken; his hunting sword with a point like a spear; another rich suit of armour of his, curiously carved into figures of horsemen, worth 100,000 florins; archduke Albert's rich armour, and his fighting armour, his spear, standard and sword; the sword Henry IV. of France sent him as a challenge to war, which was requited with a suit of armour which the archduke sent Henry IV.; the skin of the horse which brought the archduke out of the battle of Nieuport. This horse was then shot thro' the neck, and the mark may be still seen; a year after, on the same day the fight was, this horse died, and hath a Latin epitaph, which we observ'd to be as Golnitz hath transcrib'd it. The perspective the archduke us'd to view the enemy thro'; the armour, spear, and lance of Philip le Bon, two suits of armour of prince Ernest's, two of duke d'Alva's, and two suits of armour of prince Parma; one hath five shots in it; the armour of Leopold, prince cardinal, and Don John of Austria; the armour of one of the house of Lorrain shot thro' and kill'd; 36 suits of armour of several princes; the effigies of Isabella in armour on the horse she rode on when she entred her Brussels; her stirrup. The history of Pyrrhus is curiously carved with a diamond on a shield. A gun that will kill 600 foot distance, the length whereof is indifferent, which was presented by the king of Hungary to the prince cardinal; a spear-head with two little pistols; Indian armour made of whale-bone, and cover'd with fine work; Indian bow and arrows; the great Turk's quiver; a great sword sent from Nurenburgh, from whence, they say, is sent one every year to the magistrates of Brussels.

INEFFICIENT PIRATES

From

SIR WILLIAM MONSON'S

NAVAL TRACTS

Sir William Monson, to quote Churchill's preface, "was a gentleman well descended, but of small fortune, as he confesses, which made him take to the sea, where he served many years in several capacities, till merit raised him to the degree of an admiral, first under Queen Elizabeth, and then under King James and King Charles the first; for he lived till the civil wars, with an untainted reputation for conduct and bravery."

He was born in 1569, and went up to Balliol in 1581: he was a lieutenant in the fleet that defeated the Armada; Essex knighted him for his conduct in the expedition to Cadiz in 1596, and in 1604, having had several independent commands, he was made Admiral of the Narrow Seas. Among his duties was that of suppressing the pirates of Broad-Haven in Ireland, and it is from his remarks on piracy that this extract is taken.

His manuscript *Naval Tracts* were first published in Churchill; those of the tracts which deal with naval administration have been republished, a recent reprint being in volumes 22, 23, 43, 45 and 49 of the Navy Records Society, 1902-4.

I AM at last arrived in a safe and secure port, where I have leisure to recollect my self, and think of my errors past, in taking so great pains to so little purpose, as to write so many lines and leaves of the sea only, few gentlemen delighting in it, or making profession of it: but before I end, as in my former navigation I have spoke of the profit of fishing, I will set down the enemy to fishermen and fishing in this that followeth.

There is no action at sea, be it great or small, that brings not with it both charge and danger; nor no business so easy that can be done, without pains and difficulty: and this subject we are now upon, that is, fishing, the only thing that is required in it, is labour and pains; for danger is little to be regarded, considering it is not far from home we are to seek our profit, nor our harbours so few, but they may be entered for our safeties both day and night, by erecting lights.

But indeed the greatest danger that may be feared to our fishermen, is interruption of pirates, who are the very scum of a commonwealth and people to be abhorred by all honest and laborious men. It is usual, when these miscreants fail of relief of victuals, and are made desperate by want of it, to place all their hopes of food upon the poor painful fishermen, who, we may truly say, get their living with more hazard, with more pains, with more cold and watching, than any other trade or people whatsoever: their labour produces nothing that is ill, but the best help for man, which is food to live on.

Husbandmen and fishermen are the upholders of commonwealths; all other people live by their labours. They are stewards to provide sustenance to feed on; and yet comparing them together, there is great difference betwixt their lives and pains: the husbandman's work is without danger or hazard; and if he be wet, he has present help of fire to dry him; he is allowed a bed instead of the other's board to lie on; his diet is certain, and in a quiet manner, when the others are tost to and fro without a stedfast standing: if the one be cold, he may recover himself with exercise and work; if the other be cold, he is made colder, his labour being in the cold water; the one keeps his certain hours for sleep, the other has no certain time to rest, but must attend his danger, which he is never free from: every hour he must be ready to look out for his shoal of fish, and watch his opportunity of weather and tide to take them: the one has pleasure on holidays, and is free from labour; all days are alike to the other; and the Sunday can give no more content or comfort, than the rest of the week.

What heart can be so hardened, or pirate so pitiless, as to disturb those harmless and innocent creatures, that make pains their pleasure, and labour their countries plenty, procuring good for it by their own toils. And because such wickedness will never escape unpunished or unavenged, as these pirates commit upon such harmless people, I will a while digress from the subject I have in hand, and relate a strange and tragical accident that deservedly befel two pirates that were disturbers of the innocent fishing.

A STORY OF TWO PIRATES

After my return from Ireland, in 1614, where I had been imploy'd to suppress the arrogance and insolence of pirates, and where I punished the conniving that was betwixt those people and the inhabitants of that kingdom, I once again sent a bark for that coast, to be informed how things stood after

I left them, and whether the severe course I had taken against them, in doing justice by death upon one of them, wrought better effect than before.

The first harbour my bark arrived in, she met a pirate named Tucker, a seaman bred from his youth, and continual practice made him excellent in his art and profession: he was very glad upon this occasion of meeting my bark to insinuate into my man's acquaintance, thinking thereby it would be a means for him to bewail himself to me, and to obtain the thing next to life he desired which was his pardon, though he departed with the best part of his spoils, which were things of good value.

His persuasion prevailed so far with my servant, that though his directions were to view the northern parts of Ireland, where I had lately been, and there to inquire after the behaviour of pirates, and the entertainment the country gave them; yet, as I have said, by the importunity of Tucker, my man was diverted from his imployment, and persuaded to return with his letter of submission to me, on whom he wholly cast himself to dispose of, with promise there to stay a certain time to expect my answer; and to sweeten me the more, he presented me with a token worth accepting, but that I was always cautious in such cases how to connive with pirates, as in my letter I expressed. I mistrusted, before he could receive my answer, the winds then hanging contrary, he would depart from Ireland; whereupon I directed divers letters to one effect, and sent them by several ships, if they should chance to meet Tucker upon their way in their voyages. But as I have shewed the last refuge pirates have for victuals, is to feed upon the fishermen; and Tucker finding that Ireland could not supply him, by the strict course I had formerly taken, was forced to go to the northward, to seek succour of the poor fishermen, a contrary course to the ships that carry'd my letters: and coming the north Farro, there he met with another pirate of the same sort, but far less honest, as it proved. These two concerted together, as thieves use to do in mischief.

The islands of Farro are dangerous, by reason of the great tides and their setting; and it happened that Tucker's ship was wrecked upon one of them, in company of his companion, the other pirate; who seeking it, did not degenerate from his kind, for all spoils were alike to him, friend or foe; instead of help in that case of distress, play'd the part of a hawk over his prey, and had no more pity of him than of a Spaniard, who were most obnoxious to pirates in those days.

To be short, this pirate, who falsly called himself Monnocho, suddenly possessed himself of Tucker's ship, himself, his wealth and company; and used them with that rigorous cruelty, as though his action had been lawful, and allowed by authority to punish delinquents and offenders, and rather out of fear than pity, he shewed mercy to their lives; and mistrusting if he should detain them in his own ship, they might make a party and faction; for the conditions of such people, is never to be constant, or honest, no longer than their devilish humours hold; therefore to avoid any such tumult, Monnocho seized upon an English fisherman, amongst many others he had taken, and put Tucker and his company into her, to seek a new fortune; which you must think was like to thrive, if you consider their course of life. And here they parted company like two wolves that should separate themselves to seek their prey, they care not where, nor of whom, purposing never to see one another, unless the gallows gave them a meeting. Monnocho was a fellow of as base a condition as his present profession made him, being not long before a surgeon's mate, in a pinnace serving under me. And now hovering about those islands, it was his hap to meet a ship of the king of Denmark's, to whom the islands belong: this ship, after a little encounter, apprehended him, and knew well what to do with him, so just that nation is to the detestable course of sea-rovers.

Here Monnocho found worse usage than he gave Tucker; for the time was not long before his ship made a return into Denmark, and in as short a while after he tasted deserved death upon the gallows; where he hung a spectacle for all men to behold.

Now Monnocho is brought to the destiny by right due to him; I will go scour the seas, and look if I can spy Tucker, being out of hope to find his ship put to that use for which she was first designed; I mean fishing.

After Tucker had spent some time at sea, domineering over the poor fishermen; they now tired with the usurping tyranny of the pirates, and being desirous to live by honest labour, rather than by evil pains, privately practised, and watching their opportunity, effected that they had determined to put in execution; which was, suddenly to surprize and seize upon the pirates persons, when they should least suspect it.

The attempt proved fortunate; for some they slew, and others they hurt; and Tucker they took prisoner, and insulted over him, as he had done before over them.

This lucky accident made the fishermen repair to shore, to supply their wants, their provisions being consumed by the pirates; as also to deliver the men, as delinquents, into the hands of justice, who were after conveyed to the Marshalsea in Southwark, where they daily expected the doom of death.

The poor man, captain Tucker, being hopeless and friendless, sent me word of his misfortunes after his departure from Ireland, bewailing his hard hap and heavy chance, not to meet with any of my letters, written to him as aforesaid; He shewed the comfort of life was taken from him, and confessed his offences were above satisfaction; and that I was the only sheet-anchor he was to rely on; otherwise he was to perish.

I confess I was much moved and grieved with his calamity, when I remember'd how his penitency appeared in his former letter to me, repenting his misdoings, and detesting his kind of life, with a desire of pardon and forgiveness of his offences past.

This complaint came at an unlucky hour, both for him and me, it being in the midst of the time that malice set herself against me; for in a few days after I was unjustly committed to the Tower; and yet I thank God by his providence, not an hour before I was imprisoned, I had finished and ended his pardon, that I might say the ending of his trouble was the beginning of my own; but not through his cause or occasion.

Tucker being set at liberty, was to dispose of himself as he should be guided by grace. And to give some sign of his thankfulness for the favour I did him, he resolved not to depart London, what shift soever he made to live, till he had acknowledged his life from me; and though at that time there was a general restraint of all people's resorting to me in the Tower, yet that prohibition was no sooner taken off, but Tucker was one of the first that repaired to visit me, with that protestation of thankfulness, and vows of amendment of his life, that he gave me satisfaction it proceeded from a penitent heart. It joy'd me much to see his reformation, and I held myself happy for the deed I had done in regaining a lost sheep that had stray'd out of the flock.

His credit being lost, which made him unfit for employment, moved pity in me what course to put him into; for no beginner can set up a trade without a stock to enable him: and to requite his remembrance of me, by the token he sent me from Ireland, I returned him the better part of that gift, wishing that good fortune would attend his happy beginning.

He was not long determining with himself, but immediately took a voyage to Denmark, whither he had often before traded. Arriving there, and having occasion to go about his affairs, it happened, that passing a river, the ferryman of the boat knew him by an infallible token; for not long before the man was taken by Tucker at sea. The fellow had no sooner landed him and his fare, but speedily he hastened to the magistrate, requiring a warrant for his apprehension, alledging the cause; which was no sooner demanded than granted, all people of that country being naturally bent to revenge themselves upon offenders in that kind.

Being thus arrested, he was carried to prison, where he received the rigour of justice; and upon trial, by the witness of the ferryman was sentenced to die. The gibbet was erected near joining to that where Monnocho, his former companion, was still hanging for him to behold, which was very odd; for it is not the greatness of the person, nor of the accident, makes a wonder the greater; for all things, be they great or little, are at the disposal of God alone, who many times advances the mean, and casts down the mighty. And it is worthy of observation, how in many cases he gives light to men, to discern his just punishment to some, for example of amendment of life to others.

And amongst the rest, this accident of these mean and ungodly pirates is no less strange, if we call to mind God's justice towards them, if you will consider the first progress of their beginning, till death cut them off, as it does all people that commit unnatural crimes; for such men never escape without cruel revenge; for a father of the church saith, *He ceases to be a man, and becomes a brute beast, that leaves the rules of reason and honesty, and gives his mind to mischief and sensuality.*

These two mens cursed courses are not unlike a novel; first in their unexpected meeting in remote islands, where they were both strangers; secondly, that upon their meeting they protested and vowed friendship, though I must say, that the agreement of ill men in mischief cannot be called friendship: but call it what you will, it did not long continue; for there was a bone cast betwixt them, as it were, betwixt two ravenous mastiffs, to strive for, and the stronger to carry it away.

After these two pirates had parted company, the one stood to the northward, the other to the southward, a quite opposite course to one another, and where there was never likelihood of meeting more; but rather to avoid and eschew each other, their quarrel was so mortal: and yet both of them tasted one fortune alike; first in their apprehension, and after in their manner of execution; but above all, the place never doubted or feared by them; and where perhaps, in many ages the like will not happen again, it being out of the road-way for such people to resort to.

This shall suffice for God's justice by example of these two miscreant pirates, and his detestation to their wicked courses against the silly and innocent fishermen, who, we may truly affirm and say, of all other people, get their living with the painful sweat of their brows.

From

ROBERT EVERARD'S

RELATION OF THREE YEARS SUFFERINGS UPON THE ISLAND OF ASSADA NEAR MADAGASCAR IN A VOYAGE TO INDIA IN THE YEAR 1686

MY FATHER, Mr. William Everard, put me an apprentice to Capt. John Crib, by my consent, in the ship *Bauden*, bound for Bombay in India, and from thence to Madagascar for blacks to Achin, back to India.

I departed from London August the 5th, 1686, and we sail'd out of the Downs the same month for the Madeira. In the channel we met with a small pink, from which we receiv'd aboard M. Salway a merchant, and then we proceeded on our voyage, till we arrived and anchor'd in Madeira road; and from thence sail'd for the isle of May, where we took in salt, and bought five or six beasts. The blacks told us there had been there a pirate, who had taken away some of their cattle.

Sailing from the isle of May to St. Jago, just as we got into port, the pirate follow'd us. But it happened at the same time, that the wind blew right off shore, so that he could not get in; so he was forc'd to bear away, and came to an anchor on the other side of the isle.

Two or three days after, he came out again, trying to get in, our fore-mast being unrigg'd at the same time: and had he got in (as pleased God he could not) he had certainly taken us; but was forc'd to bear away again for the town.

On the Lord's day following, there came aboard two men in habit like padres, and the capt. made them very welcome.

They desir'd of him to shew them the ship, which he order'd the gunner to do. By some of their questions and behaviour we suppos'd them to be the pirate's men; but our capt. order'd the boat to be mann'd to put them on shore.

The next morning the ship came about, and strove to get to us, but could not: yet they haled us, but we could not tell what he said; so he fell to leeward again.

Four or five days after, we sail'd out of St. Jago; and the next day we espy'd a ship to windward early in the morning, about two or three leagues distant, and a small breeze of wind, but it presently prov'd quite calm; and we saw him row with about twelve oars on a side toward us. Our capt. presently order'd the boatswain to call up all hands to be ready for him. His boat made toward us, and hal'd us, and asked, Where we were bound? Our capt. answer'd, To Whitehall. We also hal'd him, and asked him, Where he was bound? He answered, To Brasil. Then bid us hoist out our boat; but our capt. told him, If he had any business, his boat being out, might as well come on board us. But it returned, and went on board his own ship, which rowed up with us; and about eight or nine in the morning she came under our stern, ranging up our starboard quarter. Then our capt. ask'd, Where he was bound? He answer'd, Aboard us, the drummer beating a point of war. The captain told him, Win her, and have her. He thereupon boarded us for four or five hours, cutting our poop and ensign-staff; and his shot cut many of our shrouds. Our ship being very much pester'd, we play'd but three or four of our guns; yet we beat his gunnel in, and made him put off, and lie upon the careen.

As soon as she was gone we came out of our close quarters, and found one of his men almost dead upon our poop, with a fuzee, an axe, a cartouch-box, a stink-pot, a pistol, and a cutlass. In the fight, our captain chief mate, and four men more were kill'd, and sixteen wounded, whereof one was myself. So by the brave courage of our captain and men the pirate was forc'd to leave us.

COLONEL NORWOOD'S

VOYAGE TO VIRGINIA

When first I read Colonel Norwood's voyage I found it difficult to believe that it was not exceedingly good fiction. It was in a curious little volume called *An Entertaining Account of all the Countries of the Known World . . . adorn'd, occasionally, with Cuts . . . .* printed in 1752 by one R. Goadby, at Sherborne. This book (the Sherborne edition appears to be unrecorded, by the way) is little more than an unlicenced rehash of some of Churchill's better voyages, shortened and sometimes unwarrantably altered, together with an abbreviation of Anson's circum-navigation and one or two other travels. The "occasional cuts" have nothing whatsoever to do with the text, but they are very entertaining.

I tried to trace the Colonel's narrative back to the original, but I could get no further than Churchill, who gives no account of the man or the manuscript. However, it is probable that Churchill had the manuscript and transcribed it faithfully; it can be shown that he did on other occasions, and there is no reason to doubt him this time.

The only comparatively recent reprinting of the voyage was in Force's Tracts, published between 1836 and 1846 in America.

THE month of August, Anno 1649, being the time I engag'd to meet my two comrades, Major Francis Morrison, and Major Richard Fox, at London, in order to a full accomplishment of our purpose to seek our fortunes in Virginia, (pursuant to our agreement the year before in Holland) all parties very punctually appear'd at the time and place assign'd, and were all still in the same mind, fully bent to put in practice what we had so solemnly agreed upon, our inclinations that way being nothing abated, but were rather quicken'd, by the new changes that we saw in the state of things, and that very much for the worse: For if our spirits were somewhat depress'd in contemplation of a barbarous restraint upon the person of our king in the Isle of Wight; to what horrors and despairs must our minds be reduc'd at the bloody and bitter stroke of his assassination, at his palace of Whitehall?

This unparallel'd butchery made the rebels caste away the scabbards of their swords with both their hands, in full resolution never to let them meet again, either by submission or capitulation; so that the sad prospect of affairs in this juncture, gave such a damp to all the royal party who had resolved to persevere in the principle which engaged them in the war, that a very considerable number of nobility, clergy, and gentry, so circumstanc'd, did fly from their native country, as from a place infected with the plague, and did betake themselves to travel any where to shun so hot a contagion, there being no point on the compass that would not suit with some of our tempers and circumstances, for transportation into foreign lands.

Of the number who chose to steer their course for America, such of them as inclin'd to try their fortunes at Surinam, Barbados, Antigua, and the Leeward Islands, were to be men of the first rate, who wanted not money or credit to balance the expence necessary to the carrying on the sugar works: And this consideration alone was enough to determine our choice for Virginia, had we wanted other arguments to engage us in the voyage. The honour I had of being nearly related to Sir William Barkeley the governor, was no small incitation to encourage me with a little stock to this adventure: Major Morrison had the king's commission to be captain of the fort; and Mr. Fox was to share in our good or bad success: But my best cargaroon was his majesty's gracious letter in my favour, which took effect beyond my expectation, because it recommended me (above whatever I had or could deserve) to the governor's particular care.

To proceed then, without any further exordium, to the subject of this narrative: It fell out to be about the first day of September, Anno 1649, that we grew acquainted on the Royal-Exchange with Capt. John Locker, whose bills upon the posts made us know he was master of a good ship, (untruly so call'd) *The Virginia Merchant*, burden three hundred tons, of force thirty guns, or more: We were not long in treaty with the captain, but agreed with him for ourselves and servants at six pounds a head, to be transported into James River; our goods to be paid for at the current price.

About the fifteenth day, we were ordered to meet the ship at Gravesend, where the captain was to clear with his merchants, and we to make our several payments; which when we had performed, we staid not for the ship, but took post for the Downs, where, with some impatience, we expected her coming there. About the sixteenth ditto, we could see the whole fleet under sail, with a south-west wind; which having brought them to that road, kept them there at anchor, until our money was almost spent at Deal.

September 23. the wind veered to the east, and we were summoned by signs and guns to repair on board. We had a fresh large gale three days, which cleared us of the channel, and put us out of soundings. With this propitious beginning we pursued our course for about twenty days, desiring to make the western islands; at which time the cooper began to complain, that our water-cask was almost empty, alledging, that there was not enough in hold, for our great family (about three hundred and thirty souls) to serve a month.

Our early want of water gave the master an alarm, and an occasion to consult with his officers for a remedy to so important an evil as that might be, if not timely helped. We were now, by all accounts, very near the western islands: Fyall was that we were likely first to see, and our captain resolved to touch there to supply this defect, as the most commodious port for our purpose; and this was good news to the passengers, who are always glad at sight of land.

The day-break of October 14th, shewed us the peek of that island, the highest and most conspicuous land of any I have heard the seamen mention for land-marks, except that of Teneriff. We stood directly for the harbour, which is also a good road, land-lock'd by the peek, which stands easterly about a mile distant from the town.

Assoon as we had saluted the castle, and returned thanks for being civilly answered, captain John Tatam, our countryman, did the same from aboard his goodly ship the *John*. He was newly returned from Brasil, in the kingdom of Portugal's service, and now bound for Lisbon, with a rich freight, and some lady of great note, who with her family took passage with him.

The English merchants from the town came soon on board our ship, and gave us a very civil welcome. Of them, one Mr. Andrews invited me, with my two comrades, to refresh our selves with fruit and meat such as the island produced. Our captain dined with us at his house, and so did captain Tatam, who in like courteous manner engaged us all to dine on board his ship the next day. We visited the peach-trees for our desert, of which I took at least a double share, and did not fail to visit and revisit them in the dead of night, to satisfy a ravenous appetite nature has too prodigally given me for that species.

The next morning we surveyed the island, and thought the castle well fortified, especially on the sea-barr'd parts. The governor very civilly declared, he had lately received command from his majesty the king of Portugal, to treat all ships that belonged and were faithful to the king of Great Britain, with more than common courtesy, as he, for his part, did in all we could desire.

A little before the time of dinner captain Tatam had sent his boats to bring us on board his ship; and it was well for us he did so, our ship's long-boat having been staved in pieces the night before, by the seamen's neglect, who had all tasted so liberally of new wine, by the commodiousness of the vintage, that they lay up and down dead drunk in all quarters, in a sad pickle.

The loss of our long-boat, as it was likely to make our watering tedious, and chargeable to the owners, so did it expose us to the hazard of many inconveniencies and perils in the whole course of our voyage, wherein frequent occasions occur that render that boat necessary to preserve the whole fabrick and lives of the ship and company; but to this breach no other reparation was applicable, but by recourse to that great stock of patience we were to be furnished withal for our support in the mighty straights we must encounter before we come to safe port.

Our captain disabled hereby to take the best course for our dispatch, made choice of the next best way to effect it, by the island boats; and having ordered his officers to use all diligence, and greater care than before, he led the van into Tatam's boat which brought us safe on board the *John*.

At our arrival we were welcomed with a whole tyre of guns, and with a very kind aspect in the captain. He gave us excellent wines to drink before dinner, and at our meat as good of other sorts for concoction. There was a handsome plenty of fish and fowl, several ways cooked, to relish the Portuguese's and the English palates; and, which made our entertainment more complete, he had prevailed with that great lady, with her pretty son of about twelve years old (tho' contrary to the custom even of the meaner sort at land) to sit at the table with us. She was taller than the ordinary stature of that nation, finely shap'd, had a very clear skin; her eyes and hair vying for the blackness and beauty of the jet; her modesty served, without any other art, to put a tincture of red upon her face; for when she saw herself environed with a company of strange faces, that had or might have had beards upon them, her blushes raised in her face a delicate complexion of red and white.

The captain was our interpreter to tell her how much we esteemed our selves honoured with her presence, which (for her better justification) she was in a manner forced to grant us, the ship affording her no other place fit for her retreat whilst we were there. Her young son sat by her, on whom all our eyes were fix'd; and our minds united with one opinion, that the air and lineaments of his face, full of sweetness, made him so like our king when he was of that age, that, every one whispering his thoughts to his neighbour, we all broke out at length in an open admiration of so great resemblance.

The healths of the two kings were passing about with thundering peals of cannon; the youth was permitted by his mother to kiss the cup, and drink a small portion to that of our king; and she was in so pleasant an humour at this honour done to her son, that, to close our feast, she ordered the table to be covered anew, and a handsome banquet placed upon it, which we must partake of before we parted. To conclude this rare treat, she repeated the health of our king in a sort of choice rich wine that they make in Brasil, and drank the proportion she would take, without the allay of water, which till then she drank with little or no wine.

The approaching night made us take leave sooner than our inclinations would have led us ashore, the merchants having told us, there was no safe walking the streets in the night, for fear the Pycaroes (a sort of land-pyrates) should snatch away our hats and looser garments, as they use to treat strangers.

When we had paid our thanks to the captain, we desired his best language to make our compliments to the lady and her son, which she returned with her wishes for our happy voyage.

Whilst we were caress'd in this manner on shipboard, the seamen on shore continued in their debauchery, with very little advance of our dispatch; the getting water was so tedious in itself for lack of our boat, and so full of delays by drunken contests of ours with the islanders, and with themselves, that, after some days stay upon the island, when our captain resolved to sail away, he found the ship in worse condition for liquors, than when we came on shore; for if we got a new supply of water, the proportion was hardly enough to balance the expence of beer that was spent in the time we got it.

Some days before we parted, we saw the *John* under sail, bound for Lisbon; where the captain no sooner arrived and discharged his ship, but he listed himself as a man of war in a squadron of ships then there, under command of the prince Rupert: which I mention for his honour, because I have heard the prince acknowledge in his favour, that he did his duty very well when there was like to be an occasion of trying his valour.

It was about the 22nd of October that we took leave of our landlord and Fyal. We had store of black pigs for fresh meat, and I carry'd peaches without number. We parted with an easterly wind a topsail gate, which soon brought us at fifty or sixty leagues in twenty-four hours, till we came to the height of Bermudas. In that latitude it is the general observation of seamen, that the seas are rough, and the weather stormy. It was my fortune to have a curiosity to look out, when the officer on the watch shewed me a more than ordinary agitation of the sea in one particular place above the rest; which was the effect of what they call a spout, a raging in the bowels of the sea (like a violent birth) striving to break out, and at last springs up like a mine at land, with weight and force enough to have hoised our ship out of her proper element, into the air (had the helm been for it) and to have made her do the supersalt; but God's providence secured us from that danger.

The sight of the island was welcome to all: the mariners learned thereby our true distance from cape Hatteras; and the passengers were relieved with hopes to be soon at shore from a hungry pester'd ship and company.

The gale continued fair till November 8: then we observed the water changed; and heaving the lead, we had thirty-five fathom of water, which was joyful news; our want of all things necessary for human life, made it so.

Towards break of day, weary of my lodging, I visited mate Putts on the watch, and would have treated him with brandy, but he refused that offer, unless I could also give him tobacco, which I had not. He said, it was near break of day, and he would look out to see what change there was in the water. No sooner were his feet upon the deck, but with stamps and noise he calls up the seamen, crying out, *All hands aloft! Breaches, breaches on both sides! All hands aloft!*

The seamen were soon on deck with this dismal alarm, and saw the cause thereof; but instead of applying their hands for their preservation (through a general despondency) they fell on their knees, commending their souls as at the last gasp. The captain came out at the noise to rectify what was amiss; but seeing how the case stood, his courage failed. Mate Putts (a stout seaman) took heart again, and cryed out, Is there no good fellow that will stand to the helm, and loose a sail? But of all the ship's crew there were but two foremast men that would be perswaded to obey commands, namely, Thomas Reasin and John Smith, men of innate courage, who, for their good resolution on that and divers other occasions in the various traverses of this voyage, deserve to have their names kept in lasting remembrance.

One of them got up and loosed the fore top-sail, to put the ship (if possible) in steerage way, and under command; the other stood to the helm, and he shifted it in a nick of time; for the ship was at the point of dashing on the starboard breach: and altho', in the rest of the voyage, she was wont to be blamed for the ill quality of not feeling the helm, she did, in this important instance, redeem her credit, and fell round off for our rescue from that danger. But the sense of this escape lasted but a moment; for no sooner was she fallen from that breach, but another on the larboard-bow was ready to receive her. The ship's crew, by this time (reproached by the courage of Reasin and Smith) were all at work; and the helm shifting opportunely, she fell off again as before. The light of the day (which now broke forth) did discover our condition to be altogether as perillous as possible; for we now saw our selves surrounded with breaches; scarce any water like a channel appeared for a way to shun them. In this sad condition the ship struck ground, and raised such a war of water and sand together, which fell on the main-chains, that now all hopes of safety were laid aside; but the ship being still afloat, and the seamen all of them now under command, nothing was omitted for our preservation that was in their power.

Tom Reasin, seeing the ship go a-head in the likeliest water for a channel, and ordering the helm accordingly, heaved the lead; and after a little further advance into that new channel, wholly against his hopes, he had a good deal of water more than the ship drew, which soon mended upon us, the next cast of the lead affording eighteen or twenty foot. We stood to this channel, and the light of the morning enabling the quarter-masters to con the ship, we were by this miraculous mercy of God, soon clear of the breaches at cape Hatteras, and got out to sea.

No sooner was the ship freed of this danger, and gotten a little into the offing, but the seamen (like so many spirits) surveyed each other, as if they doubted the reality of the thing, and shook hands like strangers, or men risen from the other world, and did scarce believe they were, what they seemed to be, men of flesh and blood. As they recovered force, they made what sail they could to stand to sea-ward.

The gale came fresh at north-west, and this fresh gale did soon grow up to a violent storm, which increased to so great a rigour, separating us from the land at the rate of eight leagues a watch, merely with our fore-courses, insomuch that the master thought it necessary to stop that career; and, in order thereunto, he did advise with his officers to bring the ship about, to furl all sails, and to try with the mizzen.

The mountainous towring north-west seas that this storm made, were so unruly, that the seamen knew not how to work the ship about. We were already at a great distance from land, and something must be done to hinder our running off at that excessive rate. The first thing they did, was to lower the main-yard, to give some ease to that mast, by laying it on the ship's waste. Our great difficulty was, how to deal so with the fore-sails, that the ship might work about with as little hazard as possible. All hands were too little to hale the sheet close, in order to bring the ship about. Many great seas were shipp'd as she came to work thro' the trough of the sea: amongst the rest one chanc'd to break upon the poop (where we were quartered) and that with so sad a weight, that we guess'd a tun of water (at the least) did enter the tarpaulin, and set us all on float who were in the round-house. The noise it made by discharging itself in that manner, was like the report of a great gun, and did put us all into a horrible fright, which we could not soon shake off. This shock being past, the ship about, and our fore-sail handled, we now lay trying with our mizzen.

I cannot forget the prodigious number of porpoises that did that evening appear about the ship, to the astonishment of the oldest seamen in her. They seemed to cover the surface of the

sea as far as our eyes could discern; insomuch that a musket
bullet, shot at random, could hardly fail to do execution on
some of them. This the seamen would look upon as of bad
portent, predicting ill weather; but in our case, who were in
present possession of a storm, they appeared too late to gain the
credit of foretelling what should come upon us in that kind.

The seas enraged, and all in foam, the gale still increasing
upon us, the officers on the watch made frequent visits to the
round-house, to prepare the captain for some evil encounter
which this mighty tempest must bring forth: and their fears
proved reasonable; for, about the hours of ten or eleven, our
new disasters did begin with a crash from aloft. All hands were
summon'd up with loud cries, that the fore-topmast was come
by the board, not alone, but in conjunction with the fore-mast
head broken short off, just under the cap.

This was a sore business, and put all to their wits end to
recover to any competent condition; what could be done was
done to prevent further mischiefs; but the whole trim and
rigging of a ship depending much upon stays and tackle fixed
to that mast, we had reason to expect greater ruins to follow,
than what had already befallen us. Mate Putts was then on the
watch, and did not want his apprehension of what did soon
ensue, which in all likelihood was to end in our utter perdition;
for about the hours of twelve or one at night, we heard and felt a
mighty sea break on our fore-ship, which made such an inunda-
tion on the deck where the mate was walking, that he retired
back with all diligence up to his knees in water, with short
ejaculations of prayers in his mouth, supposing the ship was
foundering, and at the last gasp. This looked like a stroke of
death in every seaman's opinion: the ship stood stock still, with
her head under water, seeming to bore her way into the sea.
My two comrades and myself lay on our platform, sharing
liberally in the general consternation. We took a short leave of
each other, men, women, and children. All assaulted with the
fresh terror of death, made a most dolorous outcry throughout
the ship, whilst mate Putts perceiving the deck almost freed of
water, called out aloud for hands to pump. This we thought a
lightning before death, but gave me occasion (as having the best
sea legs) to look out and learn the subject of this astonishing
alarm, which proved to arise from no less cause than the loss
of our forecastle, with six guns, and our anchors (all but one

that was fastened to a cable) together with our two cooks, whereof one was recovered by a strange providence.

This great gap, made by want of our forecastle, did open a passage into the hold for other seas that should break there before a remedy was found out to carry them off, and this made our danger almost insuperable; but it fell out propitiously, that there were divers land-carpenter passengers, who were very helpful in this distress; and, in a little time, a slight platform of deal was tack'd to the timbers, to carry off any ordinary sea in the present straight we were in; every moment of this growing tempest cutting out new work to employ all hands to labour.

The bowsprit, too top-heavy in itself, having lost all stays and rigging that should keep it steady, sway'd to and fro with such bangs on the bows, that at no less rate than the cutting it close off, could the ship subsist.

All things were in miserable disorder, and it was evident our danger increas'd upon us: the stays of all the masts were gone, the shrouds that remained were loose and useless, and it was easy to foretel, our main-topmast would soon come by the board. Tom Reasin (who was always ready to expose himself) with an ax in his hand, ran up with speed to prevent that evil, hoping thereby to ease the main-mast, and preserve it; but the danger of his person in the enterprize, was so manifest, that he was called down amain; and no sooner was his foot upon the deck, but what was feared came to pass with a witness, both main and topmast all came down together, and, in one shock, fell all to the windward clear into the sea, without hurt to any man's person.

Our main-mast thus fallen to the broadside, was like to incommode us more in the sea, than in her proper station; for the shrouds and rigging not losing the hold they had of the ship, every surge did so check the mast (whose but-end lay charg'd to fall perpendicular on the ship's side) that it became a ram to batter and force the plank, and was doing the last execution upon us, if not prevented in time by edge-tools, which freed the ship from that unexpected assault and battery.

Abandon'd in this manner to the fury of the raging sea, tossed up and down without any rigging to keep the ship steady, our seamen frequently fell overboard, without any one regarding the loss of another, every man expecting the same fate, tho' in a different manner. The ceilings of this hulk (for so it was no better) were for the same cause so uneasy, that, in many tumbles, the deck would touch the sea, and there stand still as if she would never make another. Our mizzen mast only remained, by which we hoped to bring the ship about in proper season, which now lay stemming to the east.

In this posture did we pass the tenth and eleventh days of November; the twelfth in the morning we saw an English merchant, who shewed his ensign, but would not speak with us, tho' the storm was abated, and the season more fit for communication. We imagined the reason was, because he would not be compelled to be civil to us: he thought our condition desperate, and we had more guns than he could resist, which might enable us to take what he would not sell or give. He shot a gun to leeward, stood his course, and turn'd his poop upon us.

Before we attempted to bring the ship about, it was necessary to refresh the seamen, who were almost worn out with toil and want of rest, having had no leisure of eating set meals for many days. The passengers, overcharged with excessive fears, had no appetite to eat; and (which was worst of all) both seamen and passengers were in a deplorable state as to the remaining victuals, all like to fall under extreme want; for the storm, by taking away the forecastle, having thrown much water into the hold, our stock of bread (the staff of life) was greatly damnified; and there remained no way to dress our meat, now that the cook-room was gone: the incessant tumbling of the ship (as has been observ'd) made all such cookery wholly impracticable. The only expedient to make fire betwixt decks, was, by sawing a cask in the middle, and filling it with ballast, which made a hearth to parch pease, and broil salt beef; nor could this be done but with great attendance, which was many times frustrated by being thrown topsy-turvy in spite of all circumspection, to the great defeat of empty stomachs.

The seas were much appeas'd the seventeenth day, and divers English ships saw, and were seen by us, but would not speak with us; only one, who kept the pump always going, for having tasted too liberally of the storm, he was so kind as to accost us. He lay by till our wherry (the only surviving boat that was left us) made him a visit. The master shewed our men his leaks, and proposed, that ours would spare him hands to pump in lieu of any thing he could spare for our relief. He promised however to keep us company, and give us a tow to help to weather the cape, if occasion offered; but that was only a copy of his countenance; for in the night we lost each other, and we never heard more of him, tho' he was bound to our port.

The weather now invited us to get the ship about with our mizzen; and having done so, the next consideration was, how to make sail. The fore mast, all this while (as much as was of it) stood its ground: and as it was without dispute, that a yard must in the first place be fixed to it, so was it a matter of no small difficulty how to advance to the top of that greasy slippery stump, since he that would attempt it, could take no hold himself, nor receive any help for his rise, by other hands. This was a case that put all the ship's crew to a nonplus; but Tom Reasin (a constant friend at need, that would not be baffled by any difficulty) shewed by his countenance, he had a mind to try his skill to bring us out of this unhappy crisis. To encourage him the more, all passengers did promise and subscribe to reward his service, in Virginia, by tobacco, when God should enable us so to do. The proportions being set down, many were the more generous, because they never thought to see the place of payment, but expected to anticipate that by the payment of a greater debt to nature, which was like to be exacted every hour by an arrest of the merciless sea, which made small shew of taking bail for our appearance in Virginia.

The manner of Tom Reasin's ascent to this important work, was thus. Among the scatter'd parcels of the ship's stores he had the luck to find about half a dozen iron spikes fit for his purpose. His first onset was to drive one of them into the mast, almost to the head, as high as he could reach; which being done, he took a rope of about ten foot long, and having threaded the same in a block or pulley, so as to divide it in the middle, he made both ends meet in a knot upon the spike, on both sides of the mast; so that the block falling on the contrary side, became a stirrup to mount for driving another spike in the same manner: and thus from step to step, observing the best advantage of striking with his hammer in the smoothest sea, he got aloft, drove cleats for shrouds, to rest upon, and was soon in a posture of receiving help from his comrades, who got a yard and sails (with other accommodation) such as could be had, and thus we were enabled, in few hours time, to make some sail for our port.

The main-yard, that in the storm had been lowered to the waste to lie out of harm's way, was now preferred to the place of a main mast, and was accordingly fitted and accoutred, and grafted into the stump of what was left in the storm, some eight or ten foot from the deck. It was a hard matter to find out rigging answerable to that new-fashioned mast and yard; top-gallant sails and yards were most agreeable to this equipage, and was the best part of our remaining stores. The seas grew every moment smoother; so that for a while we began to shake off the visage of utter despair, as hoping ere long to see our selves in some capacity to fetch the cape. We discovered another ship bound to Virginia, who as frankly promised to stand by us, the wind at N. N. W. We did what could be done by a ship so mangled, to get the weather-gage of the cape Henry, conceiving our selves to the southward of cape Hatteras: but by taking an observation on a sun-shine day, we found our selves carryed by a current we knew not of, to the windward, much beyond all our dead reckonings and allowances for sailing, insomuch that when we thought we had been to the southward of the cape, we found our selves considerably shot to the north of Achomat, and that in the opinion of mate Putts, who was as our north star.

We passed this night with greater alacrity than we had done any since we had left Fyall; for mate Putts, our trusty pilot, did confidently affirm, that, if the gale stood, there would be no question of our dining the next day within the capes. This was seasonable news, our water being long since spent, our meat spoiled (or useless) no kind of victuals remaining to sustain life, but a bisket cake a day for a man; at which allowance there was not a quantity to hold out many days. In the dark time of the night, in tacking about, we lost our new comrade, and with much impatience we expected the approaching day; the wind N. W.

The morning appeared foggy, as the wind veered to the east, and that did cover and conceal the land from our clearer sight; howbeit we concluded by mate Putts's computation, we were well to the northward of the capes. Many times he would mount the mizzen top for discovery, as the weather seemed to clear up, and would espy and point at certain hum-works of trees that used to be his several land-marks in most of the twenty-two voyages he had made to that plantation. Under this confidence he made more sail, the day-light confirming him in what he thought was right.

All the forenoon we lost the sight of land and marks by trees, by reason of the dark fogs and mists that were not yet dispelled; but as soon as the sun, with a north-west gale, had cleared all the coast (which was about the hours of two or three o'clock) mate Putts perceived his error from the deck, and was convinced, that the hum-works of trees he had seen and relied on for sure land-marks, had counter points to the south cape, which had misguided him; and that it was the opening of the bay which made the land at distance out of sight.

This fatal disappointment (which was now past human help) might have met an easy remedy, had our sails and rigging been in any tolerable condition to keep the windward gage (for we had both the capes in our sight) but under our circumstances it was vain to endeavour such a thing; all our equipage, from stem to stern, being no better than that of a western barge, and we could not lie within eleven or twelve points of the wind.

Defeated thus of lively hopes we had the night before entertain'd to sleep in warm beds with our friends in Virginia, it was a heavy spectacle to see our selves running at a round rate from it, notwithstanding all that could be done to the contrary. Nothing was now to be heard but sighs and groans thro' all that wretched family, which must be soon reduced to so short allowance, as would just keep life and soul together. Half a bisket cake a day to each (of which five whole ones made a pound) was all we had to trust to. Of liquors there remained none to quench thirst: Malaga sack was given plentifully to every one, which served rather to inflame and increase thirst, than to extinguish it.

The gale blew fresh (as it uses to do) towards night, and made a western sea that carry'd us off at a great rate. Mate Putts, extremely abash'd to see his confidence so miserably deluded, grew sad and contemplative, even to the moving compassion in those whom his unhappy mistake had reduc'd to this misery. We cherish'd him the best we could, and would not have him so profoundly sad, for what was rather his misfortune than his fault.

The wind continued many days and nights to send us out into the ocean, insomuch that until we thought our selves at least an hundred leagues from the capes, the north-west gale gave us no truce to consider what was best to do. All little helps were used by top-gallant sails, and masts placed where they could be fixed, to keep the windward gage; but, for lack of borolins and other tackle to keep them stiff to draw, every great head-sea would check them in the wind, and rend and tear them in pieces; so that it was an ordinary exercise with us to lie tumbling in the sea a watch or two together, driving to leeward, whilst the broken sails were in hand to be repaired.

It would be too great a trial of the reader's patience to be entertain'd with every circumstance of our sufferings in the remaining part of this voyage, which continued in great extremity for at least forty days from the time we left the land, our miseries increasing every hour: I shall therefore omit the greatest number of our ill encounters, which were frequently repeated on us, and remember only what has in my thoughts been most remarkable, and have made the deepest impression in my memory.

To give us a little breathing, about the nineteenth day the wind shifted to the east, but so little to our avail (the gale so gentle, and the seas made against us like a strong current) that, with the sail we were able to make, we could hardly reckon the ship shortened the way, but that she rather lost ground. In less than two watches the gale faced about; and if we saved our own by the change, it was all we could pretend unto.

Our mortal enemy, the north-west gale, began afresh to send us out to sea, and to raise our terrors to a higher pitch. One of our pumps grew so unfix'd, that it could not be repair'd; the other was kept in perpetual motion; no man was excus'd to take his turn that had strength to perform it. Amongst the manifold perils that threatened every hour to be our last, we were in mortal apprehension, that the guns which were all aloft, would shew us a slippery trick, and some of them break loose, the tackle that held them being grown very rotten: and it was another providence they held so long, considering how immoderately the ship rolled, especially when the sails were mending that should keep them steady, which was very near a third part of our time, whilst we plyed to the windward with a contrary gale.

To prevent this danger which must befal when any one gun should get loose, mate Putts found an expedient by a more than ordinary smooth water; and by placing timber on the hatchway, to supply the place of shrouds, he got them safe in hold; which tended much to our good, not only in removing the present danger, but by making the ship (as seamen say) more wholesome, by having so great weight removed from her upper works into her centre, where ballast was much wanted.

But the intolerable want of all provisions, both of meat and drink, jostled the sense of this happiness soon out of our minds. And to aggravate our misery yet the more, it was now our interest to pray, that the contrary gale might stand; for whilst the westerly wind held, we had rain water to drink, whereas at east the wind blew dry.

In this miserable posture of ship and provision, we reckoned our selves driven to the east, in less than a week's time, at least two hundred leagues, which we despaired ever to recover without a miracle of divine mercy. The storm continued so fresh against us, that it confounded the most knowing of our ship's company in advising what course to take. Some reckoned the ship had made her way most southerly, and therefore counselled we should put our selves in quest of the Bermudas islands, as to the nearest land we could hope to make: but that motion had great opposition in regard of the winter season, which would daily produce insuperable difficulties, and give greater puzzle in the discovery of it, than our circumstances would admit. Others would say, The furthest way about, in our case, would prove the nearest way home; and judged it best to take advantage of the westerly winds, and impetuous seas made to our hands, to attempt returning back to the western islands, as a thing more likely to succeed (tho' at a great distance) than thus to strive against the stream without any hopeful prospect of gaining the capes. But that motion met with a more general aversion, because the run was so long, that, tho' the gale had been in our own power to continue it, we could not have subsisted. Backwards we could not go, nor forwards we could not go in the course we desired: it followed then of consequence, that we must take the middle way; and it was resolved, that, without further persisting in endeavouring to gain our port by a close hale, we should raise our tackle, and sail tardy for the first American land we could fetch, tho' we ran to the leeward as far as the coast of New England.

Whilst this determination was agreed and put into practice, the famine grew sharp upon us. Women and children made dismal cries and grievous complaints. The infinite number of rats that all the voyage had been our plague, we now were glad to make our prey to feed on; and as they were insnared and taken, a well grown rat was sold for sixteen shillings as a market rate. Nay, before the voyage did end (as I was credibly inform'd) a woman great with child offered twenty shillings for a rat, which the proprietor refusing, the woman died.

Many sorrowful days and nights we spun out in this manner, till the blessed feast of Christmas came upon us, which we began with a very melancholy solemnity; and yet, to make some distinction of times, the scrapings of the mealtubs were all amassed together to compose a pudding. Malaga sack, sea water, with fruit and spice, all well fryed in oyl, were the ingredients of this regale, which raised some envy in the spectators; but allowing some privilege to the captain's mess, we met no obstruction, but did peaceably enjoy our Christmas pudding.

My greatest impatience was of thirst, and my dreams were all of cellars, and taps running down my throat, which made my waking much the worse by that tantalizing fancy. Some relief I found very real by the captain's favour in allowing me a share of some butts of small claret he had concealed in a private cellar for a dead lift. It wanted a mixture of water for qualifying it to quench thirst; however, it was a present remedy, and a great refreshment to me.

I cannot forget another instance of the captain's kindness to me, of a like obligation. He singled me out one day to go with him into the hold to seek fresh water in the bottoms of the empty casks. With much ado we got a quantity to satisfy our longing, tho' for the thickness thereof it was not palatable. We were now each of us astride on a butt of Malaga, which gave the captain occasion to taste of their contents. We tasted and tasted it again; and tho' the total we drank was not considerable, yet it had an effect on our heads that made us suspend (tho' we could not forget) our wants of water. The operation this little debauch had upon the captain, was very different from what it wrought on me, who felt myself refresh'd as with a cordial; but the poor captain fell to contemplate (as it better became him) our sad condition; and being troubled in mind for having brought so many wretched souls into misery, by a false confidence he gave them of his having a good ship, which he now thought would prove their ruin; and being conscious, that their loss would lie all at his door, it was no easy matter to appease his troubled thoughts. He made me a particular compliment for having engaged me and my friends in the same bottom, and upon that burst into tears. I comforted him the best I could, and told him, We must all submit to the hand of God, and rely on his goodness, hoping, that the same providence which had hitherto so miraculously preserved us, would still be continued in our favour till we were in safety. We retired obscurely to our friends, who had been wondering at our absence.

The westerly wind continued to shorten our way to the shore, tho' very distant from our port; but this did not at all incline us to change our resolution of sailing large for the first land; it did rather animate and support us in our present disasters of hunger and thirst, toil and fatigue. The hopes of touching land was food and raiment to us.

In this wearisome expectation we pass'd our time for eight or nine days and nights, and then we saw the water change colour, and had soundings. We approach'd the shore the night of January 3d. with little sail; and, as the morning of the fourth day gave us light, we saw the land; but in what latitude we could not tell, for that the officers, whose duty it was to keep the reckoning of the ship, had for many days past totally omitted that part; nor had we seen the sun a great while, to take observations, which (tho' a lame excuse) was all they had to say for that omission. But in truth it was evident, that the desperate estate of the ship, and hourly jeopardy of life did make them careless of keeping either log or journal; the thoughts of another account they feared to be at hand, did make them neglect that of the ship as inconsiderable.

About the hours of three or four in the afternoon of the twelfth eve, we were shot in fair to the shore. The evening was clear and calm, the water smooth; the land we saw nearest was some six or seven English miles distant from us, our soundings twenty-five fathoms in good ground for anchor-hold.

These invitations were all attractive to encourage the generality (especially the passengers) to execute what we had resolved on for the shore: but one old officer who was husband for the ship's stores whilst there were any, would not consent on any terms to trust the only anchor that was left us for preservation, out of his sight at sea. His arguments to back his opinion were plausible; as, first, The hazard of losing that only anchor by any sudden storm, bringing with it a necessity to cut or slip, on which every life depended. 2dly. The shortness of the cable, very unfit for anchorage in the ocean: And 3dly. The weakness of the ship's crew, many dead and fallen over board, and the passengers weakened by hunger, dying every day on the decks, or at the pump, which with great difficulty was kept going, but must not rest.

Against the old man's reasonings was urged the very small remains of bisket, at our short allowance, which would hardly hold a week; the assurance of our loss by famine if we should be forced to sea again by a north-west storm, and the great possibility of finding a harbour to save our ship, with our lives and goods, in some creek on the coast. These last reasons prevailed upon the majority against all negatives: and when the anchor was let loose, mate Putts was ordered to make the first discovery of what we might expect from the nearest land. He took with him twelve sickly passengers, who fancied the shore would cure them; and he carry'd major Morrison on shore with him in pursuit of such adventures as are next in course to be related; for according to the intelligence that could be got from land, we were to take our measures at sea, either to proceed on in our voyage in that sad condition that has been in some proportion set forth, or to land our selves, and unload the ship, and try our fortunes amongst the Indians.

In four or five hours time we could discover the boat returning with mate Putts alone for a setter, which we look'd upon as a signal of happy success. When he came on board his mouth was full of good tidings, as namely, That he discovered a creek that would harbour our ship, and that there was a depth of water on the bar, sufficient for her draught when she was light. That there was excellent fresh water, (a taste whereof major Morrison had sent me in a bottle.) That the shore swarm'd with fowl, and that major Morrison stayed behind in expectation of the whole ship's company to follow.

I opened mine ears wide to the motion, and promoted the design of our landing there with all the rhetorick and interest I had. The captain was no less forward for it, hoping thereby to save the lives of the passengers that remained: and that he might not wholly rely on mate Putts's judgment in a matter wherein he was most concern'd, he embark'd with me in the wherry, with a kinsman of his, and some others; and the seamen were glad of my help to put the boat to shore, my hands having been very well season'd at the pump, by taking my turn for many weeks at the rate of three hours in twenty-four. My passionate desires to be on shore at the fountain head to drink without stint, did not a little quicken me, insomuch that the six or seven miles I rowed on this occasion, were no more that the breadth of the Thames at London, at another time, would have been toilsome to me.

In our passage to the shore, the darkness of the evening made us glad to see the fires of our friends at land, which were not only our beacons to direct us to their company, but were also a comfortable relief to our chill bodies when we came near them, the weather being very cold (as it ever is) the wind north-west on that coast.

Assoon as I had set my foot on land, and had rendred thanks to almighty God for opening this door of deliverance to us, after so many rescues even from the jaws of death at sea, major Morrison was pleased to oblige me beyond all requital, in conducting me to the running stream of water, where, without any limitation of short allowance, I might drink my fill. I was glad of so great liberty, and made use of it accordingly, by prostrating myself on my belly, and setting my mouth against the stream, that it might run into my thirsty stomach without stop. The rest of the company were at liberty to use their own methods to quench their thirst; but this I thought the greatest pleasure I ever enjoyed on earth.

After this sweet refreshment, the captain, myself, and his kinsman crossed the creek in our wherry, invited thither by the cackling of wild-fowl. The captain had a gun charged, and the moon shining bright in his favour, he killed one duck of the flock that flew over us, which was roasted on a stick out of hand by the seamen, whilst we walk'd on the shore of the creek for further discovery.

In passing a small gullet we trod on an oyster bank that did happily furnish us with a good addition to our duck. When the cooks had done their parts, we were not long about ours, but fell on without using the ceremony of calling the rest of our company, which would have been no entertainment to so many, the proverb telling us, *The fewer the better chear*. The bones, head, legs, and inwards were agreed to be the cook's fees; so we gave God thanks, and return'd to our friends, without making boast of our good fortunes.

Fortify'd with this repast, we inform'd our selves of the depth of water at the bar of the creek, in which the captain seem'd satisfy'd, and made shews in all his deportment, of his resolution to discharge the ship there in order to our safety. Towards break of day he ask'd me in my ear, If I would go back with him on board the ship? I told him, No, because it would be labour lost, in case he would persist in his resolution to do what he pretended, which he ratify'd again by protestations, and so went off with his kinsman, who had a large coarse cloth gown I borrow'd of him to shelter me from the sharpest cold I ever felt. That which had sometimes been a paradox to me, was by this experience made demonstrable, (viz.) That the land on the continent is much colder than that of islands, tho' in the same latitude; and the reason is evident to any who shall consider the many accidents on the continent that cool the air by winds that come from the land; as in those parts of America, the mighty towring mountains to the north-west, covered all the year with snow, which does refrigerate the air even in the heat of summer; whereas winds coming from the sea are generally warm: and this hath proved a fatal truth to the inhabitants of Virginia, who, in the south-east winds, have gone to bed in sultry heat and sweat, without any covering, and have awaked in the night stiff and benumb'd with cold, without the use of their limbs, occasion'd by a shifting of the wind in the night from sea to land.

No sooner had the captain cleared himself of the shore but the day-break made me see my error in not closing with his motion in my ear. The first object we saw at sea was the ship under sail, standing for the capes with what canvass could be made to serve the turn. It was a very heavy prospect to us who remained (we knew not where) on shore, to see our selves thus abandon'd by the ship, and more, to be forsaken by the boat, so contrary to our mutual agreement. Many hours of hard labour and toil were spent before the boat could fetch the ship: and the seamen (whose act it was to set sail without the captain's order, as we were told after) car'd not for the boat whilst the wind was large to carry them to the capes. But mate Putts, who was more sober and better natur'd, discovering

237

the boat from the mizzen-top, lay by till she came with the captain on board.

In this amazement and confusion of mind that no words can express, did our miserable distress'd party condole with each other being so cruelly abandon'd and left to the last despairs of human help, or indeed of ever seeing more the face of man. We entred into a sad consultation what course to take; and having, in the first place, by united prayers, implored the protection of Almighty God, and recommended our miserable estate to the same providence which, in so many instances of mercy, had been propitious to us at sea; the whole party desired me to be as it were the father of this distressed family, to advise and conduct them in all things I thought might most tend to our preservation. This way of government we agreed must necessarily reside in one, to avoid disputes, and variety of contradictory humours, which would render our deliverance the more impracticable; and it was thought most reasonable to be placed in me, for the health and strength it had pleased God to preserve unto me above my fellows, more than for any other qualification.

At the time I quitted the ship my servant Thomas Harman, a Dutchman, did, at parting, advertise me (for I left him on board to look to my goods) that, in the bundle I ordered to be carry'd with me on shore, I should find about thirty bisket cakes, which he, by unparallel'd frugality, had saved out of his own belly in the great dearth and scarcity we lived in. The thoughts of these biskets entring upon me at the time I was press'd to accept this charge, I thought myself obliged, in christian equity, to let every one partake of what I had; and so dividing the bread into nineteen parts (which was our number) perhaps I added the fraction to my own share.

It was, to the best of my remembrance, upon the fifth day of January, that we entred into this method of life, or rather into an orderly way unto our graves, since nothing but the image of death was represented to us: but that we might use our outmost endeavours to extract all the good we could out of those evil symptoms that did every way seem to confound us, I made a muster of the most able bodies for arms and labour; and, in the first place, I put a fowling-piece into every man's hand that could tell how to use it. Amongst the rest, a young gentleman, Mr. Francis Cary by name, was very helpful to me in the fatigue and active part of this undertaking. He was strong and healthy, and was very ready for any employment I could put upon him. He came recommended to me by Sir Edward Thurlan, his genius leading him rather to a planter's life abroad, than to any course his friends could propose to him in England; and this rough entrance was like to let him know the worst at first.

All our woodmen and fowlers had powder and shot given them, and some geese were killed for supper. Evening came on apace, and our resolution being taken to stay one night more in these quarters, I sent my cousin Cary to head the creek, and make what discovery he could as he passed along the shore, whether of Indians or any other living creatures that were likely to relieve our wants, or end our days. To prepare like men for the latter, we resolved to die fighting, if that should be the case; or if, on the contrary, the Indians should accost us in a mien of amity, then to meet them with all imaginable courtesy, and please them with such trivial presents as they love to deal in, and so engage them into a friendship with us.

My cousin Cary was not absent much above an hour, when we saw him return in a contrary point to that he sallied out upon. His face was clouded with ill news he had to tell us, namely, that we were now residing on an island without any inhabitants, and that he had seen its whole extent, surrounded (as he believed) with water deeper than his head; that he had not seen any native, or any thing in human shape, in all his round, nor any other creature besides the fowls of the air, which he would, but could not, bring unto us.

This dismal success of so unexpected a nature, did startle us more than any single misfortune that had befallen us, and was like to plunge us into utter despair. We beheld each other as miserable wretches sentenc'd to a lingering death, no man knowing what to propose for prolonging life any longer than he was able to fast. My cousin Cary was gone from us without notice, and we had reason (for what followed) to believe he was under conduct of an angel; for we soon saw him return with a chearful look, his hands carrying something we could not distinguish by any name at a distance; but by nearer approach we were able to descry they were a parcel of oysters; which in crossing the island, as he stept over a small current of water, he trode upon to his hurt; but laying hands on what he felt with his feet, and pulling it with all his force, he found himself possessed of this booty of oysters, which grew in clusters, and were contiguous to a large bank of the same species, that was our staple subsistence whilst we remained there.

Whilst this very cold season continued, great flights of fowl frequented the island, geese, ducks, curlieus, and some of every sort we killed and roasted on sticks, eating all but the feathers. It was the only perquisite belonging to my place of preference to the rest, that the right of carving was annexed to it. Wherein, if I was partial to my own interest, it was in cutting the wing as large and full of meat as possible; whereas the rest was measured out as it were with scale and compass.

But as the wind veered to the southward, we had greater warmth and fewer fowl, for they would then be gone to colder climates. In their absence we were confined to the oyster bank, and a sort of weed some four inches long, as thick as houseleek, and the only green (except pines) that the island afforded. It was very insipid on the palate; but being boiled with a little pepper (of which one had brought a pound on shore) and helped with five or six oysters, it became a regale for every one in turn.

In quartering our family we did observe the decency of distinguishing sexes: we made a small hut for the poor weak women to be by themselves; our cabbin for men was of the same fashion, but much more spacious, as our numbers were. One morning, in walking on the shore by the sea side, with a long gun in my hand loaden with small shot, I fired at a great flight of small birds called ox-eyes, and made great slaughter among them, which gave refreshment to all our company. But this harvest had a short end; and as the weather by its warmth, chased the fowl to the north, our hunger grew sharper upon us. And in fine, all the strength that remained unto us was employed in a heartless struggling to spin out life a little longer; for we still deemed our selves doom'd to die by famine, from whose sharpest and most immediate darts tho' we seemed to be rescued for a small time, by meeting these contingent helps on shore, yet still we apprehended (and that on too great probability) they only served to reprieve us for a little longer day of execution, with all the dreadful circumstances of a lingering death.

For the south-west winds that had carry'd away the fowl, brought store of rain, which meeting with a spring-tide, our chief magazine, the oyster bank, was overflown; and as they became more accessible, our bodies also decayed so sensibly, that we could hardly pull them out of their muddy beds they grew on. And from this time forward we rarely saw the fowl; they now grew shy and kept aloof when they saw us contriving against their lives.

Add to this, our guns most of them unfix'd and out of order, and our powder much decayed, insomuch that nothing did now remain to prolong life, but what is counted rather sauce to whet, than substance to satisfy the appetite; I mean the oysters, which were not easily gotten by our crazy bodies after the quantity was spent that lay most commodious to be reach'd, and which had fed us for the first six days we had been on the island. And thus we wish'd every day to be the last of our lives (if God had so pleased) so hopeless and desperate was our condition, all expectation of human succour being vanished and gone.

Of the three weak women before-mentioned, one had the envied happiness to die about this time; and it was my advice to the survivors, who were following her apace, to endeavour their own preservation by converting her dead carcase into food, as they did to good effect. The same counsel was embrac'd by those of our sex: the living fed upon the dead; four of our company having the happiness to end their miserable lives on Sunday night the —— day of January. Their chief distemper, 'tis true, was hunger; but it pleased God to hasten their exit by an immoderate access of cold, caused by a most terrible storm of hail and snow at north-west, on the Sunday aforesaid, which did not only dispatch those four to their long homes, but did sorely threaten all that remained alive, to perish by the same fate.

Great was the toil that lay on my hands (as the strongest to labour) to get fuel together sufficient for our preservation. In the first place I divested myself of my great gown, which I spread at large, and extended against the wind in nature of a screen, having first shifted our quarters to the most calm commodious place that could be found to keep us, as much as possible, from the inclemency of that prodigious storm.

Under the shelter of this traverse I took as many of my comrades as could be comprehended in so small a space; whereas those who could not partake of that accommodation, and were enabled to make provision for themselves, were forced to suffer for it. And it was remarkable, that notwithstanding all the provision that could possibly be made against the sharpness of this cold, either by a well-burning fire consisting of two or three loads of wood, or shelter of this great gown to the windward, we could not be warm. That side of our wearing cloaths was singed and burnt which lay towards the flames, whilst the other side that was from the fire, became frozen and congeal'd. Those who lay to the leeward of the flame, could not stay long to enjoy the warmth so necessary to life, but were forced to quit and be gone to avoid suffocation by the smoke and flame.

When the day appeared, and the sun got up to dissipate the clouds, with down-cast looks and dejected, the survivors of us entred into a final deliberation of what remained to be done on our parts (besides our prayers to Almighty God) to spin out a little longer time of life, and wait a further providence from heaven for our better relief. There were still some hands that retained vigour, tho' not in proportion to those difficulties we were to encounter, which humanly did seem insuperable. The unhappy circumstance of our being coop'd up in an island, was that which took from us all probable hopes of escaping this terrible death that did threaten us every hour. Major Morrison, on whose counsel I had reason to rely most, was extremely decayed in his strength, his legs not being able to support him. It was a wonderful mercy that mine remained in competent strength, for our common good, which I resolved, by God's help, to employ for that end to the last gasp.

In this last resolution we had to make, I could not think on any thing worthy my proposal, but by an attempt to cross the creek, and swim to the main (which was not above an hundred yards over) and being there to coast along the woods to the south-west (which was the bearing of Virginia) until I should meet Indians, who would either relieve or destroy us. I fancied the former would be our lot when they should see our conditions, and that no hurt was intended to them; or if they should prove inhuman, and of a bloody nature, and would not give us quarter, why even in that case it would be worth this labour of mine to procure a sudden period to all our miseries.

I open'd my thoughts to this purpose to the company, who were sadly surprized at the motion; but being fully convinc'd in their judgment, that this was the only course that could be depended on (humanly speaking) for our relief, they all agreed it must be done.

To fortify me for this expedition, it was necessary that some provision should be made for a daily support to me in this my peregrination. Our choice was small; our only friend the oyster bank was all we had to rely on; which being well stew'd in their own liquor, and put up into bottles, I made no doubt, by God's blessing, but that two of them well filled, would suffice to prolong my life in moderate strength, until I had obtain'd my end. To accomplish this design, my cousin Cary laboured hard for oysters, hoping to make one in the adventure.

About the ninth day of our being in the island, I fell to my oyster cookery, and made a good progress that very day; when in the heat of my labour my cousin Cary brought me word, That he had just in that instant seen Indians walking on the main. I suspended my cookery out of hand, and hastened with all possible speed to be an eye-witness of that happy intelligence; but with all the haste I could make I could see no such thing, but judg'd it a chimera that proceeded from some operation in my cousin's fancy, who was more than ordinary of a sanguine nature, which made him see (as it were by inchantment) things that were not, having many times been deluded (as I judg'd) by the same deception.

Defeated in this manner of my hopes to see Indians without the pains of seeking them, I returned to my work, and continued at it till one bottle was full, and myself tired: wherefore, that I might be a little recreated, I took a gun in my hand; and hearing the noise of geese on our shore, I approach'd them privately, and had the good hap to be the death of one. This goose, now in my possession without witnesses, I resolved to eat alone (deducting the head, bones, guts, &c. which were the cook's fees) hoping thereby to be much the better enabled to swim the creek, and perform the work I had upon my hand. I hung my goose upon the twist of a tree in a shrubby part of the wood, whilst I went to call aside our cook with his broach, and a coal of fire to begin the roast. But when we came to the place of execution, my goose was gone all but the head, the body stolen by wolves, which the Indians told us after, do abound greatly in that island.

The loss of this goose, which my empty stomach look'd for with no small hopes of satisfaction, did vex me heartily. I wish'd

I could have taken the thief of my goose to have serv'd him in the same kind, and to have taken my revenge in the law of retaliation. But that which troubled me more, was an apprehension that came into my mind, that this loss had been the effect of divine justice on me, for designing to deal unequally with the rest of my fellow-sufferers; which I thought, at first blush, look'd like a breach of trust: but then again when I consider'd the equity of the thing, that I did it merely to enable myself to attain their preservation, and which otherwise I could not have done I found I could absolve myself from any guilt of that kind. Whatever I suffer'd in this disappointment, the cook lost not all his fees; the head and neck remained for him on the tree.

Being thus over-reach'd by the wolf, it was time to return to my cookery, in order to my sally out of the island; for I had little confidence in the notice frequently brought me of more and more Indians seen on the other side, since my own eyes could never bear witness of their being there.

The next morning, being the ninth or tenth of our being there, I fell to work afresh, hoping to be ready to begin my journey that day; and being very busy, intelligence was brought, that a canoe was seen to lie on the broken ground to the south of our island, which was not discovered till now, since our being there: but this I thought might be a mistake cast in the same mould of many others that had deceived those discoverers, who fancy'd all things real according to their own wishes. But when it was told me, That Indians had been at the poor women's cabbin in the night, and had given them shellfish to eat, that was a demonstration of reality beyond all suspicion. I went immediately to be inform'd from themselves, and they both avowed it for truth, shewing the shells (the like whereof I ne'er had seen) and this I took for proof of what they said.

The further account these women gave of the Indians, was, that they pointed to the south-east with their hands, which they knew not how to interpret, but did imagine by their several gestures, they would be with them again to morrow. Their pointing to the south-east was like to be the time they would come, meaning nine o'clock to be their hour, where the sun will be at that time. Had the women understood their language, they could not have learned the time of the day by any other computation than pointing at the sun. It is all the clock they have for the day, as the coming and going of the *Cahuncks* (the geese) is their almanack or prognostick for the winter and summer seasons.

This news gave us all new life, almost working miracles amongst us, by making those who desponded, and totally yielded themselves up to the weight of despair, and lay down with an intent never more to rise again, to take up their beds and walk. This friendly charitable visit of the Indians did also put a stop to my preparations to seek them, who had so humanely prevented me, by their seeking ways to preserve and save our lives.

Instead of those preparations of my march which had cost me so much pains, I passed my time now in contriving the fittest posture our present condition would allow us to put on when these angels of light should appear again with the glad tidings of our relief; and the result was, that every man should have his gun lying by his side, laden with shot, and as fit for use as possible, but not to be handled unless the Indians came to us like enemies (which was very unlikely, the premises considered) and then to sell our lives at as dear a rate as we could; but if they came in an amicable posture, then would we meet them unarm'd, chearfully, which the Indians like, and hate to see a melancholy face.

In these joyful hopes of unexpected deliverance by these Indians, did we pass the interval of their absence. Every eye look'd sharply out when the sun was at south-east, to peep thro' the avenues of the wood to discover the approaches of our new friends. When the sun came to the south we thought our selves forgotten by them, and began to doubt the worst, as losing gamesters, at play for their last estate, suspect some stabcast to defeat the hopes of the fairest game. We feared some miscarriage, either from their inconstancy by change of their mind, or that some unlook'd-for misfortune that our evil fates reserved for us, had interposed for our ruin.

Scouts were sent out to the right and left hands, without discovery of any body all the forenoon: and then, considering our case admitted no delay, I began to resume my former resolution of swimming to them that would not come to us. But how wholesome soever this counsel might seem in itself, it was most difficult to be put in practice, in regard of the cold time.

The northerly wind that in these climates does blow very cold in the heat of summer, does much more distemper the air in the winter season (as our poor comrades felt that Sunday night to their cost) and did send so cold a gale upon the surface of the water in the creek I was to pass, that, in the general opinion of all the concern'd, it was not a thing to be attempted; and that if I did, I must surely perish in the act. I was easily perswaded to forbear an action so dangerous, and the rather, because I verily believed the Indians would bring us off, if our patience would hold out.

About the hours of two or three o'clock it pleased God to change the face of our condition for the best; for whilst I was busy at the fire in preparations to wait on them, the Indians, who had placed themselves behind a very great tree, discovered their faces with most chearful smiles, without any kind of arms, or appearance of evil design; the whole number of them (perhaps twenty or thirty in all) consisting of men, women and children; all that could speak accosting us with joyful countenances, shaking hands with every one they met. The words *Ny Top*, often repeated by them, made us believe they bore a friendly signification, as they were soon interpreted to signify my friend.

After many salutations and *Ny Tops* interchang'd, the night approaching, we fell to parley with each other; but perform'd it in signs more confounded and unintelligible than any other conversation I ever met withall; as hard to be interpreted as if they had expressed their thoughts in the Hebrew or Chaldean tongues.

They did me the honour to make all applications to me, as being of largest dimensions, and equip'd in a camlet coat glittering with galoon lace of gold and silver, it being generally true, that where knowledge informs not, the habit qualifies.

The ears of Indian corn they gave us for present sustenance, needed no other interpreter to let them know how much more acceptable it was to us than the sight of dead and living corpses, which raised great compassion in them, especially in the women, who are observed to be of a soft tender nature. One of them made me a present of the leg of a swan, which I eat as privately as it was given me, and thought it so much the more excellent, by how much it was larger than the greatest limb of any fowl I ever saw.

The Indians stayed with us about two hours, and parted not without a new appointment to see us again the next day: and the hour we were to expect them by their pointing to the sun, was to be at two o'clock in the afternoon. I made the chief of them presents of ribbon and other slight trade, which they lov'd, designing, by mutual endearment, to let them see, it would gratify their interest as well as their charity, to treat us well. *Ha-na Haw* was their parting word, which is farewel, pointing again at the place where the sun would be at our next meeting. We took leave in their own words *Ha-na Haw*.

The going away of the Indians, and leaving us behind, was a separation hard to be born by our hungry company, who nevertheless had received a competent quantity of corn and bread to keep us till they returned to do better things for our relief; we did not fail to give glory to God for our approaching deliverance, and the joy we conceiv'd in our minds in the sense of so great a mercy, kept us awake all the night, and was a cordial to the sick and weak to recover their health and strength.

The delay of the Indians coming next day, beyond their set time, we thought an age of tedious years: At two o'clock we had no news of them, but by attending their own time with a little patience, we might see a considerable number of them, women and children, all about our huts, with recruits of bread and corn to stop every mouth. Many of them desir'd beads and little truck they use to deal in, as exchange for what they gave us; and we as freely gave them what we had brought on shore; but to such of us as gave them nothing, the Indians failed not however to give them bread for nothing.

One old man of their company, who seem'd, by the preference they gave him, to be the most considerable of the party, apply'd himself to me by gestures and signs, to learn something (if possible) of our country, and occasion of the sad posture he saw us in, to the end that he might inform his master, the king of Kickotank, (on whose territories we stood) and dispose him to succour us, as we had need.

I made return to him in many vain words, and in as many insignificant signs as himself had made to me, and neither of us one jot the wiser. The several nonplus's we both were at in striving to be better understood, afforded so little of edification to either party, that our time was almost spent in vain. It came at last into my head, that I had long since read Mr. Smith's travels thro' those parts of America, and that the word *Werowance* (a word frequently pronounced by the old man) was in English the king. That word, spoken by me, with strong emphasis, together with the motions of my body, speaking my desire of going to him, was very pleasing to the old man, who thereupon embrac'd me with more than common kindness, and by all demonstrations of satisfaction, did shew that he understood my meaning. This one word was all the Indian I could speak, which (like a little armour well plac'd) contributed to the saving of our lives.

In order to what was next to be done, he took me by the hand and led me to the sea side, where I embark'd with himself and one more Indian in a canoe, that had brought him there, which the third man rowed over to that broken ground, where, not long before, we made discovery of a canoe newly laid there, and (as they told us) was lodg'd there on purpose to be ready for our transport, at such time as they thought fit to fetch us off; and the reason of their taking me with them was to help launch this weighty embarkation, as being made of the body of an oak or pine, some twenty-two foot in length, hollowed like a pig-trough, which is the true description of a canoe. The manner of its being put into motion is very particular; the labourers with long booms place their feet on the starboard and larboard sides of the boat, and with this fickle footing do they heave it forward.

I cannot omit a passage of one major Stephens, who had been an officer in the late civil war, under Sir William Waller, and was now one of our fellow-sufferers. He could not be persuaded by any means to give his vote for prosecuting the way we were in for our relief, but differ'd as much in judgment with us, in this our design of going to the king of this country, as he had done in England, by engaging against his natural sovereign; he cry'd out these rogues would draw us into their power, and take away our lives, advising, rather than to put our trust in this king, we should put ourselves into one of these canoes, and taking advantage of the calm time, we should try to get the north cape.

His fears and objections were so unreasonable, that they were not worth an answer, and his project of going thus by sea was so ridiculous, that it did exceed all chimera's of knight-errantry, and his apprehending the king would ensnare us, was all esteemed vain, as nothing could be more childish: We had been in the king's power (though we knew it not) ever since we set foot on that ground, so that had his mind been that way bent, he need use no other stratagem to end our lives, than to have forborn the sending us relief; every one dissented to the main project, and I did unfeignedly profess, for my own part, that I would much rather expose my life to the honour of a king (tho' never so mean) than to the billows of the sea, in such a bottom; which would be to tempt God to destroy us, and punish our presumption by his justice, at the same time that he was saving us by a miracle of his mercy.

I should not have remembred this passage of major Stephens, had he only shew'd his antipathy in this single instance, but because he repeated the rancor of his mind, in two other very small occasions, which will follow, 'tis just that the malignity of so ill an humour should suffer some reprimand.

The canoes being fitted to take us in and waft us to the main, I made a fair muster of the remnant we had to carry off, and found we wanted six of the number we brought on shore (*viz.*) four men and two women: five of those six we knew were dead, but missing one of our living women, we made the Indians understand the same, who as readily made us know that she was in their thoughts, and should be cared for assoon as we were settled in our quarters.

In passing the creek that was to lead us to an honest fisherman's house, we entred a branch of it to the southward, that was the road-way to it. The tide was going out, and the water very shoal, which gave occasion to any one that had a knife, to treat himself with oysters all the way. At the head of that branch we were able in a short time to discover that heaven of happiness where our most courteous host did, with a chearful countenance, receive and entertain us. Several fires were kindled out of hand, our arms and powder were laid up in safety, and divers earthen pipkins were put to boil with such varieties as the season would afford. Every body had something or other to defend and save them from the cold; and my obligation to him, by a peculiar care that he had of me, exceeded all the rest. I had one intire side of the fire, with a large platform to repose on, to myself; furrs and deer skins to cover my body, and support my head, with a priority of respect and friendly usage, which, to my great trouble, I was not able to deserve at his hands, by any requital then in my power to return.

Our kind entertainment in the house of this poor fisherman, had so many circumstances of hearty compassion and tenderness in every part of it, that as it ought to be a perpetual motive to engage all of us who enjoyed the benefit of it, to a daily acknowledgement of the Almighty's goodness for conducting us in this manner by his immediate hand, out of our afflictions, so may it ever be look'd upon as a just reproach to christians, who, on all our sea-coasts, are so far from affording succour to those who, by shipwreck and misfortunes of the sea, do fall into their power, that they treat with all inhuman savage barbarity, those unhappy souls whom God hath thus afflicted, seizing on their goods as their proper perquisites, which the waves of the sea (by divine providence) would cast upon the shore for the true proprietors; and many times dispatching them out of the world to silence complaints, and to prevent all after-reckonings. And the better to intitle themselves to what they get in this way of rapine, they wickedly call such devilish acquests by the sacred name of God's good, prophaning and blaspheming at the same time that holy name, as they violate all the laws of hospitality and human society: whereas, on the contrary, our charitable host, influenced only by natural law, without the least shew of coveting any thing we had, or prospect of requital in the future, did not only treat in this manner our persons, but did also, with as much honesty, secure for us our small stores of guns, powder, &c. as if he had read and understood the duty of the gospel, or had given his only child as a hostage to secure his dealing justly with us; so that I can never sufficiently applaud the humanity of this Indian, nor express the high contentment that I enjoyed in this poor man's cottage, which was made of nothing but mat and reeds, and bark of trees fix'd to poles. It had a loveliness and symmetry in the air of it, so pleasing to the eye, and refreshing to the mind, that neither the splendour of the Escurial, nor the glorious appearance of Versailles were able to stand in competition with it. We had a boiled swan for supper, which gave plentiful repasts to all our upper mess.

Our bodies thus refresh'd with meat and sleep, comforted with fires, and secured from all the changes and inclemencies of that sharp piercing cold season, we thought the morning (tho' clad in sunshine did come too fast upon us. Breakfast was liberally provided and set before us, our arms faithfully delivered up to my order for carriage; and thus in readiness to set forward, we put our selves in a posture to proceed to the place where the king resided. The woman left behind at the island, had been well look'd to, and was now brought off to the care of her comrade that came with us, neither of them in a condition to take a journey, but they were carefully attended and nourished in this poor man's house, till such time as boats came to fetch them to Virginia, where they did soon arrive in perfect health, and lived (one or both of them) to be well married, and to bear children, and to subsist in as plentiful a condition as they could wish.

In beginning our journey thro' the woods, we had not advanced half a mile till we heard a great noise of mens voices, directed to meet and stop our further passage. These were several Indians sent by the king to order us back to our quarters. Major Stephens (not cured of his jealous humour by the experience of what he felt the night before) took this alarm in a very bad sense, and as much different from the rest of the company as in his former fit. He was again deluded with a strong fancy, that these violent motions in the Indians who approach'd us, were the effect of some sudden change in their counsels to our detriment, and that nothing less than our perdition could be the consequence thereof, which he feared would immediately be put in practice by the clamorous men that made such haste to meet us, and (as he would apprehend) to kill and destroy us.

This passion of major Stephens, cast in the same mould with that other he discovered in the island, had not (as we all thought and told him) whereon to raise the least foundation of terror to affright a child; for besides the earnest we had received of their good intentions the night before, these men who came so fast upon us, were all unarm'd; nor was it likely, that king would now possibly imbrew his hands in our blood, and provoke he knew not how powerful a nation to destroy him, after such kind caresses, and voluntary expressions of a temper very contrary to such cruelty. In fine, we saw no cause in all the carriage of the Indians on which I could ground any fear, and therefore I long'd with all impatience to see this king, and to enjoy the plenty of his table, as we quickly did.

When these Indians came up to us, this doubt was soon cleared. The good-natur'd king being inform'd of our bodily weakness, and inability to walk thro' the woods to his house, on foot (which might be about four miles distant from our setting out) had a real tenderness for us, and sent canoes to carry us to the place nearest his house, by the favour of another branch of the same creek; and to the end we might take no vain steps (as we were going to do) and exhaust our strength to no purpose, these Indians made this noise to stop us.

We entred the canoes that were mann'd, and lay ready to receive us. We had a pleasant passage in the shallow water, eat oysters all the way: for altho' the breakfast we had newly made, might well excuse a longer abstinence than we were like to be put to, our arrear to our stomachs was so great, that all we swallowed was soon concocted, and our appetite still fresh and craving more.

Having pass'd this new course for some three English miles in another branch of the creek, our landing place was contriv'd to be near the house of the queen then in waiting. She was a very plain lady to see to, not young, nor yet ill-favour'd. Her complexion was of a sad white: but the measures of beauty in those parts where they are exposed to the scorching sun from their infancy, are not taken from red and white, but from colours that will better lie upon their tawny skins, as hereafter will be seen.

The beauty of this queen's mind (which is more permanent than that of colour) was conspicuous in her charity and generosity to us poor starved weather-beaten creatures, who were the object of it. A mat was spread without the house, upon the ground, furnish'd with *Pone, Homini*, oysters, and other things. The queen made us sit down and eat, with gestures that shewed more of courtesy than majesty, but did speak as hearty welcome as could in silence be expected: and these were the graces that, in our opinion, transcended all other beauties in the world, and did abundantly supply all defects of outward appearance in the person and garb of the queen. The southerly wind made the season tolerable; but that lasted but little, the north-west gale coming violently on us again.

When this collation of the queen was at an end, we took leave of her majesty with all the shews of gratitude that silence knew how to utter. We were now within half an hour's walk of the king's mansion, which we soon discovered by the smoak, and saw it was made of the same stuff with the other houses from which we had newly parted, namely, of mat and reed. Locust posts sunk in the ground at corners and partitions, was the strength of the whole fabrick. The roof was tied fast to the body with a sort of strong rushes that grow there, which supply'd the place of nails and pins, mortises and tenants.

The breadth of this palace was about eighteen or twenty foot, the length about twenty yards. The only furniture was several platforms for lodging, each about two yards long and more, plac'd on both sides of the house, distant from each other about five foot; the space in the middle was the chimney, which had a hole in the roof over it, to receive as much of the smoak as would naturally repair to it; the rest we shared amongst us, which was the greatest part; and the sitters divided to each side, as our soldiers do in their *corps de guarde*.

Fourteen great fires, thus situated, were burning all at once. The king's apartment had a distinction from the rest; it was twice as long, and the bank he sat on was adorn'd with deer skins finely dress'd, and the best furrs of otter and beaver that the country did produce.

The fire assign'd to us was suitable to our number, to which we were conducted, without intermixture of any Indian but such as came to do us offices of friendship. There we were permitted to take our rest until the king pleased to enter into communication with us. Previous to which he sent his daughter, a well-favour'd young girl of about ten or twelve years old, with a great wooden bowl full of *homini* (which is the corn of that country, beat and boiled to mash). She did in a most obliging manner give me the first taste of it, which I would have handed to my next neighbour after I had eaten, but the young princess interposed her hand, and taking the bowl out of mine, delivered it to the same party I aimed to give it, and so to all the rest in order. Instead of a spoon there was a well-shap'd muscle-shell that accompanied the bowl.

The linen of that country grows ready made on the branches of oak trees (or pine), the English call it moss. It is like the threads of unwhited cotton-yarn ravelled, and hangs in parcels on the lower boughs, divine providence having so ordered it for the conveniency and sustenance of the deer, which is all the food they can get in times of snow. It is very soft, sweet and cleanly, and fit for the purpose of wiping clean the hands, and doing the duty of napkins.

About three hours after this meal was ended, the king sent to have me come to him. He called me *Ny a Mutt*, which is to say, My brother, and compelled me to sit down on the same bank with himself, which I had reason to look upon as a mighty favour. After I had sat there about half an hour, and had taken notice of many earnest discourses and repartees betwixt the king and his *crotemen* (so the Indians call the king's council) I could plainly discover, that the debate they held was concerning our adventure and coming there. To make it more clear, the king address'd himself to me with many gestures of his body, his arms display'd in various postures, to explain what he had in his mind to utter for my better understanding. By all which motions I was not edify'd in the least, nor could imagine what return to make by voice or sign, to satisfy the king's demands in any thing that related to the present straights of our condition. In fine, I admir'd their patient sufferance of my dulness to comprehend what they meant, and shew'd myself to be troubled at it; which being perceiv'd by the king, he turn'd all into mirth and jollity, and never left till he made me laugh with him, tho' I knew not why.

I took that occasion to present the king with a sword and long shoulder-belt, which he received very kindly; and to witness his gracious acceptance, he threw off his Mach coat (or upper covering of skin), stood upright on his bank, and, with my aid, did accoutre his naked body with his new harness, which had no other apparel to adorn it, besides a few skins about his loyns to cover his nakedness. In this dress he seem'd to be much delighted; but to me he appear'd a figure of such extraordinary shape, with sword and belt to set it off, that he needed now no other art to stir me up to laughter and mirth, than the sight of his own proper person.

Having made this short acquaintance with the king, I took leave, and returned to my comrades. In passing the spaces betwixt fire and fire, one space amongst the rest was blinded with a traverse of mat; and by the noise I heard from thence, like the beating of hemp, I took it to be some kind of elaboratory. To satisfy a curiosity I had to be more particularly inform'd, I edg'd close to the mat; and, by standing on tiptoe for a full discovery, I saw a sight that gave me no small trouble.

The same special queen (whose courtesy for our kind usage the other day, can never be enough applauded) was now employed in the hard servile labour of beating corn for the king's dinner, which raised the noise that made me thus inquisitive. I wish'd myself in her place for her ease: but the queens of that country do esteem it a privilege to serve their husbands in all kind of cookery, which they would be as loth to lose, as any christian queen would be to take it from them.

Several Indians of the first rank followed me to our quarters, and used their best endeavours to sift something from us that might give them light into knowing what we were. They sought many ways to make their thoughts intelligible to us, but still we parted without knowing what to fix upon, or how to steer our course in advance of our way to Virginia.

In this doubtful condition we thought it reasonable to fall upon a speedy resolution what was next to be done on our parts, in order to the accomplishment of our voyage by land, which we hop'd (by the divine aid) we might be able to effect after a little more refreshment by the plenty of victuals allowed us by the king, who was no less indulgent and careful to feed and caress us, than if we had been his children.

Towards morning we were treated with a new regale brought to us by the same fair hand again. It was a sort of spoon-meat, in colour and taste not unlike to almond-milk temper'd and mix'd with boiled rice. The ground still was Indian corn boiled to a pap, which they call *Homini*, but the ingredient which performed the milky part, was nothing but dry pokickery nuts, beaten shells and all to powder, and they are like to our walnuts, but thicker shell'd, and the kernel sweeter; but being beaten in a mortar, and put into a tray, hollow'd in the middle to make place for fair water, no sooner is the water poured into the powder, but it rises again white and creamish; and after a little ferment it does partake so much of the delicate taste of the kernel of that nut, that it becomes a rarity to a miracle.

Major Morrison, who had been almost at death's door, found himself abundantly refreshed and comforted with this delicacy; he wished the bowl had been a fathom deep, and would say, when his stomach called on him for fresh supplies, that if this princess royal would give him his fill of that food, he should soon recover his strength.

Our bodies growing vigorous with this plenty, we took new

courage, and resolv'd (as many as were able) to attempt the finding out of Virginia. We guess'd the distance could not be great, and that it bore from us S. by W. to S. W. Our ignorance of the latitude we were in, was some discouragement to us; but we were confident, from what the seamen discoursed, we were to the southward of the Menados, then a Dutch plantation, now New York: Fair weather and full stomachs made us willing to be gone. To that end we laid out for a quantity of pone; and for our surer conduct we resolved to procure an Indian to be our pilot through the wilderness, for we were to expect many remora's in our way, by swamps and creeks, with which all those sea-coasts do abound.

The king remarking our more than ordinary care to procure more bread than amounted to our usual expence, gathered thence our design to leave him, and shift for ourselves. To prevent the rashness and folly of such an attempt, he made use of all his silent rhetorick to put us out of conceit of such design, and made us understand the peril and difficulty of it by many obstacles we must meet with. He shew'd us the danger we should expose ourselves unto, by rain and cold, swamps and darkness, unless we were conducted by other skill than we could pretend to: He pointed to his fires and shocks of corn, of which he had enough, and made it legible to us in his countenance, that we were welcome to it. All the signs the king made upon this occasion, we were content to understand in the best sense; and taking for granted our sojourning there was renewed to another day, we retired to our quarters.

About midnight following, the king sent to invite me to his fire. He placed me near him as before, and in the first place shewing me quarters of a lean doe, new brought in. He gave me a knife to cut what part of it I pleased, and then pointing to the fire, I inferr'd, I was left to my own discretion for the dressing of it. I could not readily tell how to shew my skill in the cookery of it, with no better ingredients then appear'd in sight; and so did no more but cut a collop and cast it on the coals. His majesty laugh'd at my ignorance, and to instruct me better, he broach'd the collop on a long scewer, thrust the sharp end into the ground (for there was no hearth but what nature made) and turning sometimes one side, sometimes the other, to the fire, it became fit in short time to be served up, had there been a dining-room of state such as that excellent king deserved.

I made tender of it first to the king, and then to his nobles, but all refused, and left all to me, who gave God and the king thanks for that great meal. The rest of the doe was cut in pieces, stewed in a pipkin, and then put into my hands to dispose of amongst my company.

Assoon as I had dispatch'd this midnight venison feast, and sent the rest to my comrades, the king was greatly desirous to make me comprehend, by our common dialect of signs and motions, the ingenious stratagem by which they use to take their deer in the winter season, especially when the surface of the earth is cover'd with snow. He shewed me in the first place a small leather thong, in which (said he) any kind of deer should be invited to hamper himself and lie fast ty'd on his back, until the engineer (or some body else for him) should take quiet possession of him. I could not conceive the particular structure of this machine, so as to direct the making of it elsewhere; but thus much in the general I did understand; they would fasten a pine green branch at the end of a pole (such as hops grow upon) which should lie athwart an oak, like the pole of a turner's lath, and the green hanging dingle-dangle at the pole end, fastened by a string; it should be set at a heighth for a deer to reach, but not without mounting and resting on his hinder legs, that so in pulling the branch, as at a trigger, the machine discharging, his heels are struck up to fly in the air, and there he remains on his back so straitly hamper'd, that the least child may approach to touch and take him.

Before I parted, the king attack'd me again, with reiterated attempts to be understood, and I thought by these three or four days conversation, I had the air of his expression much more clear and intelligible than at first. His chief drift for the first essay seemed to be a desire to know which way we were bound, whether north or south; to which I pointed to the south. This gave him much satisfaction, and thereupon steps in the little grotman before described, who by the motion of his hand seemed to crave my regard to what he was going about. He took up a stick, with which he made divers circles by the fire-side, and then holding up his finger to procure my attention, he gave to every hole a name; and it was not hard to conceive that the several holes were to supply the place of a sea-chart, shewing the situation of all the most noted Indian territories that lay to the southward of Kickotank.

That circle that was most southerly, he called Achomack, which, tho' he pronounc'd with a different accent from us, I laid hold on that word with all demonstrations of satisfaction I could express, giving them to understand, that was the place to which I had a desire to be conducted.

The poor king was in a strange transport of joy to see me receive satisfaction, and did forthwith cause a lusty young man to be called to him, to whom, by the earnestness of his motions, he seemed to give ample instructions to do something for our service, but what it was we were not yet able to resolve. In two or three days time, seeing no effect of what he had so seriously said, we began again to despond, and did therefore resume our former thoughts of putting ourselves in posture to be gone; but the king seeing us thus ready at every turn to leave him, shewed in his looks a more than ordinary resentment; still describing (as he could) the care he had taken for us, and impossibility of accomplishing our ends by ourselves, and that we should surely faint in the way and die without help, if we would not be ruled by him.

He shewed me again his stores of corn, and made such reiterated signs, by the chearfulness of his countenance, that we should not want, whilst he had such a plenty, as made us lay aside all thoughts of stirring till he said the word. But as oft as he look'd or pointed to the coast of Achomack, he would shake his head, with abundance of grimaces, in dislike of our design to go that way till he saw it good we should do so. I was abundantly convinced of our folly in the resolution we were ready to take of going away without better information of the distance from Achomack, and way that led to it; and having so frank a welcome where we were, we resolved to stay till the king should approve of our departure, which he was not able to determine till the messenger came back, that he had sent to Achomack, who, it now seemed more plainly, was dispatch'd upon my owning that place to be our home, tho' we knew it not from any cause we could rely upon, before we saw the effect.

While we liv'd in this suspense, the king had a great mind to see our fire-arms, and to be acquainted with the use and nature of them. That which best did please his eye I presented to him, and shew'd him how to load and discharge it. He was very shy at first essay, fearing it might hurt him, but I made him stand upon his lodging place, and putting him in a posture to give fire, he presented the mouth of his gun to the chimney hole, and so let fly. The combustible nature of the king's palace not well consider'd, the fabrick was endangered by the king's own hand, for the flashing of the powder having taken hold of the roof at the smoke-hole, all was in a flame; but a nimble lad or two ran up to quench it, and did soon extinguish it without considerable damage to the building, which was of mat and boughs of oak as aforesaid.

The king's eldest son, of about eighteen years of age, was hugely enamour'd with our guns, and look'd so wistfully on me, when he saw what wonders they would do, that I could not forbear presenting him with a birding-piece. Some of our company, who knew that by the laws of Virginia, it was criminal to furnish the Indians with fire-arms, gave me caution in this case, but I resolved, for once, to borrow a point of that law; for tho' it might be of excellent use in the general, yet as our condition was, I esteemed it a much greater crime to deny those Indians any thing that was in our power, than the penalty of that law could amount to.

Father and son abundantly gratify'd in this manner, the king thought himself largely requited for the cost we put him to in our entertainment. I taught his son to shoot at fowls, to charge his gun and clean it, insomuch that in a few minutes, he went among the flocks of geese, and firing at random he did execution on one of them to his great joy, and returned to his father with the game in his hand, with such celerity, as if he had borrowed wings of the wind.

About three o'clock this afternoon, the king was pleased in great condescension to honour me with a visit, a favour which I may (without vanity) assume to myself, and my better habit, from the many particular applications that he made to me, exclusive of the rest of the company. He thought I was too melancholy, (for the Indians, as has been observ'd, are great enemies to that temper) and shew'd me by his own chearful looks, what humour he would have put me on; he would not have me in the least apprehensive of wanting any thing his country afforded, as his mien and gesture witnessed; and for the higher proof of his reality, he found me out a divertisement, that was very extraordinary. He came at this time attended by his young daughter, who had done us the good offices before-mention'd, and having first by kind words and pleasant gestures given us renewed assurance of hearty welcome, he singled me out, and pointed with his hand to a way he would have me take, but whither, or to what end, I was at liberty to guess, upon that he produced his little daughter for my conductrix to the place to which I should go, and shewed his desire that I should follow her where-ever she should lead me.

Major Stephens, not yet enough convinc'd of the Indians fidelity, would have discouraged me from leaving the company in that manner, unreasonably fancying that this was a contrivance in the king to take away my life in a private way; but this I thought did so much out-strip all his other senseless jealousies, that after I had acknowledg'd the obligation I had to his care of my person, his needless caution had no other effect on me than to turn it into ridicule. These inordinate fears of this major in three foregoing instances, might (I confess) have been very well omitted, as not worthy the mention, and so they should have been, had his humour and constitution in prosperous times been any way suitable to this wary temper; but because his habits on shore were scandalously vicious his mouth always belching oaths, and his tongue proving him the vainest hector I had seen, I thought it was pity to lose such a strong confirmation of that known truth, (*viz.*) That true innate courage does seldom reside in the heart of a quarrelling and talking hector.

The weather (as I have said) was excessive cold, with frost, and the winds blowing very fresh upon my face, it almost stopt my breath. The late condition I had been in, under a roof, with great fires, and much smoke, did conduce to make me the more sensible of the cold air: but in less than half an hour that pain was over; we were now in sight of the house whereto we were bound, and the lady of the place was ready to receive us, (who proved to be the mother of my conductrix) and to shew me my apartment in the middle of her house, which had the same accommodation to sit and rest upon, as before has been described in other instances.

The lusty rousing fire, prepared to warm me, would have been noble entertainment of itself, but attended (as it was quickly) with good food for the belly, made it to be that compleat good chear, I only aimed at; a wild turkey boiled, with oysters, was preparing for my supper, which, when it was ready, was served up in the same pot that boiled it. It was a very savoury mess, stew'd with muscles, and I believe would have passed for a delicacy at any great table in England, by palates more competent to make a judgment than mine, which was now more gratify'd with the quantity than the quality of what was before me.

This queen was also of the same mould of her majesty whom we first met at our landing place, somewhat antient (in proportion to the king's age) but so gentle and compassionate, as did very bountifully requite all defects of nature; she passed some hours at my fire, and was very desirous to know the occasion that brought us there (as her motion and the emphasis of her words did shew) but I had small hopes to satisfy her curiosity therein, after so many vain attempts to inform the king in that matter. In fine, I grew sleepy, and about nine o'clock every one retired to their quarters, separated from each other by traverses of mat, which (besides their proper vertue) kept the ladies from any immodest attempts, as secure as if they had been bars of iron.

Assoon as the day peeped in, I went out and felt the same cold as yesterday, with the same wind, N. W. I was not forward to quit a warm quarter, and a frank entertainment, but my young governess, who had her father's orders for direction, knew better than myself what I was to do: she put herself in a posture to lead the way back from whence we came, after a very good repast of stew'd muscles, together with a very hearty welcome plainly appearing in the queen's looks.

My nimble pilot led me away with great swiftness, and it was necessary so to do; the weather still continuing in that violent sharpness, nothing but a violent motion could make our limbs useful. No sooner had I set foot in the king's house to visit my comrades, but a wonderful surprize appeared to me in the change of every countenance, and as every face did plainly speak a general satisfaction, so did they with one voice explain the cause thereof, in telling me the messengers of our delivery were arriv'd, and now with the king.

I hastened to see those angels, and addressing myself to one of them in English habit, ask'd him the occasion of his coming there? He told me his business was to trade for furs, and no more; but assoon as I had told him my name, and the accidents of our being there, he acknowledg'd he came under the guidance of the Kickotank Indian (which I imagin'd, but was not sure the king had sent) in quest of me and those that were left on shore, sent by the governor's order of Virginia to enquire after us, but knew not where to find us until that Indian came to his house; he gave me a large account of the ship's arrival, and the many dangers and difficulties she encountred before she could come into James river, where she ran ashore, resolving there to lay her bones. His name was Jenkin Price, he had brought an Indian of his neighbourhood with him that was very well acquainted in those parts, for our conduct back to Achomack, which Indian was called Jack.

The king was very glad of this happy success to us, and was impatient to learn something more of our history than hitherto he had been able to extract from signs and grimaces. Jenkin Price, with his broken Indian, could make a shift to instruct Jack to say any thing he pleased, and Jack was the more capable to understand his meaning by some sprinklings of English, that he had learnt at our plantations. Betwixt them both they were able to satisfy the king in what he pleased to know. Jack told them of himself what a mighty nation we were in that country, and gave them caution not to imbezzle any goods we had brought with us, for fear of an after-reckoning. I wondered, upon this serious discourse he had with the king, to see guns and stockings, and whatever trifles we had given, offer'd to be return'd, and being told the reason of it by Jenkin Price, I was very much ashamed of Jack's too great zeal in our service, which, tho' it did proceed from a principle of honesty, and good morality in him, we were to consider that our dearest lives, and all we could enjoy in this world, was (next to divine providence) owing to the virtue and charity of this king, and therefore not only what they had in possession, but whatever else he should desire that was in my power, would be too mean an acknowledgement for so high obligations. I took care to let them know that I had no hand in the menace by which Jack brought them to refund what they had got of us; the right understanding whereof increased our good intelligence, and became a new endearment of affection betwixt us.

By better acquaintance with these our deliverers, we learn'd that we were about fifty English miles from Virginia: That part of it where Jenkin did govern, was call'd Littleton's Plantation, and was the first English ground we did expect to see. He gave me great encouragement to endure the length of the way, by assuring me I should not find either stone or shrub to hurt my feet thorow my thin-soaled boots, for the whole colony had neither stone nor underwood; and having thus satisfy'd my curiosity in the knowledge of what Jenkin Price could communicate, we deferred no longer to resolve how and when to begin our journey to Achomack.

The Indian he brought with him (who afterwards lived and died my servant) was very expert, and a most incomparable guide in the woods we were to pass, being a native of those parts, so that he was as our sheet-anchor in this our peregrination. The king was loth to let us go till the weather was better-temper'd for our bodies; but when he saw we were fully resolved, and had pitch'd upon the next morning to begin our journey, he found himself much defeated in a purpose he had taken to call together all the flower of his kingdom to entertain us with a dance, to the end that nothing might be omitted on his part for our divertisement, as well as our nourishment, which his small territory could produce. Most of our company would gladly have deferred our march a day longer, to see this masquerade, but I was wholly bent for Achomack, to which place I was to dance almost on my bare feet, the thoughts of which took off the edge I might otherwise have had to novelties of that kind.

When the good old king saw we were fully determined to be gone the next day, he desired as a pledge of my affection to him, that I would give him my camblet coat, which he vowed to wear whilst he lived for my sake; I shook hands to shew my willingness to please him in that or in any other thing he would command, and was the more willing to do myself the honour of compliance in this particular, because he was the first king I could call to mind that had ever shew'd any inclinations to wear my old cloaths.

To the young princess, that had so signally obliged me, I presented a piece of two-penny scarlet ribbon, and a French tweezer, that I had in my pocket, which made her skip for joy, and to shew how little she fancy'd our way of carrying them concealed, she retired apart for some time, and taking out every individual piece of which it was furnish'd, she tied a snip of ribbon to each, and so came back with scissars, knives and bodkins hanging at her ears, neck and hair. The case itself was not excus'd, but bore a part in this new dress: and to the end we might not part without leaving deep impressions of her beauty in our minds, she had prepared on her forefingers, a lick of paint on each, the colours (to my best remembrance) green and yellow, which at one motion she discharg'd on her face, beginning upon her temples, and continuing it in an oval line downwards as far as it would hold out. I could have wish'd this young princess would have contented herself with what nature had done for her, without this addition of paint (which, I thought, made her more fulsome than handsome); but I had reason to imagine the royal family were only to use this ornament exclusive of all others, for that I saw none other of her sex so set off; and this conceit made it turn again, and appear lovely, as all things should do that are honour'd with the royal stamp.

I was not furnish'd with any thing upon the place, fit to make a return to the two queens for the great charity they used to feed and warm me; but when I came into a place where I could be supply'd, I was not wanting that way, according to my power.

Early next morning we put our selves in posture to be gone, (viz.) major Stephens, myself, and three or four more, whose names are worn out of my mind. Major Morrison was so far recovered as to be heart-whole, but he wanted strength to go thro' so great a labour as this was like to prove. We left him with some others to be brought in boats that the governor had order'd for their accommodation; and with them the two weak women, who were much recover'd by the good care and nourishment they received in the poor fisherman's house.

Breakfast being done, and our pilot Jack ready to set out, we took a solemn leave of the good king. He inclosed me in his arms, with kind embraces, not without expressions of sorrow to part, beyond the common rate of new acquaintance. I made Jack pump up his best compliments, which at present was all I was capable to return to the king's kindness; and so, after many *Hana haes*, we parted.

We were not gone far till the fatigue and tediousness of the journey discovered itself in the many creeks we were forc'd to head, the swamps to pass (like Irish bogs) which made the way at least double to what it would have amounted to in a strait line: and it was our wonder to see our guide Jack lead on the way with the same confidence of going right, as if he had had a London road to keep him from straying. Howbeit he would many times stand still and look about for land-marks; and when on one hand and the other his marks bore right for his direction, he would shew himself greatly satisfied. As to the purpose, an old deform'd tree that lay north-west, opposite to a small hammock of pines to the south-east, would evidence his going right in all weathers. It is true, they know not the compass by the loadstone, but, which is equivalent, they never are ignorant of the north-west point, which gives them the rest; and that they know by the weather-beaten moss that grows on that side of every oak, different from the rest of the tree, which is their compass. Towards evening we saw smoak (an infallible sign of an Indian town) which Jack knew to arise from Gingo Teague. We went boldly into the king's house (by advice of his brother of Kickotank) who was also a very humane prince. What the place and season produc'd was set before us with all convenient speed, which was enough to satisfy hunger, and to fit us for repose.

I was extremely tir'd with this tedious journey; and it was the more irksome to me, because I perform'd it in boots (my shoes being worn out) which at that time were commonly worn to walk in; so that I was much more sleepy than I had been hungry The alliance I had newly made at Kickotank did already stand me in some stead, for that it qualified me to a lodging apart, and gave me a first taste of all we had to eat, tho' the variety was not so great as I had seen in other courts.

And yet (as we see in all worldly honours) this grandeur of mine was not without its allay; for as it gave me accommodation of eating and sleeping in preference to my comrades, so did it raise the hopes of the royal progeny of gifts and presents, beyond what I was either able or willing to afford them: for when I would have taken my rest, I was troubled beyond measure with their visits, and saw by their carriage what they would be at; wherefore, to free myself of further disturbance, and to put myself out of the pain of denials, I resolv'd to comply with the necessities of nature, which press'd me hard to sleep; and to that end I took the freedom by Jack, to desire they would all withdraw until I found myself refresh'd.

I pass'd the night till almost day-break in one intire sleep; and when I did awake (not suddenly able to collect who, or where I was) I found myself strangely confounded, to see a damsel plac'd close to my side, of no meaner extract than the king's eldest daughter, who had completely finish'd the rape of all the gold and silver buttons that adorn'd the king of Kickotank's coat, yet on my back. When I was broad awake, and saw this was no enchantment (like those trances knights-errant use to be in) but that I was really despoiled of what was not in my power to dispense withal, I called for Jack, and made him declare my resentment and much dislike of this princess's too great liberty upon so small acquaintance, which made me have a mean opinion of her. Jack shew'd more anger than myself to see such usage by any of his country, and much more was he scandaliz'd, that one of the blood royal should purloin.

But the king, upon notice of the fact and party concerned in it, immediately caused the buttons to be found out and returned, with no slight reprimand to his daughter, and then, all was well, and so much the better by the gift of such small presents as I was able to make to the king and princess. Break-fast was given us, and we hasten'd to proceed in our journey to Achomack.

The uneasiness of boots to travel in, made me by much the more weary of the former day's journey, and caus'd me to enter very unwillingly upon this second day's work. We reckon'd our selves about twenty-five miles distant from Jenkin's house. It pleased God to send us dry weather, and not excessive cold. We had made provision of *Pone* to bait on by the way, and we found good water to refresh us; but all this did not hinder my being tir'd and spent almost to the last degree. Jack very kindly offer'd his service to carry me on his shoulders (for I was brought to a moderate weight by the strict diet I had been in) but that would have been more uneasy to me, in contemplation of his more than double pains, and so I resolved to try my utmost strength, without placing so great a weight on his shoulders.

The hopes of seeing English ground in America, and that in so short a time as they made us expect, did animate my spirits to the utmost point. Jack fearing the worst, was of opinion, that we should call at his aunt's town, the queen of Pomumkin, not far out of the way: but Jenkin Price opposed that motion, and did assure me our journey's end was at hand. His words and my own inclination carried the question, and I resolved, by God's help, that night to sleep at Jenkin's house.

But the distance proving yet greater than had been decided, and my boots trashing me almost beyond all sufferance, I became desperate, and ready to sink and lie down. Jenkin lull'd me on still with words that spurr'd me to the quick; and would demonstrate the little distance betwixt us and his plantation, by the sight of hogs and cattle, of which species the Indians were not masters. I was fully convinc'd of what he said, but would however have consented to a motion of lying without doors on the ground, within two or three flights shot of the place, to save the labour of so small a remainder.

The close of the evening, and a little more patience (thro' the infinite goodness of the Almighty) did put a happy period to our cross adventure. A large bed of sweet straw was spread ready in Jenkin's house for our reception, upon which I did hasten to extend and stretch my wearied limbs. And being thus brought into safe harbour by the many miracles of divine mercy, from all the storms and fatigues, perils and necessities to which we had been exposed by sea and land for almost the space of four months, I cannot conclude this voyage in more proper terms, than the words that are the burthen of that psalm of providence. *O that men would therefore praise the Lord for his goodness, and for his wondrous works unto the children of men!*

Our landlord Jenkin Price, and conductor Jack took great care to provide meat for us; and there being a dairy and hens, we could not want. As for our stomachs, they were open at all hours to eat whate'er was set before us, assoon as our wearied bodies were refresh'd with sleep. It was on Saturday the —— day of January, that we ended this our wearisome pilgrimage, and entred into our king's dominions at Achomat, called by the English, Northampton county, which is the only county on that side of the bay belonging to the colony of Virginia, and is the best of the whole for all sorts of necessaries for human life.

Having been thus refresh'd in Jenkin's house this night with all our hearts could wish, on the next morning, being Sunday, we would have been glad to have found a church for the performance of our duty to God, and to have rendred our hearty thanks to him in the publick assembly, for his unspeakable mercies vouchsafed to us; but we were not yet arrived to the heart of the country where there were churches, and ministry perform'd as our laws direct, but were glad to continue our own chaplains, as formerly. As we advanced into the plantations that lay thicker together, we had our choice of hosts for our entertainment, without money or its value; in which we did not begin any novelty, for there are no inns in the colony; nor do they take other payment for what they furnish to coasters, but by requital of such courtesies in the same way, as occasions offer.

When I came to the house of one Stephen Charlton, he did not only outdo all that I had visited before him, in variety of dishes at his table, which was very well order'd in the kitchen, but would also oblige me to put on a good farmer-like suit of his own wearing cloaths, for exchange of my dirty habit; and this gave me opportunity to deliver my camlet coat to Jack, for the use of my brother of Kickotank, with other things to make it worth his acceptance.

Having been thus frankly entertain'd at Mr. Charlton's, our company were in condition to take care for themselves. We took leave of each other, and my next stage was to esquire Yardly, a gentleman of good name, whose father had sometimes been governor of Virginia. There I was received and treated as if I had in truth and reality been that man of honour my brother of Kickotank had created me. It fell out very luckily for my better welcome, that he had not long before brought over a wife from Rotterdam, that I had known almost from a child. Her father (Custis by name) kept a victualling house in that town, liv'd in good repute, and was the general host of our nation there. The esquire knowing I had the honour to be the governor's kinsman, and his wife knowing my conversation in Holland, I was receiv'd and caress'd more like a domestick and near relation, than a man in misery, and a stranger. I stay'd there for a passage over the bay, about ten days, welcomed and feasted not only by the esquire and his wife, but by many neighbours that were not too remote.

About the midst of February I had an opportunity to cross the bay in a sloop, and with much ado landed in York river, at esquire Ludlow's plantation, a most pleasant situation. I was civilly receiv'd by him, who presently order'd an accommodation for me in a most obliging manner. But it fell out at that time, that captain Wormly (of his majesty's council) had guests in his house (not a furlong distant from Mr. Ludlow's) feasting and carousing, that were lately come from England, and most of them my intimate acquaintance. I took a sudden leave of Mr. Ludlow, thank'd him for his kind intentions to me, and using the common freedom of the country, I thrust myself amongst captain Wormly's guests in crossing the creek, and had a kind reception from them all, which answered (if not exceeded) my expectation.

Sir Thomas Lundsford, Sir Henry Chickly, Sir Philip Honywood, and colonel Hamond were the persons I met there, and enjoy'd that night with very good chear, but left them early the next morning, out of a passionate desire I had to see the governor, whose care for my preservation had been so full of kindness.

Captain Wormly mounted me for James Town, where the governor was pleased to receive and take me to his house at Green-spring, and there I pass'd my hours (as at mine own house) until May following; at which time he sent me for Holland to find out the king, and to sollicite his majesty for the treasurer's place of Virginia, which the governor took to be void by the delinquency of Claybourne, who had long enjoy'd it. He furnish'd me with a sum of money to bear the charge of this sollicitation; which took effect, tho' the king was then in Scotland. He was not only thus kind to me (who had a more than ordinary pretence to his favour by our near affinity in blood) but, on many occasions, he shew'd great respect to all the royal party, who made that colony their refuge. His house and purse were open to all that were so qualify'd. To one of my comrades (major Fox) who had no friend at all to subsist on, he shew'd a generosity that was like himself; and to my other (major Morrison) he was more kind, for he did not only place him in the command of the fort, which was profitable to him whilst it held under the king, but did advance him after to the government of the country, wherein he got a competent estate.

And thus (by the good providence of a gracious God, who helpeth us in our low estate, and causeth his angels to pitch tents round about them that trust in him) have I given as faithful an account of this signal instance of his goodness to the miserable objects of his mercy in this voyage, as I have been able to call to a clear remembrance.

A LIST OF SEA-TERMS

Aft or abaft, towards the stern or rudder-end of a ship.

Anchor, there may be five anchors on a ship. The best bower and small bower are the two stowed farthest forward, the best bower being the one on the starboard bow and the small bower that on the port. The sheet anchor is of the same size and weight as either of the bowers, the stream anchor is smaller, and the kedge is the smallest of all.

Backstays are long ropes that run from the topmast and topgallantmast heads towards the stern and serve to keep the masts from pitching forwards or overboard.

Belay, to make fast.

Binnacle or bittacle, the box on deck that holds the mariner's compass.

Bob-stays are ropes that hold the bowsprit downwards.

Bolt-rope, a rope round the edge of a sail to keep it from tearing.

Bonnet, extra canvas laced to the foot of a sail.

Boom, a long spar of wood.

Bow, the fore-end of a ship from where it begins to curve inward to the cutwater or stem.

Bowlines are ropes fastened to the leeches or sides of the sails to pull them forward.

Bowse, to haul on a rope.

Bowsprit or boltsprit, a large boom or mast running out from the stem of a ship.

Braces are ropes serving to turn the sails; they are made fast to the ends of the yards.

Breeching, a stout rope holding a gun from recoiling too far.

Broaching-to is when a ship is forced round sideways on to the sea and the wind in spite of the helm.

Bulkheads are the walls or partitions in a ship.

Bunt-lines, ropes fastened to the bottom of a sail to haul it up to the yard; this eases the labour of furling.

Cap, a great block with two holes for fastening an upper mast to a lower.

Careen, to careen a ship is to make her lie right over on one side so that men may come at the other to mend or clean it.

Cat-heads, two horizontal beams, one on each bow, for raising and holding the anchors.

Chains or channels are the strong iron fastenings for the shrouds; they are fixed to the ship's sides abreast of the masts, so there are main-chains, fore-chains and mizzen-chains.

Chess-trees, small timbers, one on each side of the ship between the main and fore-chains; the main-tack passes through them.

Cleats are pieces of wood at the ends of the yards to stop ropes sliding off: also, pieces of wood to fasten ropes with or to fasten anything to.

Clue-garnets, tackles fastened to the clues or lower corners of the main and foresail to truss them up to the yard, which is termed cluing up those sails. Clue lines serve the same purpose for the other square sails.

Coamings, the borders of the hatches raised above the deck.

Companion, the frame on the quarterdeck to light the cabin.

Companion-way, the stairs down to the cabin; the covering of it is called the companion-hatch.

Counter, the curved part of the ship's stern.

Courses are the foresail, mainsail and driver.

Cross-jack-yard, the lower yard on the mizzen-mast.

Cross-trees are horizontal timbers at the top of the lower and topmasts; they support the masts above them, and the topmast cross-trees secure the topgallant-shrouds.

Cutwater, the foremost part of the ship's prow.

Davit, a piece of timber used as a crane to hoist the anchor clear of the side and for lowering boats.

Dead-eyes, round flat blocks with three holes for extending the shrouds.

Driver, the large sail suspended on the mizzen-gaff.

Earings, small ropes fastening the upper corners of the sail to the yard.

Falconet, a cannon of two inches bore, to shoot a ball of a pound and a half upwards of a thousand paces.

Forecastle, the forward parts about the foremast, where the common sailors lie.

Foremast, see Mast.

Forestay, the stay running from the foremast head to the stem.

Forward, towards the bows.

Furling is wrapping or rolling a sail close up to the yard or stay to which it belongs.

Grapnel, a clawed iron for seizing hold on another ship, or for anchoring a small boat.

Gudgeons or Gudgins, rudder irons, the sockets in which the rudder works.

Gunnel or Gunwale, is the upper edge of the ship's side.

Halser or Hawser, a large rope, somewhat less than a cable.

Halyards, the ropes or tackles for hoisting sails or yards.

Hand, to hand a sail is to take it in.

Hawse-holes are holes through the bows on each side for the cables.

Horses are ropes hanging in loops under the yards for the sailors to tread upon when they furl or reef the sails.

Jears are the tackles which hoist or lower the lower yards.

Jib, the foremost sail of a ship.

Jibboom, the continuation of the bowsprit, as a topmast is of a lower mast. A flying jibboom is a spar running out beyond the jibboom.

Jury masts are those makeshifts which replace broken or lost masts.

Lanyards are short pieces of rope used as fastenings or handles.

Larboard is the same as port, meaning the left-hand side of a ship.

Lazaretto, the part of the hold used for stores, usually aft.

Leech, the leech of a sail is its upright side. Leech-lines are fastened to the middle of the leech of the mainsail and the foresail; they serve to truss the sails up to the yards.

Lifts are ropes running from the cap and masthead to the ends of the yard below to support it.

Marline, a small thin rope with but two strands. A marline spike is a handspike for parting the strands of a rope.

Masts: the mainmast is the largest in the ship, and stands nearly in the middle between stem and stern. The foremast stands near the stem, and is next in size to the mainmast. The mizzen is the smallest, and stands about half-way between the mainmast and the stern.

Each mast has three members, the mast itself, which stands upon the keel, the topmast, which is raised at the head of the lower mast through a cap, and the topgallantmast, which is raised on the topmast in the same manner. Sometimes a fourth part, called the royal-mast, is raised above the topgallantmast.

The masts and their members, then, are called thus, the mainmast, maintopmast, maintopgallant; foremast, foretopmast, foretopgallant; mizzen, mizzentopmast, and mizzentopgallant.

Minion-guns, cannon of three-and-a-half inch bore.

Mizzen-gaff, the spar extending the top of the fore-and-aft sail set on the aft side of the mizzenmast.

Nun-buoy, is one that is round in the middle and pointed at each end.

Paterero, a small gun or swivel.

Pink, a small ship with a narrow stern.

Plat, a map or chart.

Poop, the highest and aftermost deck of a ship.

Port is the left-hand side of the ship as you look forward from the stern.

Quarter-deck, that part of the upper deck that lies between the stern and the mizzenmast.

Rattlings or Ratlines are small ropes which traverse the shrouds horizontally, forming a variety of ladders, whereby to climb to any of the mast-heads.

Reefs are parts of a sail that can be rolled up or taken in to lessen the area of the sail according to the force of the wind.

Round-house, the uppermost cabin in the stern of a ship, where the master lies.

Runner, a rope with a block or pulley at one end and a hook the other, for hoisting things.

Sails: there are two sorts of sails in a ship, four-sided sails and triangular. The former are called square sails and the latter staysails, from their being spread on the stays, or ropes that run from the mast-heads forward. The square sails are spread on yards or booms. All sails derive their names from their mast, yard, boom or stay. Thus the principal sail, extended on the mainmast, is called the mainsail; the next above, which stands upon the maintopmast, is termed the maintopsail; and that which is spread across the maintopgallantmast is named the maintopgallantsail; the sail above it is called the main-royal.

In the same manner there is the foresail, foretopsail, mizzentopgallantsail, and mizzen-royal.

Thus also there is the main-staysail, maintopmast-staysail, maintopgallant-staysail, and a middle staysail between the last two; all these staysails are between the main and foremast. The staysails between the main and mizzen are the mizzen-staysail, the mizzentopmast-staysail, and sometimes the mizzen-royal-staysail. The sails between the foremast and the bowsprit are the forestaysail, the foretopmast-staysail, the jib, and sometimes a flying-jib, and even a middle-jib. There are besides two and sometimes three square sails extended by yards under the bowsprit and jibbooms, one called the spritsail, the second the spritsail-topsail, and the third the spritsail-topgallantsail.

Studding-sails are sometimes set in calm weather; they are extended on booms run out beyond the ends of the yards that hold the square sails. Studding-sails are named from their stations, as, the topgallant-studding-sails.

Scupper holes are made through the ship's side, through which water is carried from the deck off into the sea.

Scuttles are little square holes with lids cut in the deck, enough to let a man through, they serve to let people down upon occasion: they also serve to light the cabins.

Shallop, a kind of light open boat with a mast that can be set up.

Sheets are ropes fastened to one or both of the lower corners of a sail to hold it in a particular position.

Shrouds are those ropes that come from either side of the masts, being fastened below to the chains and aloft over the heads of the masts. They serve to stay the masts sideways, and they are named (like sails) by the masts to which they belong.

Sloop, a small vessel with one mast.

Starboard is the right-hand side of a ship as you look forward from the stern.

Stays are long strong ropes, supporting the masts by running from the mast-heads towards the stem. The forestay reaches from the foremast-head towards the bowsprit end, the mainstay extends to the ship's stem, and the mizzenstay is stretched to a collar on the mainmast immediately above the quarterdeck. The foretopmaststay comes to the end of the bowsprit, and the foretopgallantstay to the end of the jibboom; the other topmasts and topgallants are all stayed forward in the same manner.

Steerage, the place in front of the bulkhead of the cabin, where the steersman stands and lodges.

Stern-post, the upright timber which carries the rudder.

Stopper, a rope or clamp to prevent the halliards or cable from running out too fast.

Tacks are ropes for holding the foremost lower corners of the courses and staysails when the wind blows across the ship's course. A tack is also the direction in which a ship goes; she is on the starboard tack when the wind blows from the starboard.

Tire, a row, as a tire of guns.

Top, a sort of platform surrounding the lower masthead serving to extend the topmast-shrouds. In ships of force the tops are furnished with swivels, musketry and other firearms.

Trennels, wooden pegs used instead of nails.

Try, a ship lies a-try when she has but her main or mizzen sail spread, and is let alone to lie in the sea.

Warps are ropes used in towing or in warping, which is the operation of carrying a rope to a fixed-point and pulling the ship up to it.

Whipstaff, a kind of tiller.

Yards are long pieces of timber suspended upon the masts of a vessel to extend the sails to the wind. They are either square, lateen, or lugsail; the first being suspended across the mast at right-angles, the two latter obliquely. The square yards are of a cylindrical form, tapering from the middle, which is called the slings, towards the extremities, which are termed the yard-arms.

The Works of Patrick O'Brian